The Yankee Mariner & Sea Power

The Yankee Mariner and Sea Power is the product of the **Center for Study of the American Experience,** which, as a part of the Annenberg School of Communications at the University of Southern California, assembled the conference from which this book sprung.

In compliance with the mandate of the Center's founders to bring the message of the American experience "to the very people who constitute the democracy," the Center pursued the identification and analysis of problems and challenges in America's past, present, and future, by sponsoring conferences and supporting visiting distinguished Scholars-in-Residence.

Edited audio and video tapes for public broadcast, and publications such as this volume, have disseminated the work of the Center beyond its physical confines. The scope and variety of the studies conducted by the Center are suggested by the list of its publications below.

John C. Weaver
Former Executive Director

The Yankee Mariner & Sea Power

America's Challenge of Ocean Space

Papers from a Conference
Sponsored by
Center for Study of the
American Experience
The Annenberg School of Communications
University of Southern California
March 1981

Foreword by **Don Walsh**
Introduction by **Athelstan Spilhaus**

Edited by **Joyce J. Bartell**

University of Southern California Press
Transaction Books • Rutgers University

Published 1982
University of Southern California Press
Los Angeles, California, 90007

Series Editor, Joyce J. Bartell
Designer, Robert Giese

Distributed by Transaction Books ![icon] Rutgers University
New Brunswick, New Jersey 08903 (U.S.A.) and London (U.K.)

Library of Congress Cataloging in Publication Data
Main entry under title:
The Yankee mariner and sea power.
    1. Sea-power—United States—Congresses.
2. Marine resources—United States—Congresses.
I. Bartell, Joyce J. II. Annenberg School of
Communications (University of Southern California).
Center for Study of the American Experience.
VA50.Y36   333.91′64′0973   82-4746
ISBN 0-88474-105-2   AACR2

Contents

Contents

Contributors

Richard T. Ackley is a retired naval officer, an authority on military strategy and defense policy, and currently Associate Dean of Academic Administration and Associate Professor of Political Science at California State College, San Bernardino. He is a graduate of the Naval Intelligence Postgraduate School and the Russian language course at the Defense Language Institute. While on active duty, he commanded the submarine *Bream* and served as Assistant Naval Attaché in Moscow, USSR.

Herbert Brand is Chairman of the Board of Trustees of the Transportation Institute, a Washington-based organization engaged in maritime industry research, education, and promotion. He is a member of the Board of Governors and the Executive Committee of the National Maritime Council; a member of the Executive Committees of the Navy League of the United States and the National Waterways Conference; and on the Advisory Board of the United States Merchant Marine Academy.

Harry C. Brockel, Director of the Port of Milwaukee from 1942 to 1969, was an international port and transportation consultant at the time of his death in 1981. A former faculty member of the Center for Great Lakes Studies at the University of Wisconsin-Milwaukee, he was for many years an advisor to the St. Lawrence Seaway Development Corporation, and served as federal port controller for Great Lakes and St. Lawrence Seaway ports. He was a past president of the American Association of Port Authorities.

John P. Craven is Dean of Marine Programs and Professor of Ocean Engineering at the University of Hawaii and has been Director of the Law of the Sea Institute since 1977. For ten years he was chief scientist in the Special Projects and Deep Submergence Systems Project Office of the U.S. Navy. He holds Distinguished Civilian Service Awards from the Departments of Navy and Defense. An engineer and lawyer, Dr. Craven is an authority on submarine design and warfare, sea resource development, and deep-ocean technology.

Contributors

John E. Flipse—marine engineer, inventor, ship designer, professor—was the first person to file a claim for deep-sea mining. With co-inventors he holds nine patents for methods and apparatuses for underwater mining. He organized and managed the first deep-sea mining company in the world, Deepsea Ventures, Inc., conducted a world leadership program in ocean mining, and served on the U.S. delegation to the U.N. Conference on Law of the Sea. In 1978 he received the Underwater Mining Institute's Award of Distinction. Professor Flipse teaches civil and ocean engineering at Texas A&M University.

John B. Hattendorf is a naval historian and Associate Professor of Strategy at the U.S. Naval War College. A former Navy lieutenant with active service at sea, he served for twelve years in the Naval History Division of the Office of the Chief of Naval Operations; he also has been research assistant to the President of the Naval War College. In mid-1981, he began a two-year visiting professorship of military history at the National University of Singapore.

Ann L. Hollick is Director of the Office of International Commodities in the U.S. Department of State. Formerly with the Department's Bureau of Oceans, International Environmental and Scientific Affairs, she headed the Policy Assessment Staff in analyzing the long-range impact of science and technology on U.S. foreign policy in energy, environment, oceans, polar regions, and space. Dr. Hollick was a member of the 1977 U.S. delegation to the U.N. Conference on Law of the Sea, and is author of *U.S. Foreign Policy and the Law of the Sea,* published in 1981. She lectures in international relations at Johns Hopkins University.

Clarence P. Idyll is a marine biologist, an educator, and a world authority on fishery biology and management, aquaculture, and international fisheries. He is Senior Marine Analyst for the National Advisory Committee on Oceans and Atmosphere, and former Chief of the Division of International Fisheries Development and Services in the National Oceanic and Atmospheric Administration. Dr. Idyll was on the faculty of the University of Miami for almost a quarter century, heading the Division of Fishery Sciences in its Institute of Marine and Atmospheric Sciences. He has also been a Senior Fisheries Consultant to the Food and Agriculture Organization of the United Nations.

L. Donald Maus is an electrical and ocean engineer, a former naval officer with background in naval nuclear propulsion, and a specialist in offshore petroleum production platforms. The group he supervises in the Offshore Structures Division of Exxon Production Research Company developed the guyed tower platform, the first of which will be installed in the Gulf of Mexico in 1983. Before Exxon, Dr. Maus was with the Naval Reactors Division of the U.S. Atomic Energy Commission (now the Nuclear Regulatory Commission).

Michael MccGwire is a Senior Fellow at the Brookings Institution, where he works on the application of cruise missiles to U.S. general purpose naval forces and on analysis of the development of Soviet strategic rocket forces. A former Commander in the British Royal Navy, he served in most parts of the world, including Moscow as an attaché; he was honored with the Order of the British Empire. For eight years before joining Brookings, he was Professor of Maritime and Strategic Studies at Dalhousie University in Halifax.

Arvid Pardo is a former diplomat and official of the United Nations, the fourth person to be employed by that body. A citizen of Malta, he served his country as U.N. Ambassador for Ocean Affairs, and in 1970 was elected Vice President of the General Assembly. He has also been Malta's ambassador to the United States and to the Soviet Union, and its High Commissioner to Canada. Ocean studies and, in particular, policy and law of the sea have been his specialty since he led the Maltese delegation to the U.N. Seabed Committee in the early 1970s. Dr. Pardo is now Professor of Political Science and Senior Research Fellow at the Institute for Marine and Coastal Studies, University of Southern California.

Contributors

Andreas B. Rechnitzer is one of America's most versatile oceanographers—a research scientist and engineer, an underwater archeological explorer, a deep submergence pioneer, and developer of ocean-related technology and systems ranging from Scuba diving methods to deep-water oil and gas production. He was scientist-in-charge of Project NEKTON, which included the Bathyscaph *Trieste*'s record dive of 35,800 feet in the Marianas Trench in 1960. Dr. Rechnitzer retired with the rank of Captain from the U.S. Naval Reserve, served for several years in the Navy Department in the Office of the Chief of Naval Operations, and is currently Manager, Lockheed Ocean Science Laboratories at Carlsbad, California.

Athelstan Spilhaus is an oceanographer, educator, author, meteorologist, and inventor, and the originator of the Sea Grant program of the National Oceanic and Atmospheric Administration, to which he has been a consultant since 1974. He was Dean of the Institute of Technology at the University of Minnesota from 1949 to 1966, and has also been Director of Research for New York University, where he started a new Department of Meteorology and Oceanography. Dr. Spilhaus was, for many years, an investigator in physical oceanography at Woods Hole Oceanographic Institution. His thirteen honorary doctorates attest to his high standing in the science and engineering communities. He was a Distinguished Scholar-in-Residence at the Center for Study of the American Experience in 1980–1981.

Craig L. Symonds is Associate Professor of History at the United States Naval Academy, Annapolis. His specialty is American naval and military history, and he has also taught strategy at the U.S. Naval War College and lectured at the Marine Corps Command and Staff College. His publications include *Charleston Blockade,* an account of the Civil War blockade of the Southern Coast, and *Navalists and Antinavalists,* a study of the early naval policy debate in the United States.

Contributors

Don Walsh, since 1975 Director of the Institute for Marine and Coastal Studies and Professor of Ocean Engineering at the University of Southern California, spent the preceding twenty-three years in the U.S. Navy, holding the rank of Captain at the time of retirement. His active service was largely in submarines in Pacific and Asian waters, and included three years as Officer-in-Charge of the Bathyscaph *Trieste.* He is a former Special Assistant for Submarines to the Assistant Secretary of the Navy for Research and Development. Among many other honors, Dr. Walsh received from the U.S. government two Legion of Merit awards and two Meritorious Service medals, and for his contributions to national programs in Antarctica had a geographic feature there named the "Walsh Spur." In 1979, the President appointed him to a three-year term as a member of the National Committee on Oceans and Atmosphere.

Foreword

This is a book about American sea power—not in the narrow traditional sense of a navy used for military advantage, but "sea power" as the sum total of all uses made of the oceans: their living and non-living resources, the energy wrested from them, their use as avenues of transport, their value and potential for recreation, as well as the vital role they play in national defense. This concept of sea power is assessed by tracing the evolution of seagoing America, the "Yankee Mariner" of our title. To some extent, then, this is a history of American experience with the sea, a history that parallels our nation's emergence as a world power in less than three hundred years.

But the book is also a "tour of the horizon" as to the total impact American sea power has had in the past and should have in the future. There have been many maritime histories, as well as many published volumes on ocean issues and politics of the sea. Few offer historical developmental background together with a clear exposition of contemporary uses of the sea. I believe we have achieved this objective and, by organization of the topic, provided a special understanding of the importance of the oceans to the future of America.

The historical development of this subject gives a sense of continuity with the past. Through the lessons of history we are helped to understand the present. In early chapters of the book, naval and maritime historians show how our nation, since the early seventeenth century, has met and overcome the manifold challenges of ocean space. The history of American sea power is seen to be uneven. Great advances have tended to cluster around periods of great national upheaval, primarily wars, only to be followed by a turn away from the sea. Some of the varied and complex reasons for this seeming reallocation of the country's priorities are explored, together with some explanation of the consequences. Ironically, the pattern continued after the end of World War II, although America had become a preeminent world power which no longer could afford to turn its back on the sea, so vital for international relations, world trade, and national defense.

As the historical development reaches the present time scale, the concept of sea power is dissected into its component parts, and it becomes evident that the present U.S. stance in ocean use leaves much to be desired. There are grave questions as to the adequacy of our naval, merchant marine, and shipbuilding capacity. Our fishing industry suffers from the aggressiveness of foreign fleets, offshore energy development faces new challenges, and the viability of deep-sea mining is problematical. The altered attitude of the U.S. government toward a law of the sea treaty raises more uncertainties in international agreements about ocean use.

In each of these areas, serious consideration is given by our authors to the scientific and technical support required for America to regain its faltering momentum in sea power. In my conclusion, I have tried to predict the state of national sea power through the end of the twentieth century.

Was there ever a "Yankee Mariner?" Or was the seagoing American simply a landsman who adapted to this environment in times of need or opportunity? I will leave this judgment for the reader.

The Yankee Mariner and Sea Power originated in a conference held at the University of Southern California in March 1981. As Director of the Institute for Marine and Coastal Studies there, I was closely involved in planning and execution of the conference, which was sponsored by the Center for Study of the American Experience, The Annenberg School of Communications. The support of the Center and active personal interest of its executive director, Dr. John Weaver, contributed greatly to success of the conference. In addition to the papers presented by the fifteen speakers (which have been edited into the chapters of this book), the Center, through the skillful editing and production of Gerald Bartell, also produced a videotape of the proceedings for public television broadcast. Both the television program and this book were created to ensure that the information presented at this stimulating meeting would survive in forms that would enlighten and instruct countless others besides those fortunate to attend in person.

It is in the spirit of helping people understand the importance of America's future in ocean space that this volume has been assembled. I should emphasize at this point that this is essentially a collection of monographs, and hence a different "voice" addresses the reader in each chapter. No extraordinary attempt was made editorially to homogenize the varied expressions of ideas. Certainly we do not have here the definitive work in each of the topical areas represented; but the book does integrate and analyze, from a variety of informed perspectives, that particular set of complex activities we call sea power. Our nation's security is absolutely dependent upon our effective uses of the oceans for resources, trade and transport, energy, and national defense. That was the reason for the conference, and it is the reason for this book.

In addition to Dr. Weaver's superb leadership, I should like to recognize the contributions of Dr. Athelstan Spilhaus, who at the time of the conference was an Annenberg Distinguished Scholar. The depth of his experience and the wisdom of his observations were always helpful in planning and arranging the event. His keynote speech is the opening chapter in this book.

A generous thank you is due our authors. All busy people, they took considerable time to write their papers and take part in the conference, and then, in many cases, rewrote their lectures into chapter formats. Each of these persons is a recognized expert in his or her field. It was somewhat remarkable that we could get so many of them into one place for a four-day meeting. I am, therefore, pleased that their words and efforts will now go beyond the limited time we were together at the University of Southern California in March 1981. Because of the substantial degree of expert opinion represented, expanded biographical data have been provided for each contributor. A review of this section will make a convincing argument for why this volume should command the reader's attention.

Finally, I would recognize the efforts of Joyce J. Bartell, editor for the Center for Study of the American Experience, who undertook the difficult (but I hope rewarding) task of compiling and editing this book. She deserves special mention for her patience and diplomacy.

I am certain *The Yankee Mariner and Sea Power* will contribute significantly to public understanding of our nation's past role and future prospects in the sea—its challenge of ocean space.

Don Walsh, *Conference Chairman*
Los Angeles, California
February, 1982

Sea Power and
the Dilemmas of Mankind

Athelstan Spilhaus

Sea power is not just navy. It involves taking fish and many other resources from the sea, and it involves the ability to carry things across the high seas.

Sea power is a three-legged stool, with a navy leg, a sea resources leg, and a marine transport leg. If sea power is to stand, no one leg of this stool can be cut shorter than the others; and the foundation on which it stands is understanding and stewardship of the oceans.

We examine the past to find out how we arrived at our present successes and dilemmas. Only then can we plan the future. The future is a large topic, so the Yankee Mariner conference zeroed in on a narrower one—the dilemmas of mankind and how the sea can contribute to solutions.

The horns of the dilemma are excessive population on one side and shortage of energy on the other. Between the horns of too many people and too little energy fall the shortages of food, water, housing, and raw materials. If we cannot control our numbers, even increased energy will not help. If we cannot increase our production of energy, even stabilizing population will not cure our ills. And in facing these forebodings, doers must start from the present, with a knowledge of the past, to plan the future.

"On-and-Off" Sea Power

In the past, the U.S. Navy has been an on-and-off proposition. Naval historians John Hattendorf and Craig Symonds attest in this book that the United States has had the remarkable ability to turn *on* naval strength rapidly when needed but turn it *off* to languish during times of peace.

Sea resource acquisition has also been an on-and-off activity. The first settlers of New England were English landlubbers who engaged in coastal fishing because they had to, for food. They also developed an admirable whaling industry because they had to, for oil. That is the *on* part.

The *off* part came as the interior of the continent, with its vast land resources, opened up. New Englanders could, by manufacture, add value to things and exchange them for food from the land. Then the discovery of oil in Pennsylvania killed the whaling industry; whale oil was no longer essential. Also, the Civil War took away many whalers. The whaling industry never recovered.

Our merchant marine was *on* at the peak of its glory carrying people and things across the seas, notably the Pacific, in the marvelous clipper ships, the fastest sea carriers in the world at that time. Professor Symonds refers to this period, 1776 to 1900, as the "laissez-faire era;" the government allowed doers to do things. The triangular clipper trade from the Pacific islands, with sandalwood for China exchanged for silks for the United States and Europe, at one time had almost every ship in Hong Kong harbor flying the U.S. flag.

Sandalwood was exhausted from the Pacific islands about the same time the British took a step-jump and moved into steam. Our merchant marine was turned *off*. It revived strongly in World War I, to carry goods to allies in Europe, after which it dwindled again, to be turned *on* once more in World War II. Interest in the seas was easily turned off because people believed the United States was protected by the great watery moats of the Atlantic and Pacific.

The Three Sea Legs Today

The U.S. Navy was preeminent in World War II and for three decades thereafter, but recently somebody has fooled with the *off* switch again. Social preoccupations have taken priority over defense, and the limitations of armaments and the SALT agreements, among other things, have contributed to this decline.

Strategist Michael MccGwire, in an earlier communication, described our Navy as "depleted husks," "paralyzed," and "overstretched." At the conference, he argued that the United States need not seek naval supremacy. I cannot share either of these extreme views.

I would remark, however, that our Coast Guard, a vital component of sea power, is indeed terribly overstretched.

But we still lead in activity under the sea. From the 1950s until today, submarines and drilling for oil in deep waters have been the things we are good at. During this time, some twenty years ago Don Walsh, head of the Institute for Marine and Coastal Studies at the University of Southern California, who helped to plan this conference, blazed the way down with man's deepest dive, as Officer-in-Charge of the Bathyscaph *Trieste*.

Our magnificent technological ability to tap oil from deeper and deeper seabeds, described so graphically by ocean engineer L. Donald Maus, does not keep up with our appetite for oil (we are indeed "gasoholics") nor keep down our dependence on foreign imports. These come to our shores in foreign bottoms, because our own merchant marine seems to be not only sick but in terminal trauma. Herbert Brand, the maritime industry's vigorous advocate, expresses little doubt that the reduction of this nation's carrying power at sea is a major danger both to its position as a world power and to its very safety.

PEOPLE PROBLEMS

The merchant marine has not, up to the present, been improved by applications of high technology, which cannot be expected always to fix self-imposed people problems. The idea in the 1950s was to compete in the Atlantic passenger and freight carrying. But the reason that people traveled on the *Queen Elizabeth* or the *Ile de France* had nothing to do with high technology, but more to do with high living. On American vessels, because of high labor costs three meals a day had to be gobbled in a span of eight hours; otherwise there had to be multiple crews. The decision to build a nuclear-powered merchant ship had no relation to the problem. When the problem is food and good service, it cannot be solved by putting a nuclear furnace under the vessel's boilers.

One fairly recent innovative transport method is the container ship. The crux of this innovation is to simplify the transfer from ship at sea to rail or truck on land with minimum handling. Yet unions are striking now because men are no longer needed for antediluvian hand stevedoring. An imaginative technical fix produced an adverse people reaction.

The maritime unions, who have contributed to the demise of the merchant marine and the increase of foreign registry of our vessels, may find themselves without maritime people to unionize. Even if we agree that men who work at sea should live as well as men who work on land, we will have to find a technological fix for the long separations from normal home life.

Designing Future Sea Use

Designing the future from past and present experience is better than just letting it happen. Let us consider some random ideas for future action.

The Navy is good underwater, and the United States is advanced in the ocean of space. Richard Ackley proposes a sensible solution to lessen the burden of military land forces overseas by putting more reliance on a combination of Navy and space. We navigate from satellites, we communicate via satellites, we launch missiles from submarines. The oceans and the vast ocean of space are linked. The future course for the Navy to chart is to add to underwater strength and develop a strong synergistic combination with the military arm in space.

Our history of subsidies shows that no amount of more money for continuing to do the same will revive our merchant marine. But, if I interpret Herbert Brand correctly, we need to remove excessive and costly hampering government regulations that protect others but not ourselves, if we are to remedy inadequacies in our Navy sea-lift capabilities and permit a revival of merchant sea-lift.

INNOVATIONS IN MARITIME TRANSPORTATION

Too often we cure one ill and spawn another. Since the British introduced steam propulsion, there has been little high technology except that the fuel of vessels has changed from wood to coal to oil to atoms. We have learned that we must avoid labor-intensive sea transport, but to avoid it we must not fall into the trap of energy-guzzling sea carriers. We can reduce manpower by automation and reduce energy consumption by using the wind. Can we design automated sailing ships?

In making the attempt, we can learn from the history of the lawnmower. Originally, the lawnmower was just a cutting reel and two wheels. The grass cuttings went all over the place. Then some smart fellow developed a bag to collect the grass cuttings, but after they had been collected he did not know where to put them. He went back to his laboratory and, after some experimentation, discovered that out of grass cuttings he could make a drinkable, whitish fluid, and that the residue was a useful humus for the lawn.

By that time, the machine had a motor on it so the man did not have to push it, but the wheels did not negotiate uneven ground so he installed caterpillar-like walking treads. The machine exuded the solid material and had a bag for the fluid with little taps. Finally, he added a modern electronic device which could sense where the grass was long, and he did not even have to guide it. He sat back, satisfied to do nothing.

He had reinvented the cow.

We must be careful not to do this. (Here is an example of such nonsense: The Soviets are designing a ship that can sieve up krill, the tiny shrimp that abound in the antarctic seas. The ship then processes the krill into useful food. But whales live on this krill and process it beautifully into whale meat. The Soviets should simply give up slaughtering whales and start breeding them, and when the herd is well established, take only the renewable harvest, an age-old practice of sensible animal husbandry.)

Just as the automated sailing vessel is an entirely new concept and not just a return to sail, so our abilities with submarines makes us think of taking another imaginative look at submarine transportation of bulk materials.

A successful submarine cargo carrier called *Deutschland* took two loads of copper to Germany from the United States in 1915 and 1916 during the blockade. Germany lost the war, and submarine cargo carriers were forgotten.

Now, 65 years later, from the tractor-trailer concept of our highways, should we not dream of nuclear tug-tractors under the sea, hitching on to submarine container-trailers carrying bulk materials?

One of the cheapest forms of transportation of materials is the pipeline, now used for water, oil, sulfur, and coal slurries. Can we not develop, for marine transport, pipelines on the seabed which could, in addition, transport slurries of fish or of neutrally buoyant ingots of metal, and so on and so on?

INDUSTRIAL RAW MATERIALS FROM THE SEA

The future of sea resources is vast. With our country becoming dependent on most of the raw materials needed by our industries, we should look into whether these materials or substitutes for them can be taken from the sea.

In 1975 I gave a talk on "The Oceans: Our Nation's Business." I cannot phrase it better nor need I bring it up-to-date, because since that time nothing has been done. I said:

> The United States is in a second War of Independence. I begin to wonder if in 1976 we will have a celebration or a wake—whether 1976 will mark the end of 200 years of independence for the United States.
>
> Will our dependence on imports of vital resources from other parts of the world make us dependent on the whims of others? I count about thirteen basic materials without which manufacturing industries cannot operate in our country. And if we define "dependence" arbitrarily as importing 50 percent of any of these, then we were dependent on four in 1950 and on six by 1970. By 1985 we will be dependent on nine. And by the year 2000 we will be totally dependent for almost all, except those things made of rock, sand, and vegetation.
>
> With these resources now coming in on foreign bottoms, do we not indeed return to the status of a colony? Others can turn off the spigot of our vital needs at the source, or they can cut off the transportation of these resources to our shores. Finally, they may impose blackmail prices constituting, if you will, taxation without representation—the thing we fought against 200 years ago.

We can indeed increase our independence through the proper use of the sea. For all the potential food resources enumerated by marine biologist Clarence Idyll, high technology has not prevented costs from rising beyond those of our competitors. For each calorie of tuna that one eats, thirteen calories of external fuels are burned to acquire it. There is far less energy cost in the labor-intensive coastal fishing of less developed nations. They eat their whole catch of fish; we throw away half of ours, calling it "trash fish."

ENTREPRENEURSHIP AND PUBLIC POLICIES

Production of oil is well underway. Mining for nodules is hampered because of the lack of a suitable sea-law framework to protect the entrepreneur in the open seas. Mining has also been hampered by over-zealous concern for the sea environment.

Professor Jack Flipse adds that entrepreneurism has been drowned by the failure of the United States to protect its own interests in the United Nations Conferences on Law of the Sea and Trade and Development.

Taking of nodules from the deep sea in the Pacific, with the accompanying stirring up of perhaps nutrient-rich deep-sea sediments, emulates the natural upwelling of nutrients in seawater, equivalent to plowing on land and, far from doing harm to the sea, could make ocean deserts fertile.

I remember being called out to a proposed site on a cape where there was a plan for a nuclear power plant. The citizens were up in arms, not for any sensible reason but because they were worried about the possibility of waste heat changing the ecology of the bay. So they called in the experts.

When I arrived I discovered that if this heat were put in at a certain depth, rich in nutrients, it would stir up, *boil* up, if you like, those nutrients to the surface, and could only increase the productivity. I explained this to the people there and added, "If you do it sensibly, you can have your cape and heat it, too." In spite of this advice, the plant—although completed—is still not warming the citizens or their food.

Nevertheless, social laws, overzealously applied, sometimes stimulate entrepreneurship. The specter of pollution fathered the Dutch idea of an island for industries with objectionable wastes. Incinerator vessels, such as *Vulcanis*, which burn harmful things completely at sea, are similarly responsive.

Professor Arvid Pardo, eminent spokesman for the necessity of law at sea, analyzes United States vacillations that sometimes bend the law of the sea to temporary national enthusiasms, or tolerate violations by others while over-regulating our own vessels.

For myself, if we are going to bend the law of the sea, let us bend it our way. Let us seek a solution that magically separates the lovely concept of common heritage from the impossible idea of common ownership, and combines it with workable ocean management practices.

Dr. Ann Hollick describes the politics of attempting to set priorities when the conflicting activities and interests of the United States engender differences within our own nation as wide as between nations at the international conference.

But stewardship has always gone hand-in-hand with ownership. When whales are in nobody's inventory, nobody protects them. When everyone owns the sea, no one looks after it.

Catching the Tide

Shakespeare wrote,

> There is a tide in the affairs of men,
> Which, taken at the flood, leads on to fortune;
> Omitted, all the voyage of their life
> Is bound in shallows and in miseries.

The tide in our nation's ocean affairs is now at a low ebb. Let us prepare for the flood that leads on to fortune, or we will indeed be bound in shallows. Three things make this time propitious.

First, we have declared a wide economic zone in the sea. When you open up a new territory like that, you must homestead it. As in the old homesteading of the American West, if we do not use our new territory, we will not hold onto it. Will we be absentee landlords? Or will we go to sea to stay?

Second, there are all kinds of ideas for multiple uses of the sea—ideas burgeoning from universities, industries, and government. Fragmented, these good ideas may never survive, but put together in a grand sea development plan, they can be fruitful.

Third, recent changes in our government may, it is hoped, switch the government from its adversary position against industry to one of partnership with it.

These three elements are mutually supportive.

IMAGINATION AND PURPOSE

To homestead and stay at sea, we will need to use and combine the many available ideas and, if we do so in a grand way, we can ensure proper protection of our investment of imagination and purpose.

Longtime port director Harry Brockel, noting that the explosion of shipping technology has challenged American dock facilities, says "the ship left the shore far behind." To homestead, we need deep water ports. We now have our first, off the coast of Louisiana.

To homestead we need "mariculture," using wastes that are nutrients for fish. This has begun.

We need power from the sea. Oil drilling has given us that. We should use the power there instead of just sending it, with great losses, to land, thus contributing to the growth of already overgrown cities on the seacoast.

We need true seaward advancement as a way of really planning new industrial complexes at sea which would combine all these ideas in a coordinated effort, forming a "platform" or island which would economically serve many uses where no one use could afford it.

PROBLEMS POLITICAL, NOT TECHNICAL

Dr. Andreas Rechnitzer tells us that the "tools, instruments, ship designs, materials, power plants" and the foundation of marine science are at our fingertips. In these we are Number One. In putting them to use, we are virtually nowhere. The problems are not technical. They are societal and political.

Can we not envisage cities at sea where energy—oil from the seabed, nuclear, coal—is used *in situ* for energy-intensive manufacture from bulk materials that come easily into offshore harbors? Around our sea complexes, can we not emulate land?

For animal husbandry in the United States, the great step in agriculture on land was the marvelous invention of barbed wire. How can we invent enclosures for husbandry of life in the sea—mariculture—and also, as the cattle guard is necessary for free passage through barbed wire, invent ways of free passage through our fences at sea?

Can we not, instead of burning fuel to make refrigeration, imagine economies of energy by using the natural freezing temperature of the deep water of the oceans for storage?

We have few technological problems today that would prevent the creation of ocean cities, but we have an abundance of people problems. The time it takes will be shortened as our purpose is strengthened. If we have no purposeful goal, it will be done anyway, but by others. Like putting man on the moon, our goal is man on, in, and under the sea. People would back it. They like imagination and challenge. They are tired of pedestrian whittling. We can help fire their imagination by paying attention to the art, literature, and music of the sea, which Professor John Craven explores in this volume. We must not allow gloomy predictions to destroy imagination. We must take a few chances. There is no "zero risk." When we cross Main Street, we take a risk but gain the benefit of reaching the other side. The sea is only a step from Main Street. Let us extend Main Street into the sea through our American ingenuity.

POTENTIAL OF "SEA GRANT"

It was for the purpose of extending Main Street into the sea that, in 1963, I conceived the national Sea Grant program to act as the transmission belt for taking our extensive marine science and know-how out of the laboratories to the productive user community.

Sea Grant has been successful in turning good ideas into good, useful products and practices for people's well-being. Yet now the whole program is endangered for reasons of economy. I have communicated my concern to the President of the United States, to the Secretary of the

Department of Commerce and members of Congress closest to consideration of the proposed cuts. I have noted four useful activities within the
National Oceanic and Atmospheric Administration that could be
trimmed to effect economies but should not under any circumstances be
cut. They are the weather service, the map and chart-making activity,
overseeing fisheries, and Sea Grant. Much of the rest of NOAA could be
eliminated completely with no loss to the nation's ocean business.

The basic intent of Sea Grant still is to translate the ideas and skills
inherent in our university system to industry. One of its founding principles was the transfer of government activity to the private sector. That the
program may appear to have moved away from this principle is not, in my
opinion, sufficient reason for terminating it. Rather, effort should be
made to put Sea Grant back on track, where it can contribute substantially
to the increase of national productivity.

To cite just one example of the worth of Sea Grant, work accomplished
under it at the University of Southern California was instrumental in
saving 1,400 jobs and millions of dollars by proving that cannery wastes
from the Southern California tuna industry can enhance rather than
pollute (as contended by the Environmental Protection Agency) the marine environment.

We in the universities should be not only scholars, however distinguished. We must also be doers. And it behooves us also, as it must all
who treasure the legacy of the Yankee Mariner, to put ourselves in tune
with the humanities of the sea, so important to the involvement of people.
John Craven helps mightily elsewhere in this book, and I add one small
sample, written especially for this conference by my wife.

THE NEW FRONTIER

> Cast off, New Pioneer, the anchor of the land,
> Sail out upon the ocean wild and wide.
> No more be tied to valley, plain or sand,
> Now turn your face to water, wind and tide.
>
> The new frontier awaits your taming hand,
> As full of life and danger as the old.
> The challenge of the deep can satisfy
> The drive once aimed at California's gold.
>
> By stately clipper ships around the Horn,
> In wagon trains across the mountains tall,

Men, not for gold but for adventure born,
Subdued a continent — beasts, savages and all,

It took stout hearts to pacify your land;
Your fathers roamed from sea to shining sea.
Now cities stretch their tentacles of steel
And concrete over land no longer free.

Return, New Pioneer, to Mother Sea,
Whose bosom held you once in ages past,
Before her children crept onto the shore,
Forsaking her to forage in the grass.

Through eons long, at last evolved a man
Whose veins still carry traces of her brine,
Whose heart must answer to her siren song,
Who meets her challenge with his hands and mind.

Return, New Pioneer, not on your knees,
The way you left, but walking tall and proud.
Your mother offers you a new frontier,
Great riches and adventure — or a shroud.

Your grave may lie on her abyssal plain,
No stone to mark the mouldering of your bones.
If so, by your own weakness you'll be slain.
None but her strongest sons may call her home.

Oh, can you meet her challenge, Pioneer?
Is your courage yet of such great worth?
You've conquered every portion of the land —
'Tis but a tiny fraction of the Earth.

Return, New Pioneer, and test your strength;
Accept the challenge of your Mother Sea.
She'll best you if she can; but if you win
She'll, like a loving mother, set you free.

THE NEW PIONEER
(A Response)

Oh, I accept your challenge, Mother Sea,
For I am Man, the Conqueror, whose sword
Has beaten down each landed enemy.
I'll bend you to my will and be your lord.

My fathers braved your fury once before,
For they had heard the call of liberty.
In storm-tossed cockleshells they gained this shore
And forged a nation destined to be free.

I stand upon this pinnacle of rock
And fling my laughter in your raging face.
"Oh, puny man," your torrents seem to mock.
You've yet to test the mettle of my race.

All riches from your watery depths I'll wrest
And take my joy in your surrendering.
I'll work my will upon your heaving breast;
Your child will be your lover and your king.

— Kathleen FitzGerald Spilhaus

The Yankee Mariner, Seventeenth to Twentieth Centuries

Craig L. Symonds

A clear understanding of the importance of sea power, past, present, and future, is an aspect of the national experience that we cannot afford to ignore. Athelstan Spilhaus, in his introduction to this book, notes, quite accurately, that America's commitment to support of its maritime endeavors—naval, commercial, and in terms of ocean resources—has been an "on again, off again" process. I would claim that this is not necessarily a bad thing, and in explanation adopt his own analogy, the three-legged stool.

Dr. Spilhaus remarks that when the legs of this stool are sheared off by neglect or as the result of poor policy decisions, we are likely to get our bottoms wet. Likewise, if one leg is much shorter than the others, we are likely to fall off the stool.

But there is a third possibility: that we make the legs too *long*. Raised on a precarious perch, created by an inappropriate commitment to these mutually dependent aspects of sea power, we may find ourselves crashing to the ground—or into deep water.

I do not think that, given the current circumstances of our national position and the international environment, this is likely, but in the past, it was often a very real possibility. An overcommitment to sea power can be as dangerous a policy decision as an undercommitment.

There is a tendency on the part of historians and non-historians alike to judge the policies of the past on the basis of how appropriate they would be today. This is clearly both unreasonable and not fair to those who made the policy in the first place. The more I study the past, the more I appreciate the insight and wisdom of those who charted our course in their own time. They were not often any less farsighted about the sea than we are today, but they made ocean policy—naval and maritime— appropriate to their own time. So must we, and further, we must recognize that the times have changed.

A summary of American ocean policy from its beginnings to the twentieth century is a broad topic, so I shall adopt a convenient device used by most historians and break it down into chapters. First I will address the genesis and development of America's dependence on the sea from the time of its founding in the early seventeenth century to its declaration of independence from Britain in 1776. This was an epoch dominated by an economic philosophy known as the mercantilist system, of which the principal tenet was that the accumulation of national wealth through a favorable balance of trade was the only sure path to national strength and national greatness. It was an economic policy that impacted decisively on the English colonies in America in two ways: first, because it involved Britain in a number of wars with her mercantilist rivals—France and Spain—wars into which the American colonists were drawn; and, second, because a primary means of accumulating the national wealth that was the goal of all seventeenth century nations was the exploitation of the material wealth of their colonies. Nevertheless, it was in this epoch that the first colonists learned to appreciate the extent of the sea's largesse and of their dependence on it.

Second, I will deal with the era of dramatic American economic growth in the hundred years after the end of the American Revolution in 1783. This era was dominated by a very different economic doctrine defined by Adam Smith in his book *The Wealth of Nations*, published in the very year of American independence. This is a policy most often referred to as *laissez-faire*. Throughout the nineteenth century, the United States encouraged the expansion of national industries through favorable domestic legislation and maintained a non-aligned posture in foreign affairs. In this century, naval power belonged to Britain. The Royal Navy patrolled the seven seas as the "cop on the beat" for Western civilization. In part it was Britain's commitment to world stability—the *Pax Britannica*—that enabled Americans to achieve their remarkable national and economic growth.

Then, finally, I will discuss the awakening of the sleeping giant in the late nineteenth century, when it found itself in a highly competitive and dangerous world as it attempted to carve out for itself a niche in the world balance of power. This movement culminated in American entry into World War I, in which it was not only a major combatant but also one of the chief architects of the peace. In 1919, however, the metamorphosis was only half complete, and it would take another world war before America became the new mistress of the seas and began an era that some future historian may well refer to as the *Pax Americana.*

In all three of these epochs—the colonial experience, the century of economic growth, and the dawn of world power—the United States, if not always a naval power, was nevertheless always a sea power. Through it all, America depended on the sea for its food, its trade, its transport, and its security. It has truly been "the gem of the ocean."

Yankee Mariner Beginnings

To begin, then, at the beginning: The history of the Yankee Mariner in the seventeenth century is the history of New England. Nothing—not even its religion—defined the political and economic geography of New England quite so much as its maritime character. Exploitation of the sea constituted its first industries, fed its earliest citizens, and employed its workers. Seaborne trade was the focus of its first cities, and the profits from that trade built the buildings, wharves, piers, shipyards, and storehouses that determined the pattern of settlement and even dictated the social structure of its classes. Throughout the seventeenth century, Americans drew on the sea as the source for most of their wealth and livelihood. Fishing, whaling, shipbuilding, and, of course, trade were the dominant industries.

FISHING, WHALING, SHIPBUILDING

Fishing was the earliest form of exploiting the wealth of the sea. But it was not until the English Civil War in the 1640s that colonial fishing became a business rather than merely a means of sustenance. For the first few decades after 1620, the fishing industry was controlled by London merchants. The management of a large fleet of fishing vessels required large-scale financing beyond the capability of New Englanders. The great fishing banks of New England and Newfoundland, therefore, were harvested by fleets out of Bristol and Liverpool rather than those of Boston or Marblehead. The disruption of the English Civil War, however, provided a break in the visits of English ships to the Grand Banks and gave American seamen their opportunity. By mid-century, most of the fishing was being done out of American ports, and the colonies had their first major export. By the end of the century there were more than 120 colonial fishing ships manned by some 2,700 men on the cod banks on a regular basis.[1]

It is significant, however, that the financial support for this endeavor continued to come from London. Americans had discovered that major financial backing was necessary to achieve major financial success, particularly in any large-scale enterprise. As Bernard Bailyn noted in his book *New England Merchants in the Seventeenth Century,*

> Without some capital with which to equip the fishermen, advance sums for catches when they became available, and buy up the necessary fishing stages, boats, line, and nets needed to expand their business, they [the Americans] could not have commanded the fish they were called upon to supply.[2]

This is, of course, no less true today than it was in 1700. Indeed the question of fishing rights and national support for fishing fleets is very much a current issue. Government-owned and -run Soviet fishing fleets are even now reaping an enormous profit from the fishing banks only a few score miles off our own coast.

Akin to fishing in terms of deriving direct wealth from the sea was the whaling industry. At first colonists merely took advantage of the sea's largesse by harvesting those few whales that were washed ashore by Atlantic storms or that drifted ashore. But by 1700, Americans were putting to sea in search of the huge mammals. Most coveted of all were the sperm whales, the oil from which would sell for as much as eight shillings an ounce in the apothecary shops of Boston and London.[3] It was a highly risky business, both financially and personally, but it was very profitable when successful. I might note, parenthetically, that it was the whaling industry that stimulated America's literary reputation as well. Herman Melville's classic *Moby Dick,* later recognized as the first great American novel, helped erase the widely held belief in Europe that all Americans were illiterate savages.

Shipbuilding was America's first successful manufacturing industry. The American seaboard was a natural factory for ships in the age of sail. The oak for the hulls and the tall pines for the masts were handy and apparently limitless. Tar to caulk the hulls and hemp to manufacture the ropes were also common on the Atlantic seaboard. In the half-century between 1675 and 1725, America built and launched more than two thousand ocean-going vessels in New England alone, and of that number at least 25 percent were sold abroad, thus reversing the traditional trading pattern where the colony produced only raw materials and the mother country did the manufacturing.[4]

THE "TRIANGULAR TRADE"

As important as fishing, whaling, and shipbuilding were in the colonial economy, the single most important business was trade. As in fishing, most early commerce had originated out of the British Isles, making the settlers dependent on the regular ships from England that brought them the manufactured goods they so desperately needed. The middleman's profits in all of this trade, both going and coming, thus went into the pockets of the Bristol and London merchants. Yankee entrepreneurs, however, were quick to catch on to the enormous profits to be made in this process. The early focus of their interest was in the West Indies, where the plantation owners were recording enormous profits by exploiting slave labor to produce huge harvests of sugar and tobacco—crops that were so profitable the plantation owners preferred to import food for the slaves rather than commit precious soil to its production. Yankee merchants were more than willing to trade them the food, and later the slaves themselves, for cargoes of sugar and tobacco that brought high prices in England. To an ever-increasing degree, American-owned and American-manned merchant ships were to be found in the famous triangular trade: transporting foodstuffs to the Caribbean, sugar and tobacco to England, and manufactured goods to America. Another more sinister and even more profitable triangular trade developed as Yankee merchants carried New England rum to West Africa, traded it for a cargo of human beings, and traded them as slaves in the Caribbean for molasses, to return to New England ports with a substantial profit at each exchange.

But as in the fishing industry, colonial merchants discovered that their trade could prosper only when the individual entrepreneur could count on two things: adequate business contacts in England and protection by the Royal Navy. Few successful shipping firms were without a permanent office in London, usually supervised by a brother, son, or cousin of the shipowner in Boston or Philadelphia.

"ENGLISH GOODS IN ENGLISH SHIPS"

Englishmen on both sides of the Atlantic recognized the critical role of the trade carrier—the middleman—in seventeenth and eighteenth century economics. So spectacular were the profits that could be made in seaborne commerce—100 percent was considered average—that Oliver Cromwell in his capacity as Lord High Protector felt constrained in 1651 to issue a law that, although based on earlier navigation acts, was then and is still referred to as simply THE Navigation Act. Its principles were clear. Based on a faith in the mercantilist economic theory, the act declared that goods carried into English ports must be carried in English ships or in ships belonging to the country of origin. Its purpose also was clear. It was designed to prevent merchants of other nations, particularly Holland, from monopolizing the lucrative carrying trade. The declaration led to a trio of wars between England and the Dutch that lasted through the 1670s and ended in a decisive English victory—a victory so decisive, in fact, that although English naval and maritime supremacy was repeatedly challenged, it remained dominant for more than two centuries afterward.

At first the Navigation Act worked to the advantage of the Yankee Mariner. The banning of foreign ships from American ports—and, after all, American ports in the seventeenth century were still British— eliminated foreign competition. Not until late in the eighteenth century did they begin to appreciate that the mercantile system could also work to their disadvantage. The crucial political and economic decisions were being made in London by Englishmen who believed that colonies existed solely for the benefit of the mother country. In a word, colonies existed in order to be exploited. If enforced rigorously, such a policy would have kept America in the status of permanent economic fealty.

But it was not enforced. Despite the passage of numerous acts designed to limit America's opportunities for domestic manufacture, the colonists ignored the laws and continued to enjoy a booming trade and, simultaneously, the development of domestic political institutions of which they became very proud and very jealous.

TRADE WARS AND NAVAL SKIRMISHES

England's mercantile policy did, however, impact very strongly on the maritime fleets of other powers—Spain and France in particular. They in turn adopted mercantilist policies of their own designed to protect their colonies from visits by foreign merchants—in other words, if any exploiting was to be done here, they wanted to do the exploiting. Enterprising Britons and Americans, however, could not resist the high prices being offered in the Spanish-American colonies, and soon Massachusetts-built ships were hawking New England wares along the coast of Central and South America. Many such merchants encountered resistance from the Spanish authorities. One English captain named Jenkins was turned back by a Spanish coastal patrol ship, and afterward Jenkins himself, brandishing the evidence which he had preserved in a jar, testified before Parliament that his ear had actually been cut off by the Spanish brute as a warning to others. Thus began the war subsequently called "the War of Jenkins' Ear" between England and Spain, and later France, for domination of colonial shipping.[5]

Americans, too, fought in these wars—a whole series of them lasting to 1763—and in the process they discovered that they could organize large expeditions on their own, like the one that captured the French fortress of Louisburg at the entrance to the St. Lawrence River. And throughout all these wars, Americans also managed to continue to reap huge profits by trading, it must be admitted, to both sides.

The point of this is that maritime power and maritime profits did not fall to Britain or America solely by virtue of favorable geography and dauntless entrepreneurs, though certainly both were important factors. Britain was dominant at sea because she had a national economic policy that fostered a favorable balance of trade as a national goal—a goal she was willing to defend even at the cost of war.

The New Nation: Maritime Growth

For Americans this era came to an end with the achievement of independence. In this new era, America embarked on a truly national experience. Free now from both the limitations and the protection of the British mercantile system, the nation was no less dependent on the sea. Whaling declined in importance, especially after the success of Drake's petroleum well at Titusville, but trade and shipbuilding continued as dominant industries. In addition, Americans now bore the responsibility for a national naval policy to protect these industries.

The need for some national direction, if not support, was made immediately manifest by the British threat to apply the restrictions of the Navigation Act to Americans and exclude them from British seaports.

This somewhat spiteful but thoroughly consistent policy denied Yankee Mariners access to their most lucrative markets. While American diplomats tried to find a political solution, American merchants sought more immediate relief by finding new markets elsewhere. As early as 1784, only a year after the end of the Revolution, a New York merchant ship aptly named *Empress of China* crossed the Atlantic, rounded the Cape of Good Hope, and proceeded across the Indian Ocean and through the Sunda Straits to Canton. She returned with a modest profit of only $30,000. But soon other ships duplicated this feat, and by 1789 one observer noted the presence of no fewer than fifteen American ships in the harbor at Canton on a single day. At the same time, Americans opened commercial ties in the Baltic, in India, and on the Northwest coast of North America where the *Columbia* claimed the land for the United States during its circumnavigation of the globe in 1787–90.[6]

Americans learned, too, that the game of restrictive maritime legislation could work both ways. In 1789 Congress passed an act which required American merchant ships to pay a duty of six cents a ton on imported cargoes, but which required foreign ships, including British, to pay *fifty* cents a ton. This act, plus the natural American advantage in shipbuilding, gave American merchant commerce a needed boost. As a result, American merchant tonnage nearly tripled in a single year.[7]

TRADE REQUIRES PROTECTION

This dramatic expansion in American merchant shipping was a responsibility as well as a blessing. Three times in two decades the United States went to war to defend its seaborne commerce from foreign threats. First it was from French privateers in the Caribbean. Bitter about the lack of gratitude displayed by Americans who refused to help them fight Britain in the wars that broke out after their own revolution, the French attacked American merchantmen trading with Britain's West Indian colonies. This was the genesis of the so-called Quasi War which, like other more recent wars, was no less violent for being undeclared. Next came a series of small but bitter naval wars between the United States and the Barbary powers of the North African coast. These conflicts ended satisfactorily for the United States. But the war that broke out with Britain in 1812 did not go well. The British Royal Navy was undisputed mistress of the seas, and by 1813 she had slapped a tight blockade on the American coast, bottling up the small American navy as well as American merchantmen.

There were some bright spots in this war—the United States won twelve of sixteen ship-to-ship duels—but on the whole the war demonstrated vividly that bravado was no substitute for strength.

The lesson of these wars was that trade required protection. But for the United States in the early nineteenth century, the difficulty was not in appreciating the lesson, but in the ability to apply it. The naval strength that would have been necessary to match Great Britain on the sea in 1812 was simply beyond America's capabilities. Though future exponents of American naval power would look back on 1812 and conclude that the nation had adopted a poor strategy by not building up a battleship navy and deploying it as a concentrated squadron, such plans in the early nineteenth century would have been purely visionary.[8]

Instead, the United States acquiesced in the fact of British domination of the sea lanes, and when in 1823 President Monroe issued the famous Doctrine that bears his name warning European powers not to attempt any political interference in the Western hemisphere, it was not America's warning but the backing of the Royal Navy that made it effective. Indeed, the nineteenth century was an era of a *Pax Britannica,* a quiescent period presided over both figuratively and literally by bewhiskered British flag officers.

GREAT SHIPBUILDING ERA

This is not to say that Americans were inactive on the sea. Far from it. American merchant commerce continued to flourish. Indeed, several factors combined to boost American merchant trade in the mid-nineteenth century. The most important of these was the discovery of gold in California in 1848. Many of the so-called 49ers trekked overland to California in search of El Dorado, but the vast majority went by sea, either around Cape Horn or by transiting the isthmus at Panama. So ferocious was the demand for transport to the gold fields that American shipbuilders could barely keep up with it. It was partly to meet this demand that John Griffiths designed a new ship-type with tall slender masts and a rakish lean hull that soon came to be known as the American clipper ship.

The age of the clipper did not last beyond the 1850's, but while it did they dominated the long runs: New York to San Francisco, San Francisco to China, and even China to London. Meanwhile, American shipbuilders continued to produce a nearly-staggering number of vessels—more than

2,600 ships of all types were constructed in the twelve years after 1843. And these vessels carried a prodigious amount of trade—$360 million in 1855 alone.[9]

A second factor that helped promote this trade was the repeal, in 1849, of the British Navigation Acts. This final renunciation of the old mercantilist system opened up British ports to all comers and thus began unfettered competition. Americans were quick to respond. Their newly-built clippers made the run from Canton to London weeks ahead of the tubby East Indiamen whose commerce had previously been protected, and the British found themselves falling behind the Americans as carriers of seaborne commerce. In the 1850's, American merchant commerce reached a peak of nearly two and one-half million deadweight tons annually.

NAVAL POLICY REFLECTS INSULAR FOREIGN POLICY

By contrast, American naval policy after a brief burst of national enthusiasm in 1816, was very modest. In part this was because of a quiescent world situation, and in part because of a foreign policy that was insular—if not quite isolationist. One by one the Navy's small squadrons were assigned to distant stations where they were expected to oversee American interests. A Mediterranean squadron kept a wary eye on the Barbary states; a Caribbean squadron tried to keep piracy there under control; a Pacific squadron watched over the American whaling fleet; and an African squadron sought to stifle the now-illegal but still highly profitable trade in human beings. This was not an ambitious naval policy by any means—indeed, commanders were expressly instructed to avoid confrontations with the great powers—but it was a policy that suited the needs of the country well enough and for a half-century afterward.

In addition, the U.S. Navy embarked on a dozen or more scientific and exploratory expeditions which brought great credit to the nation. The most spectacular was the Wilkes Expedition, named after its commander, Lieutenant Charles Wilkes, a somewhat tyrannical skipper who led a handful of American ships on an information-gathering and exploring cruise to Antarctica and the South Pacific. Everywhere they went, the scientists on the expedition gathered local flora and fauna and, when possible, named and classified it. When the expedition returned in 1842, the collected samples made up the original treasures of the now-famous Smithsonian Institution. No voyage save perhaps those of Columbus and Darwin was more fruitful in its contributions to scientific knowledge.[10]

SEA POWER IN THE CIVIL WAR

The great national trauma of the nineteenth century, of course, was the American Civil War. Modern America was molded in the cauldron of that gigantic conflict that claimed more American lives than all its other foreign wars combined, including both World Wars. At sea the Union Navy dominated the Confederate coast as easily as Britain had done in 1813, but also like Britain, the Union Navy had to attempt to run down enemy commerce raiders. Ships like the *Alabama, Florida,* and *Shenandoah* sought to so punish Northern trade that Yankee merchants would cry out to let the South go. In that goal, of course, they failed. But in a bizarre way they also succeeded; for so fearful were Northern shippers of Confederate raiders and the high maritime insurance rates they encouraged, that they either adopted British registry for their ships, or sold out to foreigners and found new avenues of investment altogether. Between 1861 and 1864, a total of 609 U.S. vessels actually changed their national registry; and this does not take into account new vessels that took up foreign registration upon launching. In 1861, more than 65 percent of all American foreign trade was carried in American vessels; by 1865 that had dropped to less than 33 percent. The American merchant fleet, which had been threatening to become the world's greatest carrier of seaborne commerce, was suddenly devastated.[11]

While the merchant marine declined, the Navy grew. For the Navy, the Civil War was a catalyst for dramatic expansion. In order to blockade the extensive Confederate coastline, some 3,500 miles in length, the Union Navy had to expand from an initial 42 ships, mostly scattered around the globe on distant station patrol, to more than 700 vessels by 1865. This was not the product of a systematic plan but of a panicky buying and building of ships of all types—sail, steam, yachts, even ferry boats. Nevertheless, many of these new warships were steam-driven ironclads, and it was a sea force of sufficient size to concern even the British.

AMERICA TURNS FROM THE SEA

They need not have been concerned. At war's end this giant Union armada was disbanded. There simply was not adequate justification for its continuation in peacetime. In the *Alabama* case, England apologized and paid an indemnity for its flirtation with the Confederacy, and as the world entered the full flower of the Victorian Age, Americans exploited their built-in empire to the west, and Britain reasserted its mastery of the seas.

A principal component of that mastery was the early British commitment to steam navigation. The British government encouraged research
and development in steamships by granting subsidies in the form of mail
contracts to shipping lines. For a while this challenge was staved off by
the American clippers, but only temporarily. By the 1870s the innovation
of the triple expansion engine had increased steam efficiency to the point
where large cargo vessels could carry very heavy bulk cargo cheaper and
faster than sailing ships.

The United States did not lack the technological skill to produce large
and efficient merchant steamers. Indeed the first successful steamer, the
Clermont, was the product of an American inventor. What the United
States lacked was a national program of public support such as existed in
Britain. A U.S. steamship line, the Collins line, operated briefly in the
1850s, thanks in part to a government mail contract. But the contract was
not renewed and the line failed. Other later attempts proved too little, too
late.

American policy makers in the post-Civil War years were not necessarily wrong, however, in their ambivalence toward both the Navy and the
merchant marine. After all, American commerce and industry had higher
priorities. If subsidies were denied merchant steamship companies, the
government was more than forthcoming with grants and subsidies to the
railroads, a form of transportation even more critical to American economic development in the 1870s than was shipping. A good case can be
made that the American policy of virtually ignoring the country's maritime frontiers in the two decades after Appomattox was a reasonable one.
Naval and maritime affairs ought, after all, to depend on national circumstances, and in the circumstances of the 1870s the American West had
a higher priority than the merchant fleet or the Navy.

MISTAKEN NAVAL POLICY?

American naval policy in the nineteenth century has often been criticized by naval historians. After all, they point out, the United States
allowed its Navy to deteriorate to that of a third-rate power. It continued
to rely on wooden-hulled, sail-powered vessels in a time when a technological revolution was leading European nations to build steam and steel
battleships.

On the surface, such facts constitute a serious indictment of American
policy-makers. But in fact there were very practical reasons for refusing to

apply the new technology to naval and maritime construction, and very few compelling reasons for such an American naval commitment. First, there was the fact that steam warships required coal to fuel the engines. Then, as now, the United States had more than adequate supplies of coal, but the problem was that we had no overseas bases where coal for U.S. ships could be stockpiled. A U.S. steam vessel on its way to Canton, for example, had to re-coal no less than seven times en route, thus making itself dependent mainly on British facilities at Capetown, Singapore, and so on—a situation that worked well enough in peacetime, but which was uncertain in time of war, especially if Britain turned out to be the enemy. In a word, the United States Navy, lacking any overseas bases, was not energy independent.

Second, America's thoughts were mostly inward, toward her developing lands in the West, to her burgeoning cities in the Northeast, and to rebuilding the war-torn South. There was no external threat. Europe's eyes, too, were turned inward: to Germany, where Otto von Bismarck, known as the Iron Chancellor, was redrawing the political map of Europe. Perhaps, then, American naval policy-makers were not so foolish after all.[12]

EVALUATION BASED ON MISSION

The key to evaluating any naval policy is a careful determination of its mission. In short, to decide what kind of navy is wanted, it must first be determined what that navy is to do. This was true in the nineteenth century; it is true today. The answers are to be found in constant and concerned evaluation of world events and of America's position in the world community, by cognizant government agencies and the public forum.

Chapter 2 of this broad survey thus ends in the 1870s with the United States caught up in a temporary miasma. Its merchant fleet was reduced by the flight from the flag during the Civil War. American merchantmen carried only 23 percent of the nation's commerce in 1880 and 12 percent in 1890. Its Navy, only a few years earlier the largest in the world, was growing obsolete. Even the New England fishing and whaling fleets had fallen on hard times. Competition from Canadian fishermen and the higher wages available in U.S. factories led men away from the sea to other occupations.

But there were straws of change in the wind: American industry was

booming; the vast natural resources of our continent were being discovered and mined; the abundance of God's gift to the land was only
beginning to be appreciated, and Americans were swift to exploit it.
Between 1870 and 1900 the GNP grew by 82 percent! Adopting the
Bessemer process, U.S. steel production outstripped that of both Britain
and Germany by the 1880s, increasing 1900 percent in the three decades
before 1900. This new and growing national wealth contributed to an era
of national awareness, and, for better or for worse, the United States
became drawn into the international power game. Chapter 3, therefore, is
an era of international involvement.

The United States Becomes a World Power

This era is characterized by a sequence of events and policy decisions
that transformed the United States into a world power, not only in economic terms, but in military and naval terms as well. Our participation in
the First World War was dramatic and unmistakable evidence of that new
status, but Americans were hard pressed to reconcile themselves to this
very real fact. Though they might seek a return to the Jeffersonian policy
of no entangling alliances, they would discover that the act of being a
world power depends less on one's own policies than it does on the
considerations of others.

Nevertheless, the first step on this road was a deliberate one: in the
1880s, the United States began to build a modern navy. In 1885 the first
steam-powered and steel-hulled battleships, the *Maine* and the *Texas*,
were authorized. And two years later, the keels for three more were laid
down in the building yards.

What is curious about this naval renaissance is that no one had, as yet,
codified the reasons why it was necessary; many people had a general,
unarticulated feeling that it was a good idea, but there was no clear body
of thought that explained the rationale of possessing naval power. That
void was filled by Alfred Thayer Mahan.

THE MAHAN INFLUENCE

As a lecturer at the newly founded Naval War College in Newport,
Rhode Island, Mahan authored a series of talks on the impact sea power
had had on world events. He based his study on the experience of
England in the century and a half after the Anglo-Dutch Wars, and came

to the not very startling conclusion that it had been sea power that had made Britain great. Wealth, he said, is the clearest measure of greatness, and Britain's wealth came mainly from its seaborne commerce. Therefore, a large merchant marine and a strong navy to protect it were the elements of national greatness. His analysis was, in fact, nothing less than a prescription. Follow these rules, he implied, and you too can be great. Not all of Mahan's conclusions have borne the test of time—he was an unrelenting defender of the battleship as queen of the sea—but his recognition of the crucial role of trade and naval forces in historical development is seldom denied.[13]

With Mahan's prescription as a semiofficial guide, the United States continued to expand its Navy in the 1890s, and at the end of the decade the nation used its new Navy to fight a naval war with Spain and gain an overseas empire. Almost immediately thereafter, an assassin's bullet led into the presidency Theodore Roosevelt, a man who wielded the big stick with relish and who sent the Great White Fleet around the world. Probably no other single event so clearly marked a turning point in American foreign policy as that voyage. Far from avoiding foreign entanglements, the United States was serving notice unmistakably that it was determined to assume the role of a major power.

At the same time, a newly unified Germany challenged Britain's control of European waters by launching a naval building program of its own. The twin threats of American and German naval expansion threatened to destroy the *Pax Britannica*. What finally ended it, of course, was World War I.

WORLD WAR I AND NAVAL EXPANSION

That catastrophe proved not to be the short war both sides had anticipated. Instead it degenerated into a war of attrition, and as the war lengthened, Britain and France—the Western Allies—became increasingly dependent on food and supplies from the United States. The Germans, of course, sought to break those supply lines. To do so, they relied on a new and very effective commerce raider—the U-boat.

Once again, as during the Napoleonic wars almost exactly a century before, the United States found itself caught in the middle of a stalemated war between a sea power and a land power. In 1812 it had been the sea power—Britain—that had so harassed American trade that the nation finally committed itself to war. This time it was the land power that broke America's patience, employing the traditional commerce raiding strategy of the weaker naval power.

America's role in World War I was decisive. Our few hundred thousand troops helped turn the tide on the Western Front, but more important, the material goods convoyed across the Atlantic by British and American escorts helped ensure the allied victory. Finally, the psychological impact of the arrival of fresh troops boosted the morale of one side and helped break that of the other.

After the war, wearied by a long struggle and burdened with debts, Britain was unable to reassert its dominant role as a stabilizing influence, and with Germany defeated, the United States was widely heralded as Britain's successor. After all, the nation's industrial plant had produced a prodigious number of new vessels during the war, and, counting the armada of battleships still on the building ways when the war ended, the United States hovered on the brink of becoming the world's foremost naval power. There was a vocal and influential group in the United States—the heirs of Mahan and Teddy Roosevelt—who argued that the nation should proceed with the building program. All Mahan's now-familiar arguments were dragged out to justify the program. But most Americans could not understand why naval expansion was necessary when "the war to end all wars" had just been fought and won. To wrest the trident of naval power from Britain's hands required more than just the material wherewithal to do so; it required a national *will* to do so. Moreover, to participate in an expensive naval building race with the nation that was our closest ally struck many Americans as particularly foolhardy. Instead, the United States hosted a naval disarmament conference in which Britain and the United States agreed to parity in capital ships and relegated the other naval powers to a lesser standard.[14]

This was an agreement often criticized by later observers who point out that the United States deliberately threw away naval preeminence and even agreed to refrain from fortifying its Pacific bases. But the key point to appreciate in this agreement is that because of financial cutbacks the United States did not even build up to the limits imposed on it by the treaty. In effect, then, the treaty did *not* limit us at all. If there had been *no* limit, we would not have built more than we did. It did, however, effectively limit Japanese naval expansion, at least into the 1930s. By then, of course, even the most optimistic observer of world affairs recognized the danger signals emanating from Germany and Japan, and the United States passed a whopping naval expansion bill in 1938.

THE RESPONSIBILITIES OF POWER

Several lessons can be drawn from this third chapter in the history of American sea power. The first is that a nation that finds itself in the front ranks of the world's powers as determined by wealth, population, and industrial production will perforce be involved in the balance of power computations of the other great powers, whether it seeks that status or not. The United States could not simply choose to remain uninvolved. It could choose to be ineffective, but not uninvolved.

The second lesson is that our ability to retain a viable alliance with our European allies—with Britain in particular—is dependent on our ability to keep open and flowing what strategists call the sea lines of communication across the Atlantic. The German U-boat threat proved that a war against these lines was a blow aimed at the very survival of the Island Empire. Winston Churchill, who was First Lord of the Admiralty in the Great War, later wrote of another war that "we must regard this struggle at sea as the foundation of all the efforts of the United Nations. If we lose that, all else will be denied us."[15]

A third lesson is that arms limitations programs can work to the advantage of the participants if a pragmatic and realistic approach is adopted and if one negotiates from strength.

In the face of new threats—economic, environmental, and military— we must remain aware of both the blessings and the dangers of our dependence on the sea. We are a sea power; we cannot be otherwise. What we must do is devise well-thought-out and practical national policies to exploit the riches of the sea, protect its environment, and guard its frontiers.

NOTES

1. Bernard Bailyn, *New England Merchants in the Seventeenth Century* (Cambridge, Mass., 1979), pp. 48–49.

2. *Ibid.*, p. 82.

3. Samuel W. Bryant, *The Sea and the States, A Maritime History of the American People* (New York, 1967), p. 46.

4. Joseph A. Goldenberg, *Shipbuilding in Colonial America* (Newport News, Virginia, 1976). See also Chapter 1 of Howard I. Chapelle, *The History of the American Sailing Navy* (New York, 1949).

5. See Walter L. Dorn, *Competition for Empire, 1740–1763* (New York, 1940).

6. Bryant, p. 112.

7. *Ibid.*, p. 115.

8. See Craig Symonds, *Navalists and Antinavalists: The Naval Policy Debate in the United States, 1785–1827* (Newark, Delaware, 1980).

9. Bryant, p. 274.

10. See William Stanton, *The Great United States Exploring Expedition of 1838–1842* (Berkeley, California, 1975). For other such expeditions see Vincent Ponko, *Ships, Seas, and Scientists* (Annapolis, Maryland, 1975).

11. G. W. Dalzell, *The Flight from the Flag: The Continuing Effect of the Civil War upon the American Carrying Trade* (New York, 1940).

12. This argument is ably presented by Lance Buhl in his chapter entitled "Maintaining an 'American Navy,' 1865–1889" in Kenneth J. Hagan, ed., *In Peace and War, Interpretations of American Naval History, 1775–1978* (Westport, Conn., 1978).

13. Alfred Thayer Mahan, *The Influence of Sea Power upon History, 1660–1783* (Boston, 1890). For a negative view of Mahan and his impact, see Robert Seager, *Alfred Thayer Mahan, the Man and His Letters* (Annapolis, Maryland, 1977).

14. See Harold and Margaret Sprout, *Toward a New Order of Sea Power, American Naval Policy and the World Scene, 1918–1922* (Princeton, New Jersey, 1940).

15. Quoted in Robert G. Albion and Jennie B. Pope, *Sea Lanes in Wartime, The American Experience, 1775–1945* (New York, 1942), p. 9.

Ocean Science and Engineering, the Foundation of Effective Use of the Sea

Andreas B. Rechnitzer

This nation and its men of the sea—the Yankee Mariner—have been linked together since the day this country was discovered by seafaring men. The early growth of the American colonies was strongly supported by trade with the old world and the transport of emigrants. As we have learned from history, the merchant marine posture of the United States has waxed and waned, but the importance of the Yankee Mariner remains high, and perhaps crucial to the future of this nation.

Just who or what is a Yankee Mariner? Clearly those who use the sea for commerce, the merchant mariners, are the first to come to mind. Those who harvest or otherwise exploit the natural resources of the sea are Yankee Mariners. Those who provide national security—our Navy, Marines, and Coast Guard—are Yankee Mariners of the seven seas. Also in the community are the scientists, engineers, technicians, and the other professionals whom we recognize collectively as "oceanographers." Then there is a hard-to-define category of those who rarely, if ever, go to sea, but derive a livelihood from the Yankee Mariners, for example, sea lawyers, insurers, naval architects, and others.

Ocean science and engineering have been used as a foundation for economic advantage in the building of our nation, including the advances of the industrial age in which we are living. Concomitantly, the building of the nation has been, at times, a great support of ocean science and engineering. In the new nation there was a strong desire to become economically successful. At the same time there was a strong desire within the scientific community to establish itself as a major force in adding to the world's knowledge.

The balanced development of our nation's sea power closely follows the perspective of theorist Alfred Thayer Mahan. He held that a state's sea power depends ultimately on three factors: the production of manufactured goods in the home country for overseas trade; commerce across the seas on its own ships; and colonies, or dependent states, on the opposite shore to provide safe ports and goods for exchange, usually raw materials to be brought back to the home country for fabrication into finished products. The function of the national navy was to advance all three elements of sea power. By dominating the sea, the navy protected the homeland from invasion and ensured that wars would be fought at sea or on other people's territory while production at home proceeded unimpeded. The nation guarded its merchant ships and drove the ships of other nations off the ocean, as necessary. The United States, in one of its proudest moments, had acquired all three elements and did indeed rise to preeminence in sea power. Although Mahan made no specific mention of the real or potential contribution marine science and engineering could make to this recipe for success, it nevertheless can be recognized that these professions were involved.

This paper deals with the practical value of marine science and engineering that served to aid the Yankee Mariner exploit the sea's resources, transport goods and people across its surface, design and fabricate superior vessels, and lead the way to new uses and management of the sea.

Beginnings: Whaling, Sealing, Fishing

The American whaling industry provided an early impetus to growth of the Yankee Mariner tradition. By 1760 the whaling industry of young America was extended to the Greenland grounds; thence to the South Pacific grounds beyond Cape Horn by 1791; and to the grounds west of Peru by 1818. In 1819 the Yankee Mariner had extended his whaling sorties to the waters off Japan. The Yankee whalemen were the frontiersmen of the sea. New England whalers were lured more by the good money and the practicality of their venture than by scientific challenge. However, logs that all kept of their voyages provide descriptions of environmental factors that often worked against them in their quest. Science would use these data to their eventual benefit and for general scientific and commercial gain.

The success of the Pacific whalers in 1817 started a whale fisheries boom that continued to the Civil War. In 1829 the whaling fleet of the United States consisted of 203 vessels, which represented about one-tenth the total tonnage of the merchant fleet that was registered for foreign trade. In 1840 the number had increased to 554, and in 1842 to 652, a fleet valued at more than twenty million dollars and providing employment for 70,000 persons.

The United States found that the southern ocean offered another valued natural resource—the fur seal. Some ninety vessels, half of them British, half American, worked the ground to such a degree that the seals rapidly disappeared. Without scientific knowledge about the population, it was beyond the sealers' comprehension that limiting the take would sustain the supply.

The deep-sea fishing of the United States was conducted entirely by New Englanders, and became known as the "Yankee monopoly." Throughout the seventeenth, eighteenth, and early nineteenth centuries, New Englanders had an unprecedented attraction to and predilection for the sea.

Early Navigation Aids

Seaborne trade became the lifeblood of the republic after the Revolution. A strong and close connection developed between seafaring men and the men of science, particularly in the subject of navigation. In the late eighteenth century, one of these men of science was Ben Franklin. While serving as Postmaster General for the colonies, he had often received complaints that mails from England were delayed. His investigations revealed that the captains of American ships were acquainted with the phenomenon of the Gulf Stream but the captains of English packets were not. Unaware of "the great river of the sea," they were bucking a four-knot current. After discussions with the most knowledgeable Yankee whalers, Franklin drew a chart of the surface current as he perceived it to exist. We recognize that this chart is a simple version of the Gulf Stream, but even today the Stream is of major interest as its characteristics continue to plague our Navy in ways of no concern to the early captains.

Nathaniel Bowditch, a distinguished American scientist of the early 1800s, produced a work of great value to mariners entitled *American Practical Navigator*. It is still available today in edited and updated form. Bowditch began his seagoing career when accurate time was not available to the average naval or merchant ship. A system of determining the elusive longitude by "lunar distance," a method not requiring an accurate timepiece, was known, but the product, in the minds of mathematicians and astronomers, was so involved as to be beyond the capabilities of the uneducated seamen of that day. Consequently, ships navigated by a combination of dead reckoning and parallel sailing (a system of sailing north or south to the latitude of destination and then east or west to the destination). A landfall accuracy of ten miles was acceptable.

Through analysis and observation, Bowditch derived a new and simplified formula, a formula that was to open the book of celestial navigation to all seamen. The first edition of his *American Practical Navigator* was published in 1802. In addition to the improved method of determining longitude, it gave a ship's officer information on winds, current, and tides; directions for surveying; statistics on marine insurance; a glossary of sea terms; instruction in mathematics; and numerous tables of navigational data. His simplified methods, easily grasped by the intelligent Yankee Mariner, paved the way for U.S. supremacy of the seas.

After Bowditch's death, his son Jonathan Ingersoll Bowditch took up the work of updating the book. In 1868 the then newly-organized U.S. Navy hydrographic office bought the copyright. Revisions kept it a best seller; by 1977, more than 850,000 copies had been sold.

Federal Agencies Established

In recognition of the scientific needs of the burgeoning merchant, whaling, sealing, and fishing fleets, President Thomas Jefferson in 1807 pushed through Congress a law establishing the first scientific agency of the federal government—the United States Coast Survey. Its first head, scientist Ferdinand Rudolph Hassler, soon found that his political problems were to be as large as his scientific ones. He faced a Congress committed to keeping the machinery of the national government as small as possible and unable to perceive any difference between the scientifically conducted surveys of professional geodesists and those of practical men without scientific training. Beginning without suitable instruments or trained personnel, and partly delayed by the War of 1812 and lack of appropriations, Hassler did not get out into the field for nine years. Then, the work barely begun was abruptly removed from civilian hands in 1818 and turned over to the U.S. Navy.

The result was seen as a setback for science. From 1818 to 1832 the civilian Coast Survey was abolished. In the same period the Congress rejected the plea of the shipping community for establishment of a national observatory, a facility claimed to be urgently needed to resolve navigational problems affecting the Yankee Mariner. In 1828 the House Committee on Naval Affairs called for an audit of the Navy's surveying activities. Secretary of the Navy Southard characterized the charts produced by the Navy as expensive and unsafe, and recommended that the law of 1807 be reinstituted. Congress had little interest in this recommendation.

DEPOT OF CHARTS AND INSTRUMENTS

In 1830 the Navy, apparently responding to earlier criticism, established the Depot of Charts and Instruments. Meanwhile, Secretary Southard kept urging re-establishment of the civilian Coast Survey, and with his help and that of the shipping lobby, it was revived in 1832. However, the naval influence was strong, inasmuch as most of the naval leaders of the day served tours of duty with the Coast Survey.

The sister government agency, the Depot of Charts and Instruments, drew heavily on officers who had gained their experience with the Coast Survey. The Depot grew rapidly in stature and influence. In 1833, Lieutenant Wilkes moved over from the Coast Survey to head the Depot. He bought a house on Capitol Hill and moved the Depot in with himself and his family. He installed a transit instrument in order to rate by the stars the chronometers which the Depot then furnished the ships of the Navy. Although this astronomical installation was a major step forward, it was not the "national observatory" for which American scientists and the shipping community had stumped. However, this was an important beginning for astronomy in the United States.

In 1836 Lt. James M. Gillis joined Wilkes at the Depot, and immediately reacted to the stinging remarks of Secretary Southard that no naval officer is capable of serious scientific work by embarking on a course to refute that opinion. He was the first scientist to make the Navy his professional base.

Introduction of the Steamboat

On page 130 of *Scientific American* for January 11, 1851, one can read:

> Let us look back to the beginning of this century and see what mighty works have been done by inventors since that time. In 1800 there was not a single steamboat in the world. Our inland seas and noble rivers were lying grand and silent in primeval loneliness except when enlivened by a clumsy batteau or the crude flatboat. In 1807 Fulton launched the *Clermont*, which made a passage to Albany in thirty-two hours. At that time the mode of travel was by schooners and sloops, which were frequently six days on the passage. The improvement was certainly great, but what would Fulton now say, to see steamboats running the same distance in eight hours—and some of them large enough to stow the *Clermont* on their forward decks. No steamboat had broken the water of the Mississippi previous to 1815; the voyage from Cincinnati to New Orleans was a tremendous undertaking, and occupied more time than a steamboat would now take to circumnavigate the globe.
>
> At present it is calculated that there are no less than 3,000 steamboats of all sizes in America, and the time saved to travellers, by the invention of the steamboat, is at least 70 percent; that is, a person can travel a greater distance in thirty days now, by steamboat, than he could in a hundred days in 1800. Just fancy Benjamin Franklin being almost wrecked in going from New York to Amboy, and the vessel in which he was, occupying thirty-two hours on the passage—a distance which is accomplished every day by our steamboats in one and one-half hours—a great change, truly.
>
> In Europe, steamboats were unknown until 1811, and no sea was regularly navigated by steamboats until 1818. The progress of marine navigation is remarkable. In 1838 no steamship had ventured across the stormy Atlantic to establish ocean navigation. Now we have communications every week with Europe, by regular steam mails; and to show the advantage of steam over mere sailing vessels, within a few days from the present date, some of our finest sailing packets have come in after a passage of fifty days, while our steamships have not been out more than sixteen days. If the last half-century had given us no other invention than the steamboat, that alone, considering its importance, is enough to immortalize it.

Great as the steamboats were, in their introduction to the shipping community they were not without need of engineering refinement. For example, on page 131 of the same issue of *Scientific American* appear these discouraging remarks under the heading of "Steamboat Explosions and the Law":

> Let me indulge myself a few moments in writing the thoughts which arose in my mind after hearing of the explosion of the *Knoxville*. I asked of myself the cause of the inefficiency of the act of Congress passed in 1838 "to provide for the better security of the lives of passengers on board a steamboat. . . ." Now, it seems to me, the appointing power should be a unit, controlled if you please, a board, and that it should be confided to a man of practical and theoretical knowledge in mechanics; one who has constant opportunities of obtaining information in relation to steam engines, navigation, explosions, manufacture of machinery—one who has time and ability to watch over the manner in which the Inspectors perform their duties. (Signed) Yankee Creole, New Orleans, Dec. 21, 1850.

The welcome call for professional scientific and engineering assistance was heeded, and standards were established by competent researchers. The ships continued to come off American shipbuilding ways. The report of the Department of the Treasury of 1850 revealed that America had 247 ships, 117 brigs, 547 schooners, 290 sloops and canal boats, and 159 steamers. In 1853, at the first meeting of the Association of Steamboat Engineers, it was revealed that in the preceding twenty-five years there had been sixty explosions and a loss of more than 3,000 lives, but that in the Cincinnati district, since enforcement of the law, not one life had been lost by explosion—a commendable improvement and one attributable to the engineering community. That there were still isolated problems is evidenced by the following sample from page 1 of the *Scientific American* for April 15, 1854 (Vol. IX, No. 31):

> We learn from the testimony taken in this remarkable case of the *Kate Kearney* that the common manner of stopping leaks in steamboat boilers is to throw in them horse dung, ropes chopped fine, potatoes, meal, etc. Sometimes lead is melted and poured in the holes, and sometimes wooden pegs answer the purpose.

The Paddle Wheel and Screw Propellor

Driving a steam vessel with the paddle wheel was quickly adopted by the Yankee Mariner, particularly for inland routes; its use on small rolling and pitching craft in the open seas left much to be desired. In 1837 American Navy Captain Robert F. Stockton saw great potential in the screw propellor for naval use, but felt that much work had to be done on the design of Swedish engineer John Ericsson before the propellor could be perfected and ready for installation on a steamship. Stockton gave Ericsson an order for two boats with steam machinery and propellors for practical demonstration in the United States. One of the vessels, bearing the name *Robert F. Stockton,* was launched in 1838. With the back-up of sails "just in case," it successfully crossed the Atlantic, the first iron vessel to do so.

In 1841 the world's first seagoing steamer driven by screw propellor to be built for either mercantile or naval service was designed and constructed in New York. Two years later forty-two vessels in America had been fitted with screws. American naval line officers, constructors, and engineers recognized the significant advantages of screw propulsion over the more primitive paddle wheel. Although they convinced the U.S. government to build three warships as propellor-driven vessels, the government was still reluctant to abandon the paddle wheel and continued to insist that government-subsidized merchant vessels built as naval auxiliaries be side-wheelers.

Despite the technological contributions of steam propulsion and the screw propellor, no steamships in the earlier years of their introduction could compete with sailing ships in deep-sea work. Big coal consumption reduced, and in some instances almost eliminated, cargo space; and the crews had not made the transition from maintaining and operating sails to managing the cantankerous steam plants.

Development of Wind and Current Charts

By the mid-nineteenth century, America's Yankee Mariner had risen from obscurity to lead the world in the engineering and construction of ships. Among the ranks of the Yankee Mariners appeared practical and technical geniuses who were to provide sound and scientifically-derived navigation products that would keep the United States in the lead. One was Navy Lieutenant Matthew Fontaine Maury. Restricted to shore duty as the result of a disabling injury, he prepared wind and current charts that proved to be a great boon to sea captains and ship owners. The sailing time for packets bound for Rio was shortened from a hundred days to seventy-five days.

The Gold Rush to California in 1849 put a premium on speed. Although fast clippers were coming on line, Maury's charts are credited with reducing their transit time by 26 percent. He generously advised British captains to circle the globe going first via Africa and returning via South America, in order to take advantage of the major ocean current systems. Maury's charts and recommended sailing tracks were recognized as "road maps of the sea."

Maury was made superintendent of the Depot of Charts and Instruments in 1842. Here he discovered long-neglected charts and records that gave him adequate material to write a paper on the Gulf Stream. From this effort he recognized the paucity of environmental data. Maury gradually enlisted the assistance of virtually every shipmaster on every sea to gather new facts for a new science.

NAVAL OBSERVATORY

In 1844 Maury's Depot of Charts and Instruments was fittingly housed in Washington, and it became known as the Naval (or National) Observatory. In 1847 he produced the first great map of its kind for guidance of ships on the open sea; five thousand copies of this chart were distributed and used to shorten sailings by days and weeks. The economic impact of his work was so impressive that thousands of captains at sea obliged him with observations and records of winds and currents, in anticipation of receiving his next improved product.

Men who could not at first share Maury's vision, such as Alexander Dallas Bache and Joseph Henry, steadfastly ignored the hard facts and sound economy of using Maury's applied science. Bache and Henry were openly critical of him. From their positions as head of the Coast Survey and Secretary of the Smithsonian Institution, they looked upon Maury as a threat to their own aspirations to serve as the national leaders in surveying and astronomy. It was unfortunate that the three would become competitors for jurisdiction over applied science functions being advanced by the government and fundamental to the interests of the Yankee Mariner. The holier-than-thou attitude of the two college-trained men toward the self-taught Maury was blatantly exhibited in persistent attacks on Maury's credibility. Their public writings placed Maury in the category of "a charlatan that should be denied recognition." Bache, in particular, feared that Maury's rising fame as a hydrographer might cause the Coast Survey to be placed again under the Navy. However, so greatly were Maury's contributions appreciated by the American seamen and scientists—and by the Europeans as well—who were away from the professional struggle, that he was neither dislodged by the chauvinist pair nor reduced in image.

Sea-Bottom Exploration

About 1850, a new step was taken toward extension of our knowledge of the sea. Science had given to the world the electric telegraph; commerce demanded that it should be laid across the ocean. For this purpose, the bed of the North Atlantic needed to be carefully examined and mapped. The configuration of the sea bottom and the nature of its material also needed to be determined. This need gave a new impetus to the art of sea-sounding.

The transatlantic cable was laid, then was broken, and the end of it was fished up from a depth of nearly two miles. A great victory was thus gained; the bottom of the sea was no longer inaccessible, and the possibility of its scientific exploration became established. It was a popular opinion, shared also by men of science of the time, that the bottom of the sea was a dark and desolate waste, subject to such tremendous pressure as to render all life impossible.

Dr. Wyville Thomson of Scotland was quoted in 1873 in *Popular Science Monthly* (Volume III, page 258) as follows:

> The enormous pressure at these great depths seemed at first sight alone sufficient to put any idea of life out of the question. There was a curious popular notion, in which I well remember sharing when a boy, that, in going down, the sea-water became gradually under pressure heavier and heavier, and that all loose things in the sea floated at different levels according to their specific weight: skeletons of men, anchors, and shot and cannon, and last of all, the broad gold pieces lost in the wreck of many a galleon on the Spanish Main, the whole forming a kind of false bottom to the ocean, beneath which there lay all the depth of clear, still water, which was heavier than molten gold.
>
> The conditions of pressure are certainly very extraordinary. At 12,000 feet, a man would bear upon his body a weight equal to twenty locomotive engines, each with a long goods-train loaded with pig iron. We are apt to forget, however, that water is almost incompressible and that, therefore, the density of sea water at a depth of 12,000 feet is scarcely appreciably increased.

Contrary to all anticipation, it was found that highly organized representatives of all the invertebrate classes do live under these conditions of enormous pressure. The bottom of the ocean was seen to be habitable, and has proved actually to be inhabited by numberless forms of animal life. A new world was thus opened to the naturalist, which, although difficult of access, was yet accessible and had to be investigated. The pioneers in exploration encountered formidable obstacles, but the field was too vast and the promise too rich to be neglected. How it was regarded by devotees of research may be gathered from the following words of Dr. Thomson:

> The bed of the deep-sea—the 140 million square miles which we have now added to the legitimate field of natural history research—is not a barren waste. It is inhabited by a fauna more rich and varied on account of the enormous extent of the area, and with organisms in many cases apparently even more elaborately and delicately formed and more exquisitely beautiful in their soft shades of coloring and in the rainbow tints of their wonderful phosphorescence than the fauna of the well-known belt of shallow water, teeming with innumerable invertebrate forms, which fringes the land. And the forms of these hitherto unknown living beings, and their mode of life and their relations to other organisms whether living or extinct, and the phenomena and laws of their geographical distribution, must be worked out.

To chart the great depths in that day posed a technical challenge. In the 1870s the ordinary system of sounding failed at great depths, and could not be depended upon for more than 6,000 feet. The weight was not sufficient to carry the line rapidly and vertically to the bottom and, if a heavier weight were used, the line was in danger of breaking. No impulse was felt when the lead struck the bottom, and the line continued running out and, if stopped, was liable to break. Sometimes the line was carried along by submarine currents, forming loops or bights, and it often continued to run out and coil itself in a tangled mass directly over the lead. These sources of error vitiated very deep soundings, so that reports of that period included measurements in the Atlantic of 39,000, 46,000, and 50,000 feet without reaching bottom; these were recognized even at the time as exaggerations. Admiralty charts of the North Atlantic in 1873 included no soundings beyond 24,000 feet.

The main theater of sounding operations had been the Atlantic Ocean which, for its relation to the leading commercial nations and for intercontinental telegraphic purposes, had been more carefully surveyed than any other great body of water. Open from Pole to Pole, subject to all conditions of climate, communicating freely with other seas, and covering thirty million square miles, the Atlantic was believed to represent general oceanic conditions and to contain depths nearly, if not quite, as great as the other ocean basins of the world (although but little was known in this respect of the Indian, Antarctic, and Pacific seas). The general result of its soundings indicated that the average depth of the Atlantic bed was not much more than 12,000 feet, and that there seemed to be few depressions deeper than 15,000 or 20,000 feet. These conclusions have been validated in the past two decades.

Oceanography Becomes a Science

The greatest oceanographic expedition of the nineteenth century, and perhaps ever, was a four-year around-the-world cruise from 1872 to 1876. This sailing of H.M.S. *Challenger* established oceanography as an integrated science. All the major oceans were visited, sampled, and measured to such a degree that the amassed wealth of information gathered required twenty-eight years for compilation in fifty quarto volumes. The success of the *Challenger* led to a series of other national oceanographic expeditions, including those of Prince Albert of Monaco, who sent his own fleet of yachts on numerous expeditions.

Late in the nineteenth century, U.S. oceanography was given increased stature and emphasis due to the energies and accomplishments of Yankee scientist Alexander Agassiz. His sailings on the first U.S. ship built especially for scientific explorations by the U.S. Fish Commission, *Albatross*, a steamer capable of making extensive cruises (16,000 kilometers in tropical seas) and working with dredge and trawls in all depths to 3,000 fathoms (6,000 meters), brought plaudits from Sir John Murray, *Challenger* biologist, who wrote:

> If we can say that we know the physical and biological conditions of the great ocean basins in their broad and general outlines—and I believe that we can do so—the present state of our knowledge is due to the combined work and observations of a great many men belonging to many nationalities, but most probably more to the work and inspiration of Alexander Agassiz than to any other single man.

Recent Advances and Future Trends

At the close of the nineteenth century, the glorious rise of American shipping and shipbuilding that had contributed to the success of the Yankee Mariner had waned. The United States had become as pathetically weak as it had been outstandingly strong. The next surge in science and engineering would be spurred by World War I. With the forests depleted and few young men following in the footsteps of their shipwright fathers, the shipbuilding community would have to turn to steel and to development of a broad and new foundation of engineering expertise to meet the challenge.

The U.S. Navy was primarily responsible for building, developing, and modernizing U.S. shipyards. This capability was used following World Wars I and II to fulfill partially the domestic needs for merchant vessels, but the U.S. position of leadership was not regained. Nevertheless, innovation continues to be brought into the industry from science and engineering.

Recently introduced are such improvements as the wave-making bulbous bow that yields power savings of 10 percent; greater strength and workability of hull materials; elimination of wood templates through the introduction of numerically controlled plate burning equipment; development of larger propellors, some contra-rotating and with controllable pitch; automatic hatch covers; containerized cargo vans; and means to reduce time both in port and at sea. The latter has been assisted by scientific weather prediction which enables ship routing that avoids transit delays from storms and permits the transport of cargo in optimum condition. This prediction capability was developed by the U.S. Navy and is now available from commercial sources. (Similar techniques of prediction are now being made available to the Yankee Mariners traversing the atmosphere.) Automatic control devices have been adopted for the engine room as well as on the bridge of a ship; navigational equipment using electro-magnetic devices have been augmented by satellite navigation aids for positive traffic control in congested areas—all enhancing safety and reducing operating costs.

TECHNOLOGICAL BREAKTHROUGHS AFLOAT

Important oceanographic prospects lie in increased drilling and core-sampling capabilities provided by improved technology. The *Glomar Challenger*, a 10,500-ton vessel built on the basis of technology available in the 1960s, can maintain an exact position for days and weeks at a time by means of an acoustical beacon dropped to the sea floor, hydrophone reception of the beacon's signals, shipboard computer calculations, and four special propulsion units. The ship is stabilized against roll by a gyroscopically-controlled system, so that drillers can effectively control, even in heavy seas, the 23,000 feet of drill pipe carried. A powerful drilling derrick operates through the bottom of the ship, extracting cores of extraordinary length from thousands of meters deep, thus making available for study clues to the history of oceans, climates, mountain building, life, and evolution.

Another example of support from the scientific community to the commercial Yankee Mariner is development of the unique vessel known as *Flip*. It is towed to its working location in a horizontal position, then flipped to the vertical. Stability, coupled with the unusually deep draft in the vertical position, makes *Flip* an ideal platform for many sea experiments. Oceanographic instruments may be mounted anywhere along the submerged hull. By use of precision equipment, the location, depth, and orientation of the instruments may be determined and controlled to a higher precision than can be achieved with any other platform. Although first developed for acoustical experiments, *Flip* has found many other uses since it was placed in operation on August 15, 1962. It has been used for experiments or studies of wave attenuation, sound propagation, sound-scattering or sound-reverberation measurements, meteorological work, and measurement of internal waves.

SUBMERSIBLES

The manned descent in the bathyscaph *Trieste* to 35,800 feet (10,740 meters) in January 1960 was a major event in man's conquest of the sea. A family of vehicles has since evolved that ranges in size from small one-man submarines for exploration of the continental shelf to vehicles capable of routine operation at great depths. In the continuing development of deep-sea research vehicles, the goal is to operate safely at any depth. In the early 1970s, materials were being fabricated and tested, and techniques of life support, navigation, communications, bottom mapping, photography, direct viewing, and in-place measuring were being studied to improve vehicle capability.

AIRCRAFT AND SATELLITES

Major advances have been made in the use of aircraft for obtaining operational oceanographic information. With development of air-dropped bathythermographs, aircraft can obtain information on subsurface as well as surface layers. The use of satellites for telemetering oceanographic data from buoy systems has been successfully demonstrated.

A recent and dramatic development is the collection of ocean data from remote platforms located in space. Earth-orbiting satellites have demonstrated a capability for collecting and transmitting oceanographic data of several types. Advances in marine science and technology depend critically upon the effective flow of information from data collectors to data consumers.

Commercial Contributions to Marine Progress

Private enterprise, particularly the petroleum industry, has become a significant participant in oceanographic exploration. Since the late 1940s, petroleum firms have developed their own oceanographic fleets and specialized instruments. The industry's special requirements have been fulfilled by innovative platform designs, sampling and measuring techniques, and handling facilities. The disciplines of geology and geophysics have benefitted most from the industry's activities. Markedly improved seismic techniques for acquiring, compiling, and processing data from which three-dimensional models of sub-bottom geological features could be made, have significantly aided geologists. Improved ship designs, open-sea anchoring techniques, ship control, navigation aids, and new tools and techniques have been adopted by the scientific oceanographer.

Marine fisheries have been closely allied to oceanography for many decades, and the industry has turned to the biological oceanographers for information about the marine environment. In contrast to the petroleum industry, the fishing industry has not established a significant private research capability, but has adopted engineering advances developed for other purposes.

Need for Research Continues

As we approach the twenty-first century, ocean science and engineering will occupy a different role in the affairs of the Yankee Mariner. Already the national and world concern for sharing and managing the resources of the ocean is influencing planning, policy, economics, and the people of the world everywhere, in coastal and inland countries alike. Existing knowledge has helped formulate new concepts on just how to preserve, conserve, and effectively manage a large, still poorly understood, portion of the planet. Ocean science and engineering have unlocked many of the ocean's secrets, but every year or decade produces new insight regarding the physical, biological, chemical, and geological character of the ocean. Each discovery invites further inquiry; often ten or more questions or avenues of additional investigation are generated by each step forward.

Environmental impact statements, preparation of regulations, and policy development and implementation lean ever more heavily on the capability of the ocean scientist to predict what will happen if one approach is selected over another. An answer is given, but almost without exception a caveat will be applied to the statement, to the effect that unknowns and absence of prediction algorithms assure that all events will not occur as forecast. Also, there will be a call for additional research to accompany the prediction in hope that monitoring of the conditions will avert any catastrophe.

Ocean science and engineering have been the foundation for a broad spectrum of Yankee Mariner activities. The bottom line is that we have come a long way since the birth of our nation. The Yankee Mariner's role in the affairs of the United States has changed with the passage of time, but it remains a vital component of the economic well-being of our country's overall national security.

Role of the United States in Development of Law of the Sea

Arvid Pardo

From the very beginning, the role of the United States in development of law of the sea has been ambivalent: pragmatic rather than principled. The United States supported, but seldom felt completely comfortable with, traditional law of the sea, that is to say, with a law of the sea based on the concept of freedom of the high seas beyond a three-mile limit. United States support for this concept both waxed and waned in the nineteenth century according to circumstances, but traditional law of the sea never received from the United States the principled support that it received from the United Kingdom or France. With some exceptions, the United States during the nineteenth century left the enforcement of traditional law of the sea at the international level to the United Kingdom.

When the maritime power of the United Kingdom declined after World War I, the United States was among the first nations to press for expanded jurisdictional powers beyond the traditional three-mile limit. After World War II, it was the United States that, perhaps inadvertently, was primarily responsible for the collapse of traditional law of the sea. More recently, at the ongoing United Nations Conference on the Law of the Sea, the United States has often appeared unable to play a role commensurate with that of leader of the Free World, and has on more than one occasion sounded an uncertain trumpet.

I shall attempt to suggest that lack of a principled approach to the law of the sea has not been in the best interests of the United States, but first I would like to trace briefly U.S. policies since independence.

From Cannon-Shot to Three-Mile Limit

The United States was born at the time when traditional law of the sea was beginning to take root in the practice of maritime states. It was in 1782 that Ferdinando Galiani, in his well-known book *Dei doveri dei principi neutrali verso i principi guerreggianti (The Duties of Neutral Princes Towards Belligerent Princes)*, suggested that the cannon-shot rule for determining the extent of coastal state maritime jurisdiction—a rule favored particularly by France—be equated with a three-mile belt of sea along the coast. The practice and the claims of states, however, remained far from uniform for a generation or more.

Within a decade of independence, the French Revolution and the ensuing Anglo-French hostilities along the American coast forced the young republic to adopt an official position with regard to maritime limits in order to maintain her neutrality. The immediate occasion was a letter, dated September 13, 1793, by Edmond Genet, the French minister in Washington, to Secretary of State Thomas Jefferson, noting that governments held different views on the extent of territorial protection along their coasts, and requesting that the United States define its position on the question. Washington and Jefferson were obliged to respond; a cautious note was sent both to Genet and to Mr. Hammond, the British Minister in Washington, fixing the exercise of the territorial protection of the United States *"for the present* to the distance of one sea league or three geographic miles from the seashore," for "this distance can admit of no opposition, as it is recognized by treaties between some of the powers with whom we are connected in commerce and navigation, and is as little or less than is claimed by any of them on their own coasts."[1]

One Sea League for Neutrality

The wording of the American note suggested, however, that the United States wished to keep the door open for a later claim to wider maritime jurisdiction. That this was the case is confirmed by John Quincy Adams, who in his *Memoirs* reveals that in 1805 Jefferson had told him "that we ought to assume as a principle that the neutrality of our territory should extend to the Gulf Stream which was a natural boundary." According to John Quincy Adams, Jefferson, when Secretary of State, had claimed a three-mile jurisdictional limit only "because Genet . . . forced us to fix on some point and we were not then prepared to assert the claim of jurisdiction to the extent that we are in reason entitled to. . . . I [John Quincy Adams] observed that it might be well, before we ventured to assume a claim so broad, to wait for a time when we should have a force competent to maintain it. But in the meantime, he said, it was advisable to squint at it and to accustom the nations of Europe to the idea that we should claim it in the future."[2]

From this statement it is apparent that Washington's and Jefferson's choice of a three-mile limit to maritime jurisdiction was made reluctantly; that it was intended to be temporary and to serve exclusively the purpose of tracing the limits of a neutrality zone. Nevertheless, seven months later, in 1794, Congress, by adopting an "Act in addition to the Act for the punishment of certain crimes against the United States," made the United States the first country to incorporate a claim to a three-mile jurisdiction for neutrality purposes into its domestic legislation; it is probable, however, that the government intended to extend the American claim in due course.[3] Circumstances, however, made this inadvisable, and twenty-four years later, in the Anglo-American Fisheries Convention of 1818, the United States accepted a narrow three-mile coastal state jurisdiction for fisheries also, because it was felt that Americans had more to gain by fishing within three miles of the Canadian coast than they might lose by permitting foreigners to fish within three miles of the American coast.

During the course of the next hundred years the United States on several occasions officially supported the view that "pursuant to public law, no nation can rightfully claim jurisdiction at sea beyond a marine league from its coast."[4] Thus the United States joined Great Britain in protesting the Russian decree of 1821 barring foreign vessels from the Bering Sea, the Gulf of Alaska and the Sea of Okhotsk, and obtained its withdrawal in 1824; in the second half of the nineteenth century the United States vigorously resisted on several occasions the Spanish claim to the right of visitation and search of American commercial vessels passing within six miles of the Cuban coast; and there were other such positions taken.

FOUR-LEAGUE CUSTOMS CONTROL

While supporting the three-mile rule for most purposes, however, the United States very soon began to draw a distinction between a claim of general jurisdiction beyond one league from the coast, which was opposed, and the enforcement of customs legislation beyond that distance, which was considered legitimate. Even before Jefferson made his reluctant response to Genet, the United States had asserted, in 1790, a limited customs jurisdiction up to four leagues (twelve nautical miles) from the coast; the statute was reenacted and sharpened in 1799, 1866, and 1878. Under these statutes, unlading of vessels within four leagues of the coast was forbidden, and American customs officials were given authority to board foreign or domestic vessels bound for United States ports within four leagues from the coast for inspection of manifests and examination of cargoes. The claim to a four-league customs and revenue jurisdiction was never reduced, even when Great Britain and some other countries in the second half of the nineteenth century abolished hovering acts and adopted a three-mile limit to maritime jurisdiction for all purposes.

The then generally recognized limits of national jurisdiction were disregarded also in other respects when immediate national interests appeared to be at stake. By the 1848 Treaty of Guadalupe Hidalgo with Mexico, for instance, the United States recognized not a one-league but a three-league limit of maritime jurisdiction. In another field—navigation—the United States Inland Rules of the Road, adopted in 1897, were made applicable to some maritime areas more than fifteen miles from shore.

A Century of Ambivalence and Pragmatism

During the second half of the nineteenth century, the heyday of traditional law of the sea, there continued to be a current of dissatisfaction with narrow maritime limits both at the governmental[5] and at the nongovernmental expert level. An influential minority of American legal experts continued to believe, like Jefferson and Madison, that the United States, because of the length and characteristics of its coasts, should seek to acquire control of a broad belt of coastal waters, particularly for security and neutrality purposes. James Kent, for instance, who eventually became chief justice of the supreme court in New York, made a suggestion startling in its modernity. He recognized that three nautical miles was the legal breadth of the territorial sea, but he suggested that the constraint of this limit could be alleviated if the government assumed control of all coastal waters "within lines stretching from quite distant headlands, as, for instance, from Cape Ann to Cape Cod, and from Nantucket to Montauk Point, and from that point to the capes of Delaware, and from the south cape of Florida to the Mississippi. . . ." It is a suggestion we may see implemented some day.

The 1893 Bering Sea Arbitration case and subsequent pelagic sealing controversy probably most clearly illustrate the fundamental ambivalence of the United States approach towards traditional law of the sea at the turn of the century. A policy declaration asserting that the United States claimed and admitted "the jurisdiction of any State over its territorial waters only to the extent of one marine league"[6] was made precisely at a time when American officials were attempting vigorously to enforce American domestic conservation laws well beyond one hundred miles from the coast.

It is also interesting to note that references to the three-mile limit, the heart of traditional law of the sea, were eliminated at the insistence of the American delegation from the eighth convention—dealing with the laying of submarine contact mines—drafted by the 1907 Second Peace Conference, with the argument that until agreement could be reached on specific rules for the drawing of baselines there was no point in fixing an exact limit to the territorial sea.[7] The conference, therefore, adopted a vaguely formulated article.

PROHIBITION EXTENDS TERRITORIAL WATERS

As the United States grew stronger and gradually took over the maritime role of the United Kingdom, it might have been expected that her interest in maintaining and, if possible, strengthening international observance of the three-mile limit to coastal state jurisdiction would grow. American attitudes however, remained highly pragmatic. Thus when the United States, with enactment of the 1919 National Prohibition Act, was faced with the difficult problem of controlling massive smuggling, there was little hesitation in adopting the Tariff Act of 1922 which unilaterally asserted American claims to broadened customs jurisdiction, *inter alia*, by authorizing federal officials *at any time* to stop and search *any* vessel within four leagues of the coast.[8] At the same time, the Supreme Court, in the case of *Cunard v. Mellon*, held that foreign vessels were not permitted to bring liquor into the United States or its territorial waters even if it were kept under seal and not intended for delivery within the country.

These developments were greeted with foreign protests. Under international law, the flag nation usually is recognized exclusive jurisdiction over its ships unless they enter a foreign port or internal waters; in the latter cases, the local sovereign may exercise concurrent jurisdiction. While it is for the local sovereign to decide whether to exercise jurisdiction in a particular case, local authorities usually refrain from doing so unless their assistance is requested or the peace or good order of the port is affected. The complaining countries did not believe that the presence of liquor under seal on their ships for passenger consumption outside U.S. territorial waters could affect the peace or good order of American ports.

The protests led to negotiation of the 1924 treaty with Great Britain, under which the three-mile limit of territorial waters was reaffirmed and it was agreed that Great Britain would not object to the boarding, search, and seizure by United States officials of privately owned British vessels attempting to import alcoholic beverages into the United States, provided that this right was not "exercised at a greater distance from the coast of the United States . . . than can be traversed in one hour by the vessel suspected. . . ." At the same time the United States agreed that British vessels would be permitted to enter American ports and territorial waters with liquor under seal[9] for passenger consumption outside territorial waters. Similar treaties were subsequently concluded with Japan and several European and South American countries. (Treaties with countries which had not accepted a three-mile jurisdictional limit for all purposes—Spain, France, Italy, Belgium, the Scandinavian countries— did not reaffirm this limit.)

"CONTIGUOUS ZONE" JURISDICTION

The Anglo-American treaty of 1924 and the similar treaties concluded with other nations provided powerful impetus to international acceptance of the concept that the coastal state could exercise jurisdiction in a zone contiguous to the territorial sea,[10] originally only for customs and fiscal purposes, but very soon also for other purposes—security, sanitation, and, significantly, fisheries. This development marked the modest beginning of a systematic expansion of coastal state jurisdiction beyond the traditional three-mile territorial sea. Expansion accelerated after failure of the 1930 Hague Conference to adopt a draft convention establishing a three-mile limit to the territorial sea, largely because of opposition by

Great Britain, which feared that acceptance of a contiguous zone would weaken "the authority of the general rule of international law whereby three miles is regarded as the limit of territorial jurisdiction."[11] (At the Hague Conference the United States claimed a certain amount of control over foreign ships up to twelve miles from the coast but otherwise generally supported a three-mile territorial sea.)

Probably the best statement of the American position at the time was made by Philip Jessup, who wrote that when the three-mile limit ceased to be convenient it would probably be changed by general convention; in the meantime the rule should be considered part of international law.

For the United States during the years between World Wars I and II, the three-mile rule was precisely a convenience to be utilized or manipulated as the national interest appeared to dictate. Because the rule was considered a convenience and not a principle, it was never as tenaciously defended as it had been by Britain.

MOBILE CUSTOMS ENFORCEMENT AREAS

Repeal of Prohibition in 1933 and the end of the liquor smuggling emergency offered an opportunity to restore—without any prejudice to the national interest—American claims to customs jurisdiction beyond the territorial sea to what they had been before 1920. Had such action been taken, United States example might have slowed the drift toward ever wider and more varied special purpose claims over high seas areas. Instead, largely to serve official convenience, the United States made even wider claims to maritime jurisdiction than before. Under the 1935 antismuggling act, Congress authorized the establishment of mobile customs enforcement areas which changed in size, shape, and location at the President's discretion, upon detection of a vessel suspected of "hovering" off the American coast for the purpose of smuggling.[12] The mobile nature of customs enforcement areas and the fact that they could be established at the discretion of the executive were virtually unprecedented at the time. Almost simultaneously, Norway issued her famous decree delimiting her territorial waters, not from the low water mark along the coast, as had been customary, but by means of arbitrary straight baselines joining points sometimes at some distance from the mainland. The United States, as distinguished from Great Britain, did not protest this action.

In the circumstances, it is not surprising that between the end of the

Hague Conference and the outbreak of World War II, at least two dozen countries advanced claims of special purpose jurisdiction, or occasionally sovereignty, beyond the territorial sea for distances ranging from five to approximately twelve nautical miles from the coast (in some cases, distances were expressed in kilometers or in sailing time from the coast), and that writers in this period increasingly took note of the fact that there existed no consensus on the limits of territorial waters.[13] Jurisdictional claims beyond the traditional three-mile limit in nearly all cases were, however, still modest both in extent and in content until 1939.

World War II marked the abandonment in the Americas, with the approval and encouragement of the United States, of traditional security and neutrality zone limits. The 1939 Declaration of Panama established a neutrality zone 500 to 1200 miles wide around the American continent, while United States "defensive sea areas" and subsequently "maritime control areas," established by executive order between 1939 and 1942, unilaterally restricted unauthorized navigation from eleven to sixty-five miles from the coast.[14]

The Truman Proclamations

Maritime control zones were abolished after the end of World War II, but they were replaced by new far-reaching American claims to jurisdiction beyond the territorial sea which, together with the decision of the International Court of Justice in the Anglo-Norwegian dispute,[15] dealt the final blow to traditional law of the sea. I refer, of course, to the 1945 Truman proclamations on the continental shelf and on fisheries, under which the United States unilaterally asserted, respectively, that (a) the natural resources of the subsoil and seabed of the continental shelf beneath the high seas but contiguous to the coasts of the United States appertained to the United States and were subject to its jurisdiction and control; and (b) it was the right of the United States unilaterally to establish conservation zones in areas of the high seas contiguous to its coasts, where fishing activities would be subject to U.S. regulation and control. Both proclamations explicitly stated that the character of the marine areas in question as high seas was in no way affected.

CONTINENTAL SHELF

The proclamations are not without international precedent, particularly with regard to the continental shelf. Cases can be quoted where nations reserved for themselves exclusive rights to some resources of the seabed beyond the territorial sea: nineteenth century British claims to Ceylon pearl banks or Irish oyster beds immediately come to mind in this connection. More recently, in 1942, Great Britain and Venezuela had divided between themselves the submarine areas of the Gulf of Paria. Nevertheless, so far as I am aware, no country since the sixteenth century made such sweeping claims over areas the limits of which were not officially defined.[16] It is a matter of continuing surprise to me that steps so clearly subversive of customary law of the sea should have been taken by the most powerful maritime power in the world at the time—a nation which had an obvious interest in supporting established law—largely for domestic political reasons, without the pressure of overwhelming economic or political necessity, without careful study of the consequences, and with little congressional or international consultation.[17]

The international community being what it is, the Truman proclamations prompted a rush by other countries to advance similar and even wider claims in the marine environment. Claims of exclusive rights over *the resources* of a variously defined continental shelf were rapidly accepted by the international community; on the other hand, claims of sovereignty over the continental shelf itself and over its superjacent waters advanced by some countries encountered resistance from the maritime powers. The result of a decade-long debate is the formula contained in the 1958 Geneva Convention on the Continental Shelf, which has been interpreted as permitting coastal states to control seabed resources beyond their territorial sea at ever increasing distances from the coast in step with their capability to exploit them.

FISHERIES

As for the fisheries proclamation, according to Ann Hollick, "the Department of State quickly recognized that the Truman proclamation on fisheries was not a suitable policy for a nation with global interests. It was soon abandoned, but not before the damage had been done. . . ."[18] Claims to exclusive fishery zones beyond the territorial sea quickly multiplied, causing violent controversies in Europe, Asia, and the Americas. In the controversies in which it was directly involved, the United States (as distinguished from Britain with respect to Iceland) avoided a show of force to protect American fishing vessels in Latin-American waters, and limited itself to offering to negotiate, to protests, and to the enactment of the 1954 Fishermen's Protective Act to compensate American fishermen who had been fined or whose boats had been seized.[19] This attitude was not particularly effective in obtaining withdrawal of claims which the United States considered to be not permissible under international law.

At the same time, the United States did not make the extraordinary efforts that would have been necessary to combat effectively the Soviet twelve-mile territorial sea claims and Soviet enclosure of maritime areas such as the Sea of Okhotsk through the manipulation of baselines.

First U.N. Conference on Law of the Sea

The decade of the 1950s was a decade of transition. Basic traditional concepts were questioned, but at the same time there was a continuing effort to maintain traditional law and to codify it with such adaptations as appeared necessary.

Since 1949, law of the sea topics believed suitable for codification had been considered by the International Law Commission of the United Nations. The work of the commission eventually led to the convening in 1958 of the first United Nations Conference on the Law of the Sea, which drafted four conventions codifying much of the current practice of nations. These were (1) Convention on the Territorial Sea and Contiguous Zone; (2) Convention on the High Seas; (3) Convention on Fishing and Conservation of the Living Resources of the Sea; and (4) Convention on the Continental Shelf. While this accomplishment was certainly useful, the conference failed to reach agreement on the crucial question of the breadth of the territorial sea;[20] a second conference in 1960 again failed to reach a decision on this question.

At the 1958 conference, the United States advocated a three-mile territorial sea against supporters of a wider limit, such as the Soviet Union; opposed the emerging claims of archipelagic states (for example, Indonesia and the Philippines claimed that archipelagic states could draw straight baselines joining the outermost points of the outermost islands of the archipelago); and attempted to restrain the more extreme claims of Latin-American and other states[21] and the trend towards wide exclusive fishery zones beyond the territorial sea.

At the 1960 conference, the United States made a well-prepared, vigorous effort, which failed by only one vote, to obtain the required two-thirds majority for a compromise proposal: a six-mile territorial sea with an additional six-mile exclusive fishery zone.[22] Yet even when U.S. policy opposed Russian claims to a twelve-mile territorial sea or Latin-American claims to a 200-nautical-mile fishery zone, it was based less on principle than on pragmatic interest: support for a narrow territorial sea and exclusive fishery zone protected American naval and long-distance fishery interests, while a broad legal continental shelf satisfied American petroleum interests. This position appeared inconsistent to many countries, and perhaps this perception may have been in part responsible for the failure of American efforts at the 1960 law of the sea conference.

EXPANSION OF COASTAL STATE CLAIMS

Just as the 1945 Truman proclamations and the failure of the 1930 Hague Conference had prompted a rash of unilateral claims, the failure of the 1958 and 1960 United Nations conferences to adopt clear limits to national jurisdiction in the marine environment encouraged the emergence of a variety of new and expansive claims. It is after the conferences that straight baselines became increasingly common; that the majority of the international community shifted from a three-mile to a twelve-mile or wider territorial sea; that coastal state claims over the continental shelf began to expand in earnest beyond the 200-meter isobath; that exclusive fishery zones multiplied; and that coastal states began to extend their jurisdiction for pollution control purposes far beyond their territorial seas.

With traditional law of the sea visibly disintegrating since 1960, the United States continued to follow essentially contradictory policies: official support was still given to the concept of a three-mile territorial sea, but it was a territorial sea stripped of its main content—security and fishery jurisdiction.[23] On the other hand, the United States has not hesitated unilaterally to extend its jurisdiction beyond the territorial sea whenever this appeared to be useful. The process started immediately after the end of the second United Nations Conference on the Law of the Sea with the enactment in 1961 of an Oil Pollution Act forbidding tankers to discharge wastes up to fifty miles from land, and it has continued at irregular intervals since.

In conclusion, United States practice, as distinguished from official rhetoric, has not differed significantly from Latin-American and Soviet contentions at the 1958 Geneva Conference on the Law of the Sea to the effect that every nation is competent to fix the breadth of its own territorial sea in accordance with its economic and security requirements.

Have U.S. Interests Been Served?

The question arises whether a more principled approach to the law of the sea would not have served the national interest better than the inconsistent and largely contradictory policies followed by the United States over the past half-century. No doubt these policies were a response to internal politics and to perceived national interests, but it is questionable whether the results of unilateral American action compensated adequately for the corresponding weakening of traditional law of the sea.

—The 1935 antismuggling act no doubt appeared to offer a convenient means to control smuggling, but were mobile customs enforcement zones necessary? According to Swarztrauber, only sixteen vessels were seized under its provisions; this is hardly an overwhelming number.

—No doubt the 1939 Declaration of Panama, protested by Great Britain, was a highly popular political gesture at the time, but was it wise? Effective enforcement of its provisions would have been more likely to embroil the United States and other American countries in avoidable controversies than to protect their neutrality; furthermore, effective enforcement would have favored the belligerent country with the weaker navy, i.e. Germany, thus contradicting other major U.S. policy objectives.

—Could not the policy objectives of the 1945 continental shelf proclamation have been attained without baldly proclaiming with minimum consultation that the continental shelf may be regarded as an extension of the landmass of the coastal nation and thus naturally appurtenant to it? The United States possessed the most advanced technology for the exploitation of the petroleum resources of the seabed, no foreign nation was threatening to exploit these resources off the American coast, there was no overwhelming political pressure to proclaim the continental shelf doctrine.

—As for the 1945 fisheries proclamation, I am sure that most people would acknowledge that it caused more trouble than it was worth. One wonders at the lack of political understanding on the part of eminent contemporary legal authors who praised the Truman proclamations as wise moves for the protection of important American interests. One is even more struck, however, by the failure of President Roosevelt and of the American political leadership at the time to understand the simple fact that with the growth of American commerce, with the primacy of American marine technology and naval power, it was a basic interest of the United States to support traditional law of the sea.

MISSED OPPORTUNITIES

As one of the major maritime powers in the interwar years and as the dominant maritime and technological power in 1945, the United States had far more to gain by maintaining access to all parts of the marine environment beyond a narrow territorial sea than by claiming exclusive control of marine areas, however extensive, near its coasts. Had the legal continental shelf doctrine not been proclaimed, and had the United States defended as tenaciously as Great Britain narrow limits to coastal state maritime jurisdiction for all purposes, it is probable that American corporations would have rapidly obtained control of the most productive portions of the continental shelf in many parts of the world; we may even speculate that American oil companies, and not the riparian nations, could now be controlling the rich, offshore, petroleum resources of the Persian Gulf.

Of course I do not pretend that consistent American example and consistently applied American influence and power could have saved traditional law of the sea from gradual disintegration. Pressure for the expansion of coastal state jurisdiction was already making itself felt in the 1930s, and the pressure could not have been indefinitely contained after World War II, with the decline in influence of the traditional maritime powers, with the emergence of a multitude of weak coastal states, with rapid technological advance leading to expanding and more intensive uses of the sea and to increased value of the marine environment for the coastal state in terms both of security and of resources. But a consistent American example would have slowed the trend and would have avoided much of the legal confusion of the past thirty years. An understanding at the political level of the totality of American interests in the marine environment might have enabled the United States to elaborate in useful time and to seek international agreement on the changes needed in traditional law of the sea, rather than following ad hoc inconsistent policies or merely reacting to events.

Needed: A National Ocean Policy

The United States still reacts on an ad hoc, often emotional, basis to events; a multitude of interests—economic, military, scientific, environmental—vie for primacy to determine United States policy in the marine environment. The result too often is inconsistency and imbalance in policy. What is so desperately required is a balanced national ocean policy based on the fundamental and permanent interests of the United States as a major maritime power with the capability to use the marine environment in an ever-increasing number of ways. One would hope a balanced national ocean policy would also aim at furthering equity, international cooperation, and peaceful settlement of disputes.

The United States has many excellent law of the sea experts—experts in virtually all aspects of marine technology and uses of the sea—and perhaps too many expert advocates of special interests; but experts, whether legal or other, while eminently capable of giving useful advice on specific aspects of a subject, have seldom been capable of developing broad national policies.

I believe that what is required is an institution capable of providing a broad, very special, interdisciplinary training in matters related to ocean space, a kind of "ocean space West Point," the graduates of which would be generalists, not specialists. They would be trained in ocean politics and economics, but they would also have an understanding of ocean law, technology, and the like. Most important, they would be trained to relate ocean space to the permanent interests of the United States and to understand the complex interrelationships between politics, law, technology, military, and other uses of the marine environment.

As far as I know, there is no place in the United States where a person can obtain the broad, interdisciplinary training in matters related to ocean space which I have so inadequately described. Perhaps the scarcity of persons with the requisite broad, interdisciplinary training, together with Washington politics, personality conflicts, and the undisciplined clash of interests at the political level, may explain in part the inconsistencies and policy uncertainties which have marked American participation in the latest law of the sea conference, the results of which are at this time uncertain.

Only with public perception of the vital importance of ocean space to the future of the United States, and with the emergence of a broadly trained cadre of public officials capable of interpreting the national interest in the oceans to politicians, will the United States exercise a role commensurate with its international standing, in development of the modern law of the sea.

NOTES

1. Quoted in Swarztrauber, *The Three-Mile Limit of Territorial Seas* (Naval Institute Press, 1972), p. 57.

2. *Memoirs of John Quincy Adams*, edited by Charles Francis Adams, Vol. II, pp. 375–76, quoted in Swarztrauber, p. 58.

3. Twelve years later, in fact, Secretary of State Madison, in instructing Messrs. Monroe and Pinckney, who had been sent to London to negotiate a treaty of commerce and navigation, showed a clear preference for wide jurisdictional limits. In his letter of May 17, 1806, he wrote: "It is proper that all armed belligerent ships should be expressly and effectually restrained from making seizures or searches within a certain distance from our coasts. . . . In defining the distance protected against belligerent proceedings it would not be unreasonable . . . to expect an immunity for the space between that limit [the Gulf Stream] and the American shore. But at least it may be insisted that the extent of the neutral immunity should correspond with the claims maintained by Great Britain around her own territory. Without any particular inquiry into the extent of these, it may be observed: first, that the British Act of Parliament in the year 1736 . . . assumes for certain purposes of trade the distance of four leagues from shore. . . . If the distance of four leagues cannot be obtained, any distance not less than one sea league may be substituted. . . ." (American State Papers, Vol. III, p. 119, in Masterson, *Jurisdiction in Marginal Seas* (Kennikat Press, 1929), pp. 254–56.) It is clear that Madison, like Jefferson, accepted a three-mile limit for neutrality purposes only reluctantly.

4. Mr. Fish, Secretary of State, to British chargé d'affaires in Washington (note of January 22, 1874), quoted in Masterson, p. 201.

5. In 1874, the United States together with Germany, Austria, Italy, Denmark, Holland, and Belgium signed a declaration providing "that if the limit of the territorial sea should be determined by an international agreement, three sea leagues should be the minimum." In 1896 Secretary of State Olney replied favorably to a Dutch letter suggesting the possibility of establishing a six-mile territorial sea for neutrality purposes. Early in the twentieth century, a U.S. Naval War College study proposed a six-mile limit to coastal state jurisdiction over its marginal sea, etc. For additional details, see Swarztrauber, p. 94.

6. *Declaration relative to the extent of jurisdiction claimed over the bordering waters of the Bering Sea, July 4, 1902*, in Swarztrauber, p. 115.

7. At the time, the United States was involved in a dispute with Great Britain on how to measure baselines on the eastern coast of Canada. The dispute was settled by the North Atlantic Coast Fishery Arbitration award of 1912, which, *inter alia*, recommended that straight baselines across the mouth of bays should not exceed ten miles.

8. Tariff Act of 1922, Section 581. It will be recalled that the Act of 1799 applied only to vessels bound for American ports.

9. *Convention between the United States of America and Great Britain*, January 23, 1924, quoted in Masterson, pp. 346–52.

10. Article 24 of the 1958 Convention on the Territorial Sea and Contiguous Zone defines the contiguous zone as a zone of the high seas (not extending beyond twelve miles from the

baseline used for measuring the territorial sea) contiguous to the territorial sea in which the coastal state may exercise the control necessary to prevent and punish infringement of its customs, fiscal, immigration, and sanitary regulations within its territory or territorial sea.

11. See Masterson, p. 341. The 1930 Hague Conference was convened under the auspices of the League of Nations, *inter alia*, to draft a convention codifying the breadth of the territorial sea.

12. There were some restrictions on this practice: for example, customs enforcement areas could not include waters more than one hundred miles from the place where the President had declared a vessel to be hovering or more than fifty miles from the outer limit of customs waters.

13. See Swarztrauber, pp. 147–51, for examples.

14. Swarztrauber notes that both defensive sea areas and maritime control areas were inconsistent with Hague Convention XIII of 1907 on the rights and duties of neutral powers in maritime war. Establishment of such areas, however, was justified by President Roosevelt in terms of "the principle of self-defense of the Law of Nations."

15. The International Court of Justice decided in 1951 that straight baselines, as defined in the Norwegian decree of 1935, were not contrary to international law. The decision decisively influenced the baseline provisions contained in the 1958 Territorial Sea Convention (Article 4). Furthermore the judgment, by giving weight to subjective factors, such as economic and social interests, and by failing to suggest any limit to the length of straight baselines and their distance from the coast, gave powerful encouragement to new claims over marine areas and offered a handy technical means to expand coastal state jurisdiction without ostensibly changing the breadth of the territorial sea.

16. However, a State Department press release described the legal continental shelf as "submerged land which is contiguous to the continent and which is covered by no more than one hundred fathoms of water." In view of the acrimonious debate on the subject at the current law of the sea conference it is also interesting to note that the Truman proclamation declared that "in cases where the continental shelf extends to the shores of another state . . . the boundary shall be determined by the United States and the State concerned on the basis of equitable principles" rather than on the basis of the equidistance criterion.

17. An excellent account of the background of the Truman proclamations may be found in Ann Hollick, *U.S. Foreign Policy and the Law of the Sea* (Princeton University Press, 1981). See pp. 18–56 for a careful account of events, including the role of Secretary of the Interior Harold Ickes.

18. Hollick, p. 62.

19. It is recalled that the CEP countries—Chile, Ecuador and Peru—under the 1952 Declaration of Santiago claimed "sovereignty and exclusive jurisdiction over the sea . . . up to a minimum distance of 200 nautical miles from their coasts."

20. The conference also failed to set limits on the length of straight baselines, and it adopted an ambiguous formula (adjacency, 200-meter isobath, and exploitability) to define the limits of the legal continental shelf.

21. The United States also strongly opposed Soviet and Latin-American contentions that every coastal state could establish its own territorial waters within reasonable limits taking into account its geographical situation and its security and economic needs.

22. With the proviso that foreign countries which had habitually fished for at least five years in the outer six miles could continue to do so for another ten years.

23. It is recalled that the United States established wide maritime control areas during World War II, and subsequently established air identification zones to monitor aircraft within a 400-mile-wide maritime zone. United States fishery jurisdiction was extended to twelve nautical miles in 1966 and more recently to one hundred nautical miles.

Politics in American Uses of the Sea, 1970–1980

Ann L. Hollick

Fairly recently in the history of man's use of the oceans, competition has arisen for limited ocean space and finite ocean resources. That competition—the "politics of the oceans"—has resulted from pressure caused by two related factors: population growth and technological change.

The expansion of the earth's population requires more resources to feed, clothe, transport, and house more people. The world's population stands at roughly four and one-half billion today. Twenty years ago there were three billions of us. Twenty years from now there will be six and one-half billions. This growing population has turned to the oceans for food, energy, minerals, transport, and waste disposal.

The second source of pressure on the oceans arises from man's inventiveness—from technological change. It is that inventiveness that now enables us to wipe out entire fish species through satellite-guided, computer-managed fishing, or simply through waste disposal. Technology has recently enabled us to reach the depths of the seas—to recover manganese nodules and to visit deep-sea mineral-rich vents.

The access to new and the pressure on traditional ocean resources have generated political problems at the national and international levels.

Indeed, given the nature of the issues involved, national and international politics of the sea necessarily go hand-in-hand. Whether a political issue falls, at least initially, into the domestic or the international political arena is itself a political question. The answer has depended on (1) the location of a resource—that is, proximity to shore—and (2) whether it could be managed on a strictly national basis.

Governments strongly prefer to keep the problems of commonly used areas within their domestic jurisdiction. Like other coastal nations, the United States has an established political system that can reconcile competing claims in determining whether an offshore area should be opened for oil and gas exploration, or be reserved exclusively for fishing purposes, or be provided with transit lanes. For example, when the states and the federal government disputed the ownership of offshore oil lands in the 1950s, the Supreme Court and then the Congress ruled on and resolved the issue. Given the option, therefore, governments prefer to convert ocean disputes into domestic political problems—most commonly by claiming larger offshore areas.

Some resources, however, cannot be managed nationally. Whaling is an example of an historic ocean use pursued by many nations in remote corners of the globe. By the 1930s, uncoordinated harvesting by whalers of different nations was severely affecting the whale populations. In response to this, the British in 1931 convened a conference of twenty-six whaling nations which sought, through a series of agreements, to reduce the pressure on whale stocks. The successive conventions for the regulation of whaling in the 1930s offer a useful example of the problems facing international approaches to ocean resource management. Indeed, the greatest boon to recovery of whale stocks was World War II, which kept whaling fleets at home—a management approach scarcely to be generally commended.

With the end of the war, nations turned to non-military uses of the oceans with renewed vigor. And the national and international political competition resumed. Two trends were evident at home and abroad. On the one hand, nations sought to expand claims to offshore areas. This took many forms; the Truman proclamations on the continental shelf and on living resources and the Latin-American claims to 200-mile zones are examples. On the other hand, nations began to meet within the United Nations framework to devise a commonly acceptable legal regime to limit political conflict in the oceans. The results of these international efforts were the four Geneva Conventions of 1958 on the Territorial Sea, the Continental Shelf, Fisheries, and the High Seas.

U.S. Ocean Interests

In the past decade, domestic and international ocean politics have continued to flourish. Indeed, the 1970s offered a culmination of ocean politics in the Third U.N. Conference on the Law of the Sea. This conference stemmed from and fed back into the American political scene.

Before turning to a discussion of the politics of the United Nations conference, let me set the stage by describing the kinds of ocean activities that are important to the United States and other nations, and the interests that these activities reflect.

In the 1970s, traditional ocean activities—fishing and shipping—bore little resemblance to their precursors of even a few decades. Ships have attained new speeds, enormous size, and great numbers. They can travel at speeds up to thirty-three knots. Five-hundred-thousand-ton tankers are in production with even larger superships being planned. With 26,000 merchant ships crossing the oceans, water transportation continues to be the cheapest way to move bulk goods. The dependence of all countries on seaborne trade was dramatically illustrated by the Arab oil embargo in 1973. With almost a billion tons of water-borne commerce, the United States has a major interest in ocean transport, even though much of that shipping is under foreign flags.

World commerce moves in international shipping lanes that often lie close to shore. The near-shore areas are attractive for many uses in addition to shipping. Navigation problems have developed in congested areas such as the Straits of Dover, the Straits of Gibralter, and the entrances to busy harbors.

FISHING

The second time-honored ocean use—fishing—has also undergone dramatic change in this century. Fishing is no longer the random, lonely hunting operation it once was. Large, modern fishing vessels are equipped with the latest sonar equipment to locate their catch. And the development of block-and-tackle and multiple processing lines has made it possible for a single vessel to harvest and process hundreds of tons of fish daily.

The world fish catch has leveled off at 70 million metric tons a year for the last three years for which figures are available. Our National Marine Fisheries Service estimates that 100 million metric tons may be the upper limit on world catch. Overfishing and climatic change have caused fishery levels to drop dramatically in some areas of the world. Careful management of fishing effort is needed if overall catch is to be maintained or increased.

As with shipping routes, the most valuable fishing grounds lie within 200 miles of shore; approximately 90 percent of world fisheries are found in this broad belt. The United States is particularly fortunate, as one-fifth of total world fisheries are to be found off North America. In these circumstances, it is not surprising that coastal fishermen in the United States and Canada succeeded in moving their governments to adopt 200-mile fishing zones in 1976. At the same time, the United States fishes for tuna off the shores of other nations and seeks a cooperative approach to such highly migratory species.

ENERGY

Among recent developments in ocean use is an extremely important role for the oceans as a source of energy. At present, the oceans offer energy in the form of offshore oil and gas. By the year 2000, we should be using the stored solar energy of the oceans. Ocean Thermal Energy Conversion (OTEC) devices will generate energy by utilizing the temperature differences between ocean surface and bottom layers. The United States is leading the development of this technology. At present, we can also use extreme tidal fluctuations in certain areas of the world to generate energy. And much farther down the road, ocean currents themselves may be harnessed to generate energy.

Our present source of ocean energy—namely oil and gas—comes from the continental margins at depths of up to 600 feet in near-shore areas. The continental margin is that part of the continent that extends underwater. It includes three geological areas: the continental shelf, the continental slope, and the continental rise.

The continental margin varies widely from country to country, as nature has not been equally generous to all. Indeed, there appears to be a correlation between onshore reserves—as in the Middle East or Venezuela—and offshore deposits.

The United States has a broad and productive gulf coast continental margin. We have been recovering oil from under the narrower California margin for years, and exploration is underway off the east coast.

Roughly 30 percent of world oil and gas comes from offshore areas. As in the case of domestic coastal fishermen, the oil industry has prompted the U.S. government to lay claim to offshore minerals beyond the territorial sea. The international community first adopted this approach in the 1958 Geneva Convention on the Continental Shelf. The convention provided that national mineral resource jurisdiction would extend initially to the depth of 200 meters, and beyond that point to a depth at which seabed resource exploitation is possible.

DEEP-SEA MINING

Technological progress has overtaken this 1958 limit. We are now able to recover mineral resources from the deepest seabeds. The resource of interest in these deep-ocean areas is manganese nodules, which range in size from pebbles to large rocks. Those of commercial interest contain significant quantities of nickel, copper, and cobalt as well as manganese. The nodules of greatest commercial interest lie at great depths in the North and South Pacific. They have been harvested experimentally by a variety of techniques including a hydraulic or air-lift system or by a continuous line of buckets. U.S. companies are at the forefront of this technology. Once it became apparent that resource exploitation was possible at great depths, and once it was learned that manganese nodules were commercially valuable, political and legal problems developed rapidly.

Other ocean uses must be noted in any catalog of ocean resources. Anyone who swims, dives, or sport fishes recognizes the importance of the oceans as a recreational resource—a multi-million dollar industry in this country.

A competing (and often incompatible) use of the ocean is not always recognized as a resource—that is, its use as a disposal medium. Our urban societies cluster along the coastline and only recently have we come to appreciate the value, and the danger, of dumping our refuse in the seas. The oceans are the ultimate sink for the world pollutants whether they arrive there via the atmosphere, rivers, or through direct disposal. We know little of the overall capacity of the oceans to absorb all our wastes. Knowledge is being gained—often the hard way—of the tolerance levels of closed seas such as the Mediterranean and of specific coastal environments. In the United States we have interest groups that want to use the absorptive capacity of the oceans as well as those that wish to preserve the seas from environmental damage.

SCIENTIFIC RESEARCH

This brings us to another important use we make of the oceans and one to which we give little thought—the oceans as a laboratory for scientific research. The capacity of the oceans to absorb our wastes is simply one of many questions to which the oceans hold the answer and which are vital to the future of civilization. The oceans are the source of our weather—of winds and storms. Ultimately our ability to prepare ourselves for ocean storms requires improved capabilities for prediction and perhaps control of the weather. Marine scientific research can advance this capability. The ocean floor holds the story of the history of our planet—the movement of the continents and the record of volcanic activity. To learn more of this history, marine scientific research is being conducted by a number of U.S. research institutions, such as Woods Hole Oceanographic Institution in Massachusetts and Scripps Institution of Oceanography in California, into the tectonic plates that comprise the outer crust of the earth. Other research on natural upwellings and various tides and currents should teach us more about the living resources of the oceans.

Other contributors to this book have discussed the importance of the oceans for military purposes. All major naval powers use the oceans as a medium for projecting influence over other countries. The seas have been used to convoy military supplies, to show the flag, to launch attacks, to evacuate nationals from the shores of other countries. More recently, the oceans have provided the United States with the means for a stable deterrence from nuclear attack. As long as the oceans remain opaque— that is, as long as submarine concealment outpaces detection capabilities—our submarine-launched deterrent should remain invulnerable.

Each of these activities—shipping, energy, deep-sea mining, recreation, waste disposal, environmental protection, scientific research, and military navigation—is pursued and promoted within the United States by an array of interest groups. Other countries have similar industry and private groups, although few have the diversity and open expression of interests that we enjoy in the United States.

Third U.N. Conference on the Law of the Sea

This review of present and prospective ocean resources and interest groups lays the groundwork for understanding the politics of the 1970s and what the United Nations Conference on the Law of the Sea is about. UNCLOS III has been the center for negotiations on resources of significant and immediate value. Because the ocean resources at issue are so valuable, negotiations have been protracted and difficult. Other reasons accounting for the difficult negotiations are to be found in the large number and diverse composition of conference participants, as well as in the size and scope of the conference agenda.

When the United Nations was founded in 1945, there were 50 member nations. At the time of the 1958 and 1960 U.N. Conferences on the Law of the Sea, just under 90 nations were represented. About 150 nations are participating in the present conference. The size of this undertaking poses enormous negotiating problems.

In the preparatory stages of the conference in the early 1970s, an agenda was drafted encompassing twenty-five issues and more than a hundred sub-items. Each country, in effect, included its priority issue. The result has been the proliferation of political groupings around each issue, with coalitions of states shifting according to the question at hand. The United States, for instance, has significant maritime interests at the same time that it has the world's largest coastline. Thus, on some issues—navigation through straits, for example—the United States has joined with other maritime nations, whereas on other issues, such as coastal fisheries or delimiting the continental margin, the United States acts with other coastal nations.

PARTICIPANTS AND POLITICAL GROUPS

The political groups at UNCLOS III often mirror domestic ocean interests in the United States. Let us look briefly at some of the major political groups and issues at the conference.

The first are the regional groups. These are important in relation to caucusing and the election of conference officers. At the 1958 and 1960 conferences, just over half the participants were from the developing world. Since then, newly independent African and Asian nations have raised the number, until two-thirds of the delegations to the present law of the sea conference are from the developing world. A group called "Western European and Others" includes most developed countries. The

United States is an observer in this group, but formally belongs to no group.

The twenty-nine landlocked (LL) nations have been joined by another group of roughly twenty-five states that consider themselves to be geographically disadvantaged. Geographically disadvantaged states (GDS) include states which have very short coastlines, or which are prevented from enjoying full 200-mile economic zones by the proximity of other states off their coasts. In general the geographically disadvantaged states enjoy few resources in the small offshore areas they acquire. West Germany, Singapore, Trinidad, and Tobago are representative members of this group, and they have sought, generally unsuccessfully, to limit coastal state offshore claims. Although the United States has extensive coastline and rich offshore resources, it has been sympathetic, because of its distant-water interests, to the LL/GDS efforts to limit coastal state rights in offshore areas.

Coastal Nations

Another major political grouping at the conference lies at the opposite end of the spectrum from the LL/GDS. These are the eighty-some nations with substantial coastlines, rich offshore resources, and/or broad continental margins. Some of these nations, such as Chile and Peru, have long coastlines rich in fishery resources fronting open ocean. Other countries, such as Australia and Canada, have wide continental margins as well as long coastlines. Their continental margins extend up to 500 miles from shore, and beyond in some places. The goal of wide margin nations in the conference has been to secure control over their entire continental margin, where it extends beyond 200 miles. The United States has generally supported the position of the wide margin states on resources because their participation in a law of the sea regime is critical, but has opposed attempts to extend jurisdiction over scientific research and navigation.

Another major political grouping within the conference is that of nations with strong maritime interests. These include shipping nations such as Greece; shipbuilding nations such as Norway; distant-water fishing nations such as Japan and West Germany; and major naval powers such as the United States and the Soviet Union.

Archipelagoes and Islands

In addition to the major conference groupings just mentioned, a number of smaller coalitions have formed around particular items on the conference agenda. States that border on international straits are one such group. Island nations that wish to be designated as archipelagoes are another such group. Countries such as Indonesia or Fiji are seeking a new legal designation for those waters that lie between their multiple islands. The waters would be called "archipelagic waters," and the ships of other nations would be freely allowed to transit them only within sea lanes designated by the island state.

Islands have been the source of a number of problems for law of the sea in addition to archipelagic questions. For instance, should all islands receive the same treatment as continental nations? That is, should islands receive a 12-mile territorial sea and a 200-mile economic zone? States such as Turkey which have the islands of other nations lying close to shore predictably oppose granting the same offshore rights to islands as to continents. Other states, such as Norway, with many offshore rocks and islands, have adopted the reverse approach and seek to use these pieces of real estate as a base point from which to extend their jurisdiction even farther to sea.

Nations with Mining Technology

One final political grouping in the conference merits special attention, and that is the constellation of forces that has evolved over the question of deep seabed mining. Those countries that have the technology to mine the seabed—the United States, Japan, and the Federal Republic of Germany—are eager to do so under a regime which allows them to mine with predictable and non-discriminatory regulations. Developing nations operating in the "Group of 77" (actually about 120 countries) want to establish an international authority they would control that would ensure them the benefits of deep-sea mining, both in technology and revenues. The Group of 77 has insisted that the international authority should mine the seabed directly through an operating arm called the Enterprise. Indeed, if it were not for the lack of technology, the Group of 77 would prefer to prevent national entities from mining the seabed altogether. In addition, they have sought a decision-making structure reflecting their greater numbers, and they have sought to limit production from the seabed. There are, of course, many nuances in view within these two groups, but this is a rough outline of their core positions.

This sketch of conference interest groups that have developed among the 150 participants may convey some sense of the difficult negotiating situation in UNCLOS III. The interest groups reflect the many items on the conference agenda. Indeed, the size of the agenda is itself an organizational problem. How is it possible to structure a negotiation on twenty-five items that are interrelated numerous ways?

The difficult political situation has made agreement at UNCLOS III very elusive. The conference began officially in December 1973 after five years of preparatory discussions. The eleventh session is due to begin in spring 1982 in New York. It will bring the length of the conference to ninety-five weeks—nearly two years of negotiation.

The Emerging Regime for the Oceans

What, after all this time, has UNCLOS produced? And what are the prospects for a comprehensive, widely accepted law of the sea treaty that will set the framework for the ocean politics of the 1980s and 1990s?

The draft treaty currently under consideration is impressive in its size and scope. It has 320 articles plus eight annexes. Although all states have problems with portions of the text, there is near consensus support for most of the treaty articles. In fact, even if the treaty does not go into effect formally, most of its provisions will become de facto law. The critical question, however, as each nation assesses the total treaty package, is whether the portions of the text that it finds objectionable are outweighed by those parts of the treaty that it favors.

Let us examine the outlines of the settlement, then, from the United States perspective. What are the major features of the present text and what is the likely treaty outcome?

Territorial Sea. There is general agreement, reflected in the text, that the universal breadth of the territorial sea should be set at twelve miles.

Straits. A twelve-mile territorial sea will overlap straits which are less than twenty-four miles wide, a number of which the United States considers vital for navigation. The United States has, therefore, pressed hard for a special regime of transit through international straits. Innocent passage would not apply in these areas of the territorial sea. Rather, the coastal state would have carefully delineated rights to designate sea lanes and to prescribe environmental regulations, but could not otherwise interfere with the right of transit passage by states passing through straits. The United States is generally satisfied with the straits regime that has emerged in the treaty text.

Archipelagoes. The draft treaty delineates a regime for archipelagoes which seems to encompass their maximal claims. Its main features include a generous land-water ratio and a liberal means of drawing straight baselines to encompass the archipelago. Territorial seas of twelve miles and 200-mile economic zones are to be measured from the baselines. Maritime nations, including the United States, have gone along with the archipelago formula because provision is made for air and sea passage routes to be specified by the archipelagic state.

Exclusive Economic Zone (EEZ). Another area in which the conference is developing new international law is that of the 200-mile Exclusive Economic Zone. In this zone, the coastal state would exercise sovereign rights over the exploitation of living and non-living resources. At issue between maritime nations and developing coastal nations have been a number of legal and practical questions. The central legal question has been that of the status of the zone. Maritime nations have argued that, except for coastal state resource rights, the area beyond the twelve-mile territorial sea should be designated as high seas. Developing coastal states, seeking greater measures of control, have countered with the argument that the EEZ is a unique zone and is not high seas. The present formulation of the text allows both sides to claim success on this issue of the legal status of the EEZ.

Practical questions that have arisen in the economic zone negotiations concern matters such as scientific research and protection of the environment. Coastal states have argued that research might adversely affect their economic resources or national security and therefore should not be conducted without the consent of the coastal state. Researching nations, including the United States, have countered with a reluctant willingness to allow the coastal state to control research in the EEZ that might be related to resources—recognizing full well that it will be extremely difficult to distinquish between research that is and is not related to resources. The outcome embodied in the treaty requires implied or explicit coastal state consent for research in the exclusive economic zone and on the continental margin where it extends beyond 200 miles. Although the United States is not happy with this outcome, there is little likelihood that further modifications can be negotiated.

ENVIRONMENTAL PROTECTION ENFORCEMENT

Another issue related to the EEZ with practical consequences for navigation has been the question of who can regulate and enforce standards for protection of the marine environment. Obviously, the state of the environment affects offshore fishery resources and recreation possibilities. Nonetheless, negotiations on environmental questions have not evoked the usual maritime-versus-coastal state groupings on both sides of the issue. Greater complexity exists because many developing nations fear that strict environmental regulations in the hands of the coastal state would be used to hamper their commercial shipping. Nations such as Brazil and the OPEC countries wish to become major shipping nations and are especially resistant to environmental concerns. In the United States, on the other hand, there has evolved a significant concern for the environment, and the government has pressed for enhanced coastal state environmental protection powers in the territorial sea.

The treaty has a complex set of provisions balancing coastal state and flag state rights with regard to the environment. In the economic zone, the coastal state may enact laws and regulations which conform to the international law developed by organizations such as the International Maritime Consultative Organization (IMCO). In other words, the coastal state may not set standards stricter than those set by the competent international organizations.

Enforcement of these regulations is shared among the port state, the coastal state in whose waters a violation has occurred, and the flag state of the vessel in question. From the U.S. perspective, the procedures stipulated in the treaty seem effectively to bridge the concerns of environmental groups and navigational interests. These kinds of practical problems are a necessary result of creating 200-mile exclusive economic zones.

NATURAL RESOURCE EXPLOITATION

Continental Shelf. The fifth major jurisdictional aspect of a law of the sea settlement is that coastal states exercise sovereign rights over the continental shelf where it extends beyond 200 miles, for the purpose of exploiting its natural resources. Although the landlocked and geographically disadvantaged states strongly resisted such a special territorial reward for the wide margin states, the treaty embodies a grant of additional rights beyond the economic zone. The coastal state is required to share with the international community a small amount of revenues realized in exploiting the margin beyond 200 miles. Coastal state claims to the entire continental margin, combined with archipelagic claims and 200-mile economic zones, will result in almost 50 percent of ocean space coming under some form of national control.

The Seabed. The final aspect of a law of the sea settlement concerns that 50 percent of ocean space that lies beyond areas of national jurisdiction—the seabed. As has been widely reported in the press, this has been one of the most intractable negotiating problems of the conference. On the one hand, a few developed states have the technology to mine the seabed; on the other hand, the vast majority of developing countries have the votes needed to accord unchallenged legitimacy to any regime for deep-sea mining. Given the fact that seabed mining is a novel and untested industry, the political and legal uncertainty may seriously retard mining.

Domestic Seabed Mining Legislation

The United States wants to assure access to the minerals of the seabed for its mining companies on a predictable basis. The mining industry in this country is prepared to begin seabed mining in the 1980s under suitable international arrangements. While the United States has a strong preference for a comprehensive mining regime, a number of provisions of the draft treaty are a source of dissatisfaction. The United States hopes to resolve these issues in the months ahead in the U.N. conference and in the context of an interim preparatory group.

Under the current draft, transfer of mining technology would be mandatory under many circumstances if firms were to gain access to seabed mining. Production limits could be so low as to limit seriously the number of mining operations. And after fifteen years of commercial production, a review conference would be held to renegotiate the mining arrangement agreed now. The United States is also unhappy with the voting provisions specified for the council—the principal administrative arm of a proposed international mining authority. In this thirty-six-member body, a one-nation, one-voice standard is applied, with the developing countries easily able to muster the required three-fourths majority needed to outvote the principal mining or mineral-consuming nations on most issues.

To assure that its mining industry is not held back by legal uncertainties, the United States is moving ahead under domestic seabed legislation to work with other mining countries to develop an interim mining regime.

Prospects for U.S. Acceptance of Draft Treaty

These, then, are the broad outlines set by the draft Law of the Sea Treaty. This framework will affect the politics of the next decade even if the treaty is not completed or ratified by the requisite number of states.

Given the U.S. problems with the seabed mining text, it is uncertain what course of action the government will take. To be sure, the United States would like to see the straits, territorial sea, and economic zone portions of the text reflected in international law. The conference has operated, however, on the basis that the draft treaty is an all-or-nothing proposition. In the course of negotiations to improve the seabed mining text, some countries have sought to reopen other sections of the text that they do not like.

Looking ahead, we see two broad areas of importance. In the first place, coastal states will be preoccupied with using more intensively the resources of their economic zones and continental margins. Domestic users will compete for priority access rights in these offshore areas.

Second, the United States will seek to preserve its distant-water interests in navigation and highly migratory fisheries as well as marine scientific research and deep-sea mining. In conjunction with these coastal and distant-water activities, the United States will carry out a number of bilateral and multilateral negotiations: with neighbors over boundaries and transboundary activities; with other countries over the exercise of resource-related rights in their offshore areas; and with developed and developing nations over the mining of deep-sea minerals.

Some Concepts in American Naval Strategic Thought, 1940–1970

John B. Hattendorf

In the years between 1940 and 1970, the United States Navy had more ships and more men than it had ever had or has had since. Looking back, one can mark the beginning of the period with the Two-Ocean Navy Act of 1940 and the ship construction programs of World War II. The period ended about thirty years later, when the ships that had come into use during the war reached the end of their useful service. By the 1970s, the Navy had returned to and even sunk below the size of the pre-World War II fleet. In statistical terms, the U.S. Navy had reached—and passed— its zenith.

Statistics, however, do not tell the story. Technology had altered the character of navies. The older ships gave way to the new. Weapons and sensors had longer ranges and greater power. Automation replaced men with machines. More could be done with less. For twenty of these thirty years, the United States Navy sailed the world's oceans unchallenged. The major naval powers of the older period were gone. The navies of Japan, Italy, France, and Germany were virtually destroyed in the war, and British naval power declined sharply in the wake of victory. By 1970, however, the United States found itself challenged at sea by the formidable power of the Soviet Union. This challenge came at a time when

American thinking about naval strategy was in the process of change. New ideas and new naval problems had undermined traditional American concepts on the function and use of naval power.

The Mahanian Concept: Command of the Sea

At the beginning of World War II, American naval strategists based their fundamental concepts on the ideas that Alfred Thayer Mahan had expressed fifty years earlier. With Mahan, they shared the belief that the essential problem in naval warfare was to obtain "command of the sea." In other words, the way to protect oneself from the dangers which threaten across the vast, neutral expanse of the ocean is to deprive an opponent of his ability to move at sea. Mahan believed that there were two effective ways to do this. One could destroy an enemy fleet in a battle at sea, or one could blockade it in port in order to prevent its use. Fundamentally the Mahanian concept of sea power was based on the idea that the best defense is an offense. "Command of the sea," which opens and assures the free use of the ocean to the victor, provides security by denying the use of the sea to the opponent.[1] The navy that the United States built up so dramatically after 1940 was designed to perform this function.

NAVAL STRATEGY IN THE SECOND WORLD WAR

The experience of World War II tended to confirm for Americans the broad features of Mahan's thought, but the World War in two separate hemispheres brought home separate lessons.

The war in the Atlantic and in the Mediterranean was fought against naval powers which did not share the concept of sea power held by the Anglo-American allies. The German and Italian navies persistently attempted to avoid the type of fleet battle sought by the Allies. Instead, Germany and Italy concentrated on a single task: severing Allied lines of communication. The Axis powers were initially in an advantageous position to undertake this. They had developed some very effective weapons, and German conquests on the continent placed Britain at a great disadvantage. Despite these initial strengths, the Allied defeat of this diametrically opposed system of strategy confirmed the basic correctness of Mahan's concept. Although naval battles seemed less important in the European theater, the battle fleet had been essential in giving constant support and protection.[2] Analysts in America believed that the Allies had defeated the Axis navies by exercising command of the sea.

In the Pacific, Japan had gone to war with the notion that she could obtain victory, as she had in earlier wars, by maintaining a local "command of the sea." Japanese leaders failed to understand the full implications of what they had initiated, and they failed to prevent the transition from a "limited war" to a "total war."[3] Surely this is what lies at the heart of Japan's defeat. Despite this, many Americans saw Mahan's ideas justified in the Pacific. The great battles of Midway and Leyte Gulf seemed conclusive proof that decisive victory in warfare was obtained through climactic battle between opposing fleets, and that these victories obtained command of the sea. This view tended to overlook the critical importance of American submarines and mines in destroying Japanese tankers and merchantmen, but Mahan had argued that this type of warfare was inconclusive.

MAHAN SINCE 1945

Mahan had been the first to explore rationally the fundamental problem of naval strategy. Despite some adverse criticism and developments which he could not foresee, his work seemed vindicated by experience up to 1945.

Professional naval officers continued to employ his ideas and to structure the Navy's use and construction around them. At the Naval War College, for example, discussions and lectures on "Mahan in the Nuclear Age" became commonplace. Many writers continued the effort to apply Mahan's ideas to the post-war world.[4] They were valiant attempts, but they raised some fundamental questions.

The questions came from a variety of sources. In the academic community, they came from both historians and political scientists. In the practical world of affairs, they came from those who were attempting to deal with the difficult problems of nuclear weapons and modern warfare, as well as from those who dealt in the day-to-day crises of cold war diplomacy.

Historians looked at the problem in two ways. One group looked at Mahan in relation to his own times while another focused on the same historical subject matter that he had studied.

As a man within his own times, Mahan came to be seen as a leader in the now unfashionable period of American imperialism. He was a "navalist" who sought to enhance his own profession at the expense of others, and he was an advocate of the elitist, racist, and social Darwinist ideas that were dominant in his day. As an individual, researchers found him to be the vaunted "apostle of sea power," yet whose personal characteristics were not those which the modern naval profession wanted to extol. To top it off, he was a naval officer who hated going to sea. None of these factors encouraged post-war students of naval strategy to regard Mahan as a prophet.[5]

Rejection of "Scientific School" of History

Only a very few serious historians were working in the same field which Mahan had drawn upon for his ideas—naval history between 1660 and 1815. However, historians in general had come to reject the so-called scientific school of history. Mahan had been a leader in the use of this nineteenth century approach to historical study founded on the idea that basic principles of human action could be deduced from a study of history in the way that scientists deduced laws from their observations of the physical world. By rejecting this approach, academic historians raised doubts about Mahan's conclusions and observations. The new schools of historians tended to study history with more attention to the factors that invited contrast rather than comparison to current situations. Students emphasized the past as a prologue rather than a pattern for the future. In general, when historical analogies were drawn, modern historians drew them with greater care and precision than Mahan had done.

Emphasis on Sea Battles Questioned

The few historians who were engaged in studying naval history of the seventeenth and eighteenth centuries began to reexamine the subject by comparing the results of their original research with Mahan's conclusions. Much of this work began to appear only in the 1970s,[6] but it showed that a careful examination of original source materials provided grounds for a much different interpretation of the use of naval power. In particular, historians questioned Mahan's stress on battles at sea as the decisive factor in overall strategy. Readers of these new works were left with the general impression that naval power was important for the way in which the sea could be used to affect affairs on land, but in itself naval power was neither decisive nor a determining factor for national greatness.

Different Uses for Navies

Many historians continued to interpret history through Mahan's eyes, but some provided new insights in the process. One book, titled with Mahan's own phrase, *Command of the Sea,* made the original observation that different types of nations had different uses for navies.[7] Continental powers, maritime-island nations, and small coastal states each valued and used navies in different functions, some playing a relatively more important role than others. Another student[8] developed these ideas further in terms of British maritime power, and explained naval dominance as a reflection of a unique system that was dependent on overseas trade in an era symbolized by "guns, sails, and empires."[9]

Mahan Evaluated

In post-World War II America, Mahan's work came to be seen as the product of a particular person at a specific time in history, and as the reflection of ideas that were somewhat inaccurately drawn from one peculiar set of historical circumstances. Yet his deeply detailed work was studded with flashes of great insight and originality. In 1953, Rear Admiral John D. Hayes, a prolific writer on strategy and naval history, acknowledged the problems with Mahan's thought, but Hayes concluded: "Until there comes another like him to dissect, analyze, and codify the experience of our day, none of us can go wrong if we study Mahan's great historical works."[10] This statement, more than any other, expresses the basic conflict in American thinking in this period. Admiral Hayes recognized the weakness of Mahan's ideas in the modern world, but saw the primary need to return to them until someone could provide a comprehensive statement that would supersede them.

Clausewitzian Theory in U.S. Maritime Strategy

Some of the faults in Mahan's work led historians to the writings of one of Mahan's British contemporaries, Sir Julian Corbett. Corbett had used Mahan's ideas, but had presaged some of the criticisms which later historians would make. Most important, he had attempted to go beyond Mahan and to formulate naval theory into a coherent statement. Although first published in 1911, his book *Some Principles of Maritime Strategy* had been largely ignored by American thinkers. In the 1950s and 1960s, however, Corbett's work came to the attention of Americans,[11] and many of his works were reprinted in the 1970s.[12]

POLITICAL POLICY AND DIPLOMACY

One of the attractions to Corbett's work for American thinkers was his use of Clausewitzian theory. Many of Carl von Clausewitz's nineteenth century German interpreters had emphasized only one aspect of his work, but Corbett had elaborated on the little emphasized ideas of limited warfare and on the relationship of strategy to broad political policy. Political theorists in America had been developing concepts along these lines since the 1930s, but they had had very little impact in practical affairs until after World War II. Americans continued, by and large, to see military and naval affairs as something quite distinct from political considerations and diplomacy. Academics imbued with Clausewitzian theory stressed the point that "the political object, as the original motive of the war, will be the standard for determining both the aim of the military force and also the amount of effort to be made,"[13] and that therefore "war is not merely a political act, but also a real political instrument, a continuation of political commerce, a carrying out of the same by other means."[14]

NAVIES IN LIMITED WARFARE

This line of thinking was developed further by many academics, and brought into practical use by a number of them who became advisers and officials in Washington. Among many others at various levels, Henry Kissinger was the most prominent of the academics who brought these ideas into practice.

Mahan and Corbett had been concerned entirely with the conduct of war at sea. The experience of the United States Navy after World War II emphasized the use of navies in limited warfare and in situations short of war. Both the Korean War and the Vietnam War had been limited wars, but there had been little opposition to American naval operations. The focus on the Navy's work moved from events at sea to the effect which it had ashore. This was paralleled in other experiences. In 1946 the battleship *Missouri* had appeared in Turkish waters when the Soviet Union seemed to be making a threatening diplomatic move in that area. Friendly governments in the Far East were bolstered by the U.S. Seventh Fleet after the collapse of Nationalist Chinese power in the Asian mainland. In another example, amphibious forces were landed in Lebanon in 1958 to support the government there. Perhaps the supreme example is the Cuban Missile Crisis of 1962 in which the threat of U.S. naval forces prevented the Soviet Union from following its own foreign policy objectives in the Caribbean.

Exploitation of Potential Force

The Clausewitzian emphasis on the relationship between military affairs and politics joined the practical naval experience to stimulate further thought in this area. Among notable works, civilian theorists such as Thomas C. Schelling began to apply the ideas of game theory to warfare.[15] In Schelling's view, the important focus was not the actual application of force, as it had been for Mahan, but the exploitation of potential force. In terms of naval power, however, no book of theoretical writing on this aspect of thinking appeared until the early 1970s. Since that time the subject has been explored by James Cable, Edward Luttwak, and Kenneth Booth.[16]

NEW ROLES FOR NAVIES

The work done by these men emphasized some additional functions of naval force. Kenneth Booth's work, *Navies and Foreign Policy*, was by far the most complete statement. He based his approach on a trinity of uses for the sea: (1) for the passage of goods and people; (2) for the passage of military force for diplomatic purposes or for use against targets on land and at sea; and (3) for the exploitation of resources in or under the sea. Navies, he argued, existed to further such ends, and it is appropriate that the military character of a navy forms the basis for two additional roles: a diplomatic and a policing role. In making this point, Booth emphasized that a navy's ability to threaten and to use force gives meaning to its other modes of action. In a policing role, a navy can extend sovereignty as well as defend offshore resources. In a diplomatic role, navies can provide the readily available strength behind negotiations, the latent and moveable force which can change the political calculations of other nations as well as promote prestige.[17]

The use of naval force in these varied roles presented some new dimensions and emphasized some traditional usages. The unique problem which Americans faced in the late 1960s was to understand how to use naval force in these ways, short of war, when the United States was faced with a rival naval force that was engaged in much the same activity. How, indeed, does one gauge the relative strength between two naval rivals who are trying to use their naval forces to influence and manipulate third parties as part of the rivalry between themselves?

Technology and Naval Strategy

The rise of the Soviet navy as a rival and as a potential enemy in this period remains the key element in understanding naval issues since the 1960s. This is treated in detail elsewhere in this book,[18] but let me just note that this rivalry is very deeply enmeshed in the relationship between technology and strategy.

When Mahan wrote his famous books, he had specifically argued that understanding of strategy transcended technological change. As he wrote, "Conditions and weapons change, but . . . respect must be had to these constant teachings of history . . . in those wider operations of war which are comprised under the name of strategy."[19] Mahan's contention was first challenged by the naval employment of aviation and the submarine, and it is presently challenged additionally by nuclear weapons and the guided missile.

In a book widely read in America during the late 1960s, L. W. Martin declared that the strategic world of Mahan and Corbett "is no longer with us." Similar battle fleets will no longer fight each other at sea; technological developments have altered the scene forever, Martin wrote.

> Developments in naval propulsion, in aircraft, missiles, explosives and techniques of computation have overthrown completely the context in which fleet actions were the focus of strategy. Submarines, aircraft and missiles have become the most dangerous enemies of the larger surface ships, while those ships find their prime targets on shore. Bombardment of the land, once one of the most humble naval tasks, has become a dominant concern of the larger navies—strategically with missiles launched from submarines, tactically with aircraft based at sea.[20]

THE NUCLEAR AGE NAVY

Nuclear weapons, of course, are supreme among the new developments in technology. Since they were first employed in 1945, many observers declared that they had completely altered the nature of warfare. During the short period when the United States was the sole owner of atomic weapons, the government spent vast sums in developing military uses for them. Both strategists and budgets stressed the Air Force's ability to deliver nuclear weapons, while the other services found waning support for their more traditional methods and roles. Many years later, observers have looked back on this period through the lens of Clausewitzian theory and have seen that the possession of this terrible weapon had only a very limited political effect on the outside world. Somewhat ironically, the possession of nuclear weapons has come to have a useful meaning only as a deterrent to the use of similar weapons by those who have now come to possess them.

Strategy of Deterrence

The complicated theory of nuclear weapons lies outside the scope of this paper, but two of its dimensions apply directly to the Navy. First of all, there is the use of submarines to carry submarine-launched Polaris missiles. This was part of the strategy of deterrence, based on a weapon that could be kept safe from attack. Oskar Morgenstern described the idea as early as 1959:

> The principal aim of shifting the weapons carrier, of putting it one moment here, the other there, below the water and in the air, is of course to hide it. . . . This is achieved by combining the properties of speed and depth of water with erratic movements, with randomization. Instead of deploying forces to carefully selected places, of giving their placement a pattern and formation such as fleets had to adopt by necessity even in the last war, probability alone should determine the geographical spot where the weapon carrier (submarine, floating missile base, seaplane) is next to appear. This is what the combination of nuclear propulsion of ships and seaplanes with nuclear weapons and solid fuel propulsion for missiles is making possible. Never before in warfare could a system be envisaged where mobile dispersal is combined with great power in each unit, the ability for all to act together from their dispersed points according to some previous plan, and be directed from a central point of command.[21]

The central purpose of all this is the ability to have a weapon which is still usable under attack. In view of the catastrophic implications of nuclear warfare, some observers doubted that such weapons could ever be used, and from this they argued that the deterrent effect of nuclear weapons was of no value:

> The trouble with this concept is faulty assumptions (for example, that civilian casualties and collateral damage can be kept to low levels); it ignores a basic lesson that the leaders of the U.S. government in all crises have learned—that when faced with the decision to start a nuclear war, almost any other alternative looked better.[22]

Despite this caveat, the submarine-launched Polaris missile remained a part of American strategy and performed a function while there was a reasonable suspicion that the United States might use nuclear weapons in retaliation against a nuclear attack.

The Tactical Nuclear Weapon

In this respect, American military power was muscle-bound. In attempting to circumvent the problem of having too much power to be useful, some strategists hit upon the idea of the so-called tactical nuclear weapon. This is a small nuclear weapon used in conjunction with a gun or torpedo which would have an effect limited to the battle area. With this in mind, some naval strategists envisaged a nuclear war fought at sea between two opposing naval forces. The concept attracted those who wished to find a viable method to use nuclear weapons and still to confine warfare to struggle between military forces without damage to civilian populations. A knockout blow could be delivered within the confines of a single battle area. It is an idealistic concept which suggests that naval forces could fight to the death in a duel which does little harm to anyone in a place which is of no great concern. The problem is that it reduces warfare to a boxing match and a sideshow while ignoring the military factor in the essential nature of international relations. The day is yet to come when weapons and force play no direct part in competing national interests and political goals.

At the same time, the increasing accuracy and explosive power of conventional naval weapons began to render unnecessary the potential use of "tactical nuclear weapons." A conventional weapon was soon able to deliver a knockout blow without the danger of causing an all-out war that might follow the use of a nuclear weapon of any kind.

INTER-AGENCY RELATIONS

While these ideas seem esoteric, they performed a very real and practical function in the matter of bureaucratic politics. In the late 1960s, academics began to explore the relationship of foreign and military policy with domestic affairs.[23] There are many aspects to this problem, but one very important side is the political relations of separate agencies inside one governmental organization. Each in its own way competes for a share of influence, position, or money. In the period following World War II, the Air Force had the primary position in defense because of its ability to deliver nuclear weapons. It became dominant in terms of money and its role in the defense establishment. The Navy's continual emphasis on its traditional roles, however correct, was not impressive when contrasted with the revolutionary innovations claimed for nuclear weapons. Submarines, amphibious forces, destroyers, cruisers, even aircraft carriers, seemed to be anachronisms. The ability of the Navy Department—either consciously or unconsciously—to connect the more traditional interests of naval power with nuclear warfare and nuclear deterrence played an important role in supporting the Navy's stake in national security affairs.

There is no doubt that the Navy lost much, in terms of politics, finance, and material, with the development of nuclear weapons. The Navy's ability to develop a credible maritime role for nuclear weapons served, additionally, a useful political purpose in stemming the Navy's losses in Congress.

COPING WITH TECHNOLOGICAL CHANGE

Nuclear weapons are only part of a much broader issue. The essence of the matter lies in the very basic problem in man's ability to cope with technological changes which alter the very fabric of tradition, custom, and society. For a century, the Western world has largely agreed with Matthew Arnold that technology and machines appear to have very little to do with sweetness and light, the essential elements that create culture and the best that humans have thought and said.[24] Our experience in the technological world has caused us to be more aware of the various ways in which machines affect society. Their impact can no longer be ignored.

> Technology tends to create its own environment and set of conditions. Put even more simply, as the mechanism steadily increases in power and scale, the tendency is to fit men into machinery rather than to fit the machinery into the contours of a human situation.[25]

As early as 1948, the president of the Naval War College observed this happening to naval strategy. "So much of the old has broken down," he wrote, "and so much of the new has been added that there no longer exists an accepted closely-knit analysis of the whole of war and strategy. Instead, theories have tended to center around new technological developments which have given rise to more or less unconnected and very often contradictory doctrines, like sprawling limbs without backbone or head."[26]

The means were stressed at the expense of the whole. Naval officers were becoming specialists in using a particular type of technology. They were aviators, surface ship officers, and submarine officers before they were specialists in the broader functions of armed force. Most naval officers saw the need for "hard" technological training and expertise more readily than for the "softer" understanding of political and military affairs. At the same time, naval men increasingly found that in order to maintain a rational continuity, they resisted certain types of technological change, and moved to develop machines along already established lines: aircraft carriers, destroyers, ordnance, nuclear power. They avoided change that would sweep everything away, reacting in a way that was only gradually being understood about technological societies.[27] The daily life of the ordinary naval officer, in this period, became increasingly a problem in the care and feeding of machines rather than the examination of their utility.

The problem was the same that Mahan had encountered in the 1890s, but his answer was the opposite extreme. Mahan ignored technology and sought a higher understanding that was unaffected by change. The course of events between 1940 and 1970 demonstrated that technology and change could not be ignored. They have a deep and abiding effect on human behavior, in both peace and war. They are necessary factors that must be considered in the rational use of armed force, yet American naval officers had not developed a balanced and systematic approach to strategic thinking that included these factors. They tended either to ignore the strategic implications of technological change or to be swept away in enthusiasm for their new machines.

Alternatives to Armed Force

The vast technological changes of these thirty years, particularly the development of nuclear weapons and the specter of mass destruction which they carry, created another effect. Military force seemed less relevant and less useful to the modern world. All around the globe, people were increasingly aware of the cost of military functions at the expense of social services. As economic issues became more and more important and budgets became tighter, many nations found less to spend on armament. Many people believed that they saw a long-term but clear trend that showed the traditional reasons for conflict disappearing. The very standards of international conduct were changing. International law and consensus among nations were slowly replacing the forceful assertion of national interests.

Yet there was a limit to change of this nature. The long-term trend had not reached its ultimate goal. Conflict and arms races continued. The nation still required protection, and potential enemies could still be deterred. The potential use of armed force still seemed to have persuasive value.

By 1970, American naval thinkers had not found a new conceptual basis upon which to formulate strategic ideas. The older ideas were still in use, but they had not been thoroughly reworked and adapted to new situations. New perceptions had been opened, and some of them suggested a viable way for the future.

As early as 1949, Rear Admiral C. R. Brown told the Naval War College that what was needed was not a new Mahan, but "brilliant strategists, not of land power, not of sea power, and not of air power, but able, broad-gauged individuals who can view the whole picture of *military* strategy."[28]

Strategy as "Comprehensive Direction of Power"

A small group of individuals responded to this challenge. Among them was Herbert Rosinski, a refugee from Nazi Germany and former lecturer at the German Naval Staff College. Rosinski's key contribution was his concept of strategy as comprehensive direction of power. Rosinski wrote:

> This definition required the recognition that there is much more to strategy than mere direction of action. It is a type of direction which takes into account the multitude of possible enemy counteractions, and thus it becomes a means of control. It is this element of control which is the essence of strategy. . . . It must be comprehensive in order to control every possible counteraction or factor.[29]

This concept was developed further by Rear Admiral Henry E. Eccles in the 1960s when he stressed the relationship between economic and industrial factors, policy, strategy, and tactics. "Military strategy is subordinate to national strategy, so the selection of weapons to be used and the choice of tactics to be employed is subordinate to strategic objectives and factors," Eccles emphasized. "Strategy must have at its disposal a variety of weapons and forces, so that the particular combination most suitable to a situation, as it actually arises, may be formed and swiftly and decisively employed in an appropriate manner."[30]

Rosinski and Eccles pointed the way out of the thicket in naval thinking. They provided the basic foundation stones for the development of a comprehensive theory of naval power. In addition, the next generation of naval thinkers must appreciate the subtle changes in human affairs which have both narrowed the usefulness of armed force and, at the same time, broadened the functions of naval power. Force has less of a role to play in international affairs, but navies have far more to do than the simple task of forcefully controlling the sea lanes. These significant changes require that clear thinking on the subject of naval strategy be expressed carefully, in precise language. New and comprehensive thought must take complete account of technology along with the capabilities and limitations of armed force to serve a useful function along the entire range of national power, both in peace and in war.

NOTES

1. B. Mitchell Simpson III, ed., *The Development of Naval Thought: Essays by Herbert Rosinski* (Newport, R.I.: Naval War College Press, 1977), p. 24.

2. *Ibid.*, pp. 34–35.

3. *Ibid.*, pp. 102–20.

4. See, for example, Bernard Brodie, *Layman's Guide to Naval Strategy* (Princeton, N.J.: Princeton University Press, 1942, and four other editions to 1965), and A. E. Sokol, *Sea Power in the Nuclear Age* (Washington: Public Affairs Press, 1961).

5. The preeminent work in the iconoclastic school is Robert Seager II, *Alfred Thayer Mahan* (Annapolis, Md.: Naval Institute Press, 1977).

6. See, for example, Geoffrey Symcox, *The Crisis of French Sea Power, 1688–1697: From guerre d'escadre to the guerre de course* (The Hague: Martinus Nijhoff, 1974); J. F. Guilmartin, Jr., *Gunpowder and Galleys: Changing Technology and Mediterranean Warfare at Sea in the Sixteenth Century* (Cambridge: Cambridge University Press, 1974); and my own unpublished Oxford D.Phil. thesis, "England in the War of the Spanish Succession" (1979). See also, Michael Howard, *The British Way in Warfare: A Reappraisal*, Neale Lecture in English History, 1974 (London: Jonathan Cape, 1975), which summarizes the general trend of recent work.

7. Clark G. Reynolds, *Command of the Sea: The History and Strategy of Maritime Empires* (New York: William Morrow & Co., 1974), pp. 12–16.

8. Paul M. Kennedy, *The Rise and Fall of British Naval Mastery* (London: Allen Lane, 1976).

9. Carlo M. Cipolla, *Guns, Sails, and Empire: Technological Innovation and the Early Phase of European Expansion, 1400–1700* (New York: Pantheon, 1965).

10. John D. Hayes, "Peripheral Strategy—Mahan's Doctrine Today," U.S. Naval Institute *Proceedings* (Nov. 1953), p. 1193.

11. Largely through the efforts of Donald M. Schurman, most notably in his book, *Education of a Navy: The Development of British Naval Strategic Thought, 1867–1914* (Chicago: University of Chicago Press, 1965).

12. For example, *Some Principles of Maritime Strategy* (Annapolis: Naval Institute Press, 1972) and *Campaign of Trafalgar* (New York: AMS, 1976).

13. Carl von Clausewitz, *On War*, edited by Anatol Rapoport (Baltimore: Penguin Books, 1968), p. 109.

14. *Ibid.*, p. 119.

15. Thomas C. Schelling, *The Strategy of Conflict* (Cambridge, Mass.: Harvard University Press, 1960); *Arms and Influence* (New Haven: Yale University Press, 1966).

16. James C. Cable, *Gunboat Diplomacy: Political Applications of Limited Naval Force* (New York: Praeger, 1971); Edward N. Luttwak, *The Political Uses of Sea Power* (Baltimore: The Johns Hopkins University Press, 1974); Kenneth Booth, *Navies and Foreign Policy* (New York: Crane Russak, 1977).

17. Booth, pp. 15–25.

18. See "The Superpowers at Sea: Two Studies in Sea Power" by Michael MccGwire.

19. A. T. Mahan, *The Influence of Sea Power Upon History, 1660–1783* (London: Methuen, University Paperbacks, 1965), p. 7.

20. L. W. Martin, *The Sea in Modern Strategy* (New York: Praeger, 1967), pp. 9–10.

21. Oskar Morgenstern, *The Question of National Defense* (New York: Random House, 1959), p. 90.

22. A. C. Enthoven and K. W. Smith, "What Forces for NATO? And from Whom?" in *Foreign Affairs* (October 1969), p. 82.

23. The most famous of these studies is Graham T. Allison, *Essence of Decision: Explaining the Cuban Missile Crisis* (Boston: Little Brown, 1971).

24. Matthew Arnold, "Sweetness and Light" (1867), printed in E. K. Brown, *Four Essays on Life and Letters* (New York: Appleton-Century-Crofts, 1947), pp. 44, 50, 52; and Elting Morison, *Men, Machines and Modern Times* (Cambridge, Mass.: MIT Press, 1966), pp. 206–7.

25. Morison, p. 211.

26. Naval War College Archives, RG8, Series II, XWAG: Enclosure B: "Reassessment of the Fields and Value of Three Elements of Land, Sea and Air Power," in President, Naval War College, letter to Chairman, General Board, April 30, 1948.

27. See Morison, Ch. 2, and Stansfield Turner, "Navies for Yesterday or Tomorrow?", a special university lecture in War Studies, King's College, London, May 4, 1976.

28. C. R. Brown, "The Role of the Navy in Future Warfare," *U.S. Naval War College: Information Service for Officers (Naval War College Review)* (April 1949) p. 16.

29. Herbert Rosinski, "New Thoughts on Strategy," in B. M. Simpson III, ed., *War, Strategy and Maritime Power* (New Brunswick, N.J.: Rutgers University Press, 1977), p. 64. This was written in 1955.

30. H. E. Eccles, *Military Concepts and Philosophy* (New Brunswick, N.J.: Rutgers University Press, 1965), p. 262.

The Superpowers at Sea: Two Studies in Sea Power

Michael MccGwire

Sea power is an imprecise term coined by Mahan for its evocative ring rather than its analytical precision, and to understand what differentiates America and Russia in this respect, we must first clarify what underlies the concept.

The sea's strategic quality derives from the access it provides to nonadjacent areas, and maritime strategy is therefore about the *use* of the sea. This type of use breaks down into the two broad categories of conveying goods and people, and projecting force ashore; sea power is generally equated with a nation's ability to pursue its interests by using the sea in these ways. Maritime strategy, however, has a broader scope and is concerned as much with preventing the sea being used to one's disadvantage as with using it for one's own purposes. Indeed, for most coastal states, that is its primary focus.

A nation's maritime policy will reflect the nature of its interests in use of the sea, which will in turn depend upon the country's geographical and economic circumstances and its political aspirations. These interests can be categorized as purposive or preventive and, as a generalization, we can say that most countries have a preventive interest in the sea being used to project force against their shores and a purposive interest in its use for the conveyance of goods and people. However, at any period of history, there has usually been a small number of states with a purposive interest in using the sea to project force, and the combination of both purposive interests brings with it the requirement for sea power to pursue them.

It is in this respect that the nature of Russia's interests has traditionally differentiated her from the maritime powers of Western Europe and, in due course, from America. Russia's interests were predominantly preventive, while those of the Western states were predominantly purposive, and this has had a major effect on the nature of their respective naval requirements. One of the questions to be addressed is whether this differentiation continues to exist.

The Derivation of Soviet Maritime Policy

The Russian navy is nearing its 300th birthday, and for the last 200 years or so it has generally been the third or fourth largest in the world. Russia used naval forces in the eighteenth century to gain control of the Baltic and Black Sea coasts, and four times between 1768 and 1827 she deployed sizable squadrons to the Mediterranean for a year or more. Three of these deployments took place during wars with Turkey, ships being drawn from the Baltic Fleet to operate against the southern side of the Black Sea exits.

But increasingly thereafter, Russia found herself confronting predominantly maritime powers. In the Black Sea, Britain used her naval strength to prevent Russian gains at the expense of the failing Ottoman Empire; in the company of France, Britain intervened directly in what we call the Crimean War, extending her naval operations against Russia to the Baltic, White Sea, and Pacific, and the subsequent peace treaty forbade Russia a Black Sea fleet. Twenty years later in the eighth Russo-Turkish War, British pressure ensured that Russia did not gain control of the Straits. In the Far East, Russo-Japanese rivalry culminated in a disastrous war and the loss of two Russian fleets. And in 1918, the Western navies provided vital support to the forces of counter-revolution. As a consequence, Russia's naval policy was increasingly dominated by the requirement to defend four widely separated fleet areas against maritime powers who could concentrate their forces at will.

It is therefore wrong to suggest that Russia has only recently awakened to the significance of sea power. She used it in the past to her own advantage, and has more often seen its long arm used against her. Over the years she committed very substantial resources to naval construction, and the major warship building program initiated in 1945 was the fourth attempt in sixty-five years to build up a strong Russian fleet. But national strategy involves setting priorities and balancing competing claims for scarce resources. Russia was predominantly a land power; the only threats to her territorial existence had come by land; the army was the basis of security at home and influence abroad. Naval forces were indeed required to defend against assault from the sea and to counter the capability of maritime powers to dictate the outcome of events in areas adjacent to Russia. But these forces were seen as an expensive necessity rather than a preferred instrument of policy. This ordering of priorities and the army's domination of military thought largely persist today, and are enshrined in the concept of a combined arms approach to military problems, including naval ones.

POSTWAR NAVAL BUILDUP

The Second World War confirmed Russia's belief that ground forces were the basis of her national security. However, at the end of the war her most likely opponents were now the traditional maritime powers, who had not only been responsible for the capitalist intervention during the Revolution, but had recently demonstrated their capacity to project continental-scale armies over vast distances of sea and to support their operations ashore. The likelihood of maritime invasion of the Baltic and Black Sea coasts was considered substantial. The Baltic gave access to the lines of communication with the Western front. The Black Sea would allow the invaders to bypass Russia's traditional defense in depth; and the rivers, instead of serving as defensive barriers, would provide the invaders with easy access to Russia's industrial heartlands. In enemy hands, the Black Sea becomes a grenade in Russia's gut.

In 1945, Russia had a powerful army but lacked a battleworthy fleet, and the navy therefore received relatively high priority in the postwar reconstruction, with force requirements largely carried over from before the war. Under the new, twenty-year naval construction program, no fewer than 1,200 submarines were to be built. They probably also planned to build some 200 escorts, 200 destroyers, about 36 cruisers, 4 battlecruisers, and 4 aircraft carriers during this period, plus a mass of torpedo boats, gunboats, and subchasers, and some 5,000 aircraft in the naval air force. Large numbers; but of course nothing compared to the size of the combined Western navies at the end of the war; and even the submarines fall into perspective when divided among the four fleet areas. The prewar concept of defense in depth and coordinated attacks by air, submarine, and surface units was carried over. About 1,000 of the 1,200 submarines were intended for the defense of the home fleet areas, and the carriers were probably intended to extend fighter cover in the Barents Sea and in the Pacific.

SHIFT IN THREAT PERCEPTIONS

However, in 1954, as a consequence of the post-Stalin policy review, the Soviet leadership downgraded the threat of seaborne invasion and gave first priority to the dangers of a surprise nuclear attack by strategic bombers. The naval threat from the West was seen in more limited terms . of nuclear strikes by carrier-borne aircraft, primarily against naval bases. This engendered a radical reappraisal of naval requirements and the decision to place primary reliance on long-range cruise missiles, which would be carried by small-to-medium surface ships, diesel submarines, and aircraft. The operational concept relied on the potential reach, the payload, and the accuracy of these weapons (which had yet to be developed), as a substitute for large numbers of weapon platforms. It appears to have been influenced by the demands of the domestic economy and the need to release shipbuilding facilities to commercial construction.

There was resistance within the navy to these ideas, so Khrushchev brought the forty-five-year-old Gorshkov to Moscow to implement these decisions. The building of cruisers was checked in mid-course; the mass production of medium-type submarines, then building at seventy-two units a year, was sharply tapered to a halt; and while the destroyer, escort, and subchaser programs ran their full course, their successor classes were put back four years. This represented a 60 percent cut in annual production tonnage, enabling substantial resources to be released from warship construction to the domestic economy. Seven of the thirteen largest building ways were reassigned from naval use to the construction of fish factory and merchant ships. This shift of resources from naval to commercial construction was an important indication of Soviet priorities in use of the sea.

The new concept of operations was predicated on engaging enemy carrier groups within range of shore-based air cover. It envisaged coordinated missile attacks by strike aircraft, diesel submarines, and large destroyers, and it was planned that these newly designed units would begin to enter service in 1962. However, by 1958 the key premise that shore-based fighter defense would be available over the encounter zone had been falsified by increases in the range of carrier-borne aircraft, which allowed U.S. carriers to strike at Russia with nuclear weapons from the Eastern Mediterranean and the southern reaches of the Norwegian Sea. To meet this threat from distant sea areas, it was decided to place primary emphasis on nuclear submarines, which would be able to operate in the face of Western surface and air superiority.

This involved a further major change in naval building programs, and to understand the full implications, we must backtrack to pick up the task of strategic interdiction. Faced with the U.S. atomic monopoly, at the end of the war the Soviet Union had the requirement to develop not only its own weapon, but also the means of delivering it. In regard to the latter the Soviets pursued three lines of development: the intercontinental missile, the long-range bomber, and the submarine. The navy had a tradition of daring attacks on enemy ports, and the torpedo-firing submarine was the only system immediately available which had the range and payload to bring atomic weapons to bear on North America; a shallow-water burst in the approaches to New York or San Francisco was a significant threat. But here, also, we see the parallel development of tried and innovative systems, with a nuclear torpedo probably being developed by 1954, and a ballistic missile being test-fired from a submarine in 1955. These were the precursors to four classes of submarine which began delivery in 1958, two of them nuclear-powered and two diesel, one of each type armed with ballistic missiles, the other relying on torpedoes. However, technical problems (the nuclear classes were noisy and the missile-armed classes had an unreliable weapon-system), coupled with advances in American antisubmarine capabilities, meant that at least three of these four classes were unable to meet planned operational requirements.

COUNTERING THE CARRIER AIR THREAT

Thus, by about 1958, we have a congruence of three separate developments: the apparent success of the Soviet intercontinental ballistic missile program, which would become the main means of delivering nuclear weapons on America; the relative failure of the submarine strategic delivery systems; and the emergence of a new strategic threat to Russia in the shape of long-range nuclear strikes by carrier-based enemy aircraft. It was this combination which justified the reallocation of nuclear propulsion from the role of strategic delivery to that of countering the carrier, the role of strategic missile strike being taken away from the navy at about the same time. The recently authorized missile-armed diesel submarine (SSG) programs were cancelled and, as an expedient, their long-range surface-to-surface missile (SSM) systems were used to reconfigure the nuclear-powered hull/propulsion units, which had originally been intended as ballistic missile submarines, as cruise missile-armed units (SSGN) for use against the carrier. Meanwhile, plans were put in hand to double the production of nuclear submarines to ten boats a year, with deliveries due to begin in 1968, and to develop new methods of attacking the carrier, including a horizon-range submerged-launch cruise missile system, with its own target location capability.

At this same period in 1957–58, a requirement to extend the range of antisubmarine warfare (ASW) coverage beyond that provided by shore-based helicopters was identified, particularly in northern waters, where the Soviets assumed that the Polaris submarines, whose program had been announced in the United States, would patrol in due course. This generated the requirement for the Moskva-class of antisubmarine helicopter carriers.

REFORMULATION OF SOVIET DEFENSE POLICY

This brings us to 1961, a year that is crucial to understanding contemporary Soviet policy, and that saw the reversal of decisions arrived at barely twenty months before. In January 1960, Khrushchev had announced the results of what appears to have been a thoroughgoing defense review, which included formation of the strategic rocket force (SRF), its designation as the primary arm of the nation's defense, a substantial reorganization of military research and development, and the cutting back of conventional ground forces. Given Khrushchev's faith in nuclear missiles and his belief that nuclear war would be suicidal, the new policy could only indicate a shift in emphasis towards the Western concept of nuclear deterrence, and away from the traditional reliance on balanced forces and a war-fighting capability.

But by October 1961 the shift had been reversed, and, at the 22nd Party Congress, Marshal Malinovskij's speech clearly indicated a return to traditional military verities. Meanwhile, a thoroughgoing reappraisal of what was involved in fighting with nuclear weapons was put in hand, as was development of a whole series of consequential policies, including a restructuring of the ballistic missile programs.

There is now substantial evidence[1] that this reversal of policy reflected a reevaluation of threat which was engendered by the range of defense decisions announced by President Kennedy shortly after taking office in January 1961. These included a very sharp acceleration of the Polaris program and a doubling of the planned production rate of solid-fuel ICBMs which would be deployed in underground silos, remote from centers of population. Perhaps equally important in Soviet threat perceptions was the crusading rhetoric of the new administration, with its willingness to go any place and pay any price, and the detached logic of tough-minded academic strategists who were busy thinking the unthinkable and developing theories of limited nuclear war.

From the Soviet viewpoint, a significant aspect of the U.S. decisions was the apparent shift in emphasis from land-based to sea-based strategic nuclear strike forces, the rapid buildup of Polaris units coinciding with the entry into service of the large attack carriers (including the nuclear-powered *Enterprise*) ordered in the wake of the Korean war. These units could be expected to survive the intercontinental exchange and could therefore be held back in order to influence the outcome of the war. In particular, these forces could deny the Soviet Union the use of Western Europe as an alternative socio-economic base. Given the Soviet doctrine of deterrence through possession of a war-fighting capability, this had major implications for the navy's roles and missions. First, it would have to develop some means of countering these American systems. And second, it would be necessary to develop matching assets so as to deny the United States a unilateral advantage, in the event they could not be countered.

This second requirement meant that, after all, the Soviet Union would have to build up a force of nuclear-powered ballistic missile submarines (SSBN), but this could be done only at the expense of hull/propulsion units originally intended for other roles, including that of countering the carrier. The latter mission would remain practicable, although at a lower level of effectiveness. Polaris, however, presented a problem of a different kind.

THE ANTI-POLARIS RESPONSE

There were three possible ways of directly countering Polaris: area exclusion, trailing, and ocean search/surveillance. The last two would require development of new systems, but a start could be made on the incremental process of excluding Polaris from the more threatening sea areas, by trying to raise to unacceptable levels the probability of their detection. This would involve an extension and elaboration of the operational concepts which had been successfully developed for defense of the Soviet offshore zone, but would require additional, purpose-designed ASW forces.

This explains the Soviet navy's shift to forward deployment in the early sixties, which took place in two stages. The initial response (lasting five years) extended the outer defense zone to the 1500-nautical mile (nm) circle from Moscow, which covered the threat from carrier strike aircraft as well as the early Polaris systems, and took in the Norwegian Sea and the Eastern Mediterranean. The interim response, starting in 1967–68 began the slow process of consolidating the newly established defense zones, while extending the area of naval concern to take in the 2500-nm circle of threat; this included the eastern half of the North Atlantic and the northwest part of the Arabian Sea. There was a progressive buildup in the number of ships on forward deployment and in ship-days deployed until 1972–73, when both levelled off.

Meanwhile, the major emphasis in surface ship capabilities was switched from anticarrier to antisubmarine systems, in part by the major conversion of two existing classes (SAM Kotlin and Kanin) and in part by modifying the design of new construction programs, one currently building and the others projected. For example, the twelve-ship Moskva program of helicopter-carrying antisubmarine cruisers was cancelled (because the ship was too small to be operationally effective in the new concept), and its weapon systems were used to switch the Kresta's characteristics from anticarrier (Kresta I) to antisubmarine (Kresta II). The Moskva was replaced by the Kiev ASW carrier, at twice the size.

As originally planned, it was probably hoped that ten years would be sufficient to develop a range of measures which, beginning in 1972–73, would allow some kind of final response to Polaris along all three lines of attack. However, not only were these hopes unduly optimistic, but other developments had meanwhile prompted a shift in operational priorities.

THE NATIONAL NUCLEAR RESERVE GOES TO SEA

The most significant was the relative failure of the SS-13 land-based solid-fueled ICBM in about 1967–68.[2] It seems likely that it had been intended to develop this as a mobile system, so that it could serve as the main element of the national strategic reserve. Faced by this failure, it would appear that the Soviets chose the alternative of achieving mobility and concealment by putting the strategic reserve to sea aboard the Delta-class SSBN, which was due to begin delivery in 1973. However, to ensure security, the SSBNs would have to operate in protected waters, which meant that the planned range of the SS-N-8 missile would have to be considerably extended. The resultant lengthening of the missile would explain the improbable humpback characteristics of this class.

At about this same period, the American press reported that the U.S. Navy was intending to develop two new classes of submarine for operations against Soviet SSBNs, one very fast and the other very silent, which would enter service at about the same time as the Delta. This focused attention on the force's security and led to the concept of deploying the submarines in defended ocean bastions in the Greenland and Barents Seas and in the Sea of Okhotsk. Meanwhile, as more antisubmarine systems became available to the Soviets aboard new surface ships, submarines, and aircraft, it must have become increasingly clear that these traditional methods had inherent limitations against Polaris. This led to a shift in ASW emphasis away from the Eastern Mediterranean and Arabian Seas, to extending the inner defense zones of the Northern and Pacific Fleet areas, and to providing them with watertight defenses.

The shift in operational priority to protecting the SSBN bastions generated a fundamental change in the design criteria for distant-water surface units. Previously, the emphasis had been on the capability to weather a preemptive attack long enough for them to be able to discharge their primary mission of striking at Western carriers and Polaris submarines, after which they were expendable. Now, the security of the SSBN bastions had to be ensured for the duration of a protracted war. Surface ships, therefore, had to be capable of the sustained operations needed to gain and maintain command of a large sea area such as the Norwegian Sea, and this required long endurance, large magazine loads, and an underway replenishment capability. Establishing command would be facilitated by seizing key stretches of coast, and in the Pacific this could involve the Japanese side of the two southern straits which give access to the Sea of Okhotsk, and might even extend to the whole northern coast of Hokkaido. In the Norwegian Sea, the requirement could include key islands as well as stretches of the Norwegian coast.

SCALING UP THE SURFACE FORCES

To meet these new requirements, the Soviets decided that they would have to scale up the whole surface force, roughly doubling the size of all major surface types. The traditional destroyer-sized unit of about 3,500 tons (Krivak) was redesignated as an escort toward the end of the seventies. The new-construction destroyer types which began delivery in 1980 (Sovremmeny and Udaloy) are about 7,000–8,000 tons, larger than the previous generation of light cruisers. The new-construction light cruiser class is expected to be 12,000–13,000 tons, while the Kirov-class heavy command cruiser (or battle cruiser) is over 20,000. There was a similar scaling-up of amphibious new construction. This represents a major increase in the allocation of resources to naval shipyards, and the Kirov program required the return to the navy of shipyard facilities which had been in civilian use since the mid-fifties.

These new classes appear to have been included in the Ninth Five-Year Plan which was approved by the Twenty-fourth Party Congress in the spring of 1971. It would also have included the various submarine programs, including the Oscar-class of SSGN, which displaces some 16,000 tons and carries the new mach 2.5 long-range SSM system fitted aboard Kirov, and the very large Typhoon-class of SSBN, which one must assume to have been purpose-designed to operate from the protection of Soviet home waters. However, despite these substantial increases, the navy still did not consider that this would be sufficient to meet the new demands being placed upon it, and took its case to a wider audience by means of the articles in *Morskoj sbornik* that have become known as "the Gorshkov series." This debate had other ramifications which will be touched on later, but a major strand concerned the importance of general purpose forces, particularly in the submarine support role, and the need for a greater diversity of surface ship types, whose characteristics should provide for long range at high speeds.

The in-house argument would have focused on the specifics of the threat to the Soviet SSBN. The direct threat would come from U.S. nuclear-powered attack submarines, but the SSNs' success would depend on suppression of Soviet ASW defenses by supporting U.S. surface forces. The Soviet navy would have had to assume that U.S. carrier groups would be deployed in support of their SSN, whereas Soviet shore-based air would cease to be available after the initial nuclear exchange. Without this air component, there would be no certainty that the Soviets would be able to prevent the carrier groups from penetrating the outer defense zones. It could be assumed that U.S. carriers would seek to establish command of the surface and the air, denying their use to Soviet ASW forces, that they would harry the defending SSN, and they might even become directly involved in hunting down Soviet SSBN. If the Soviet navy were to prevail against this kind of force, it would need a comparable capability, including effective sea-based air.

Presumably, it was the inherent plausibility of this scenario that allowed the Soviet navy to win at least part of its case, and it seems that by mid-1974 authority was given to go ahead with the design of a large air-superiority carrier, which would enter service in the second half of the eighties. It may also have been at this stage that the second of the new destroyer-sized classes was authorized, in order to allow for task specialization between classes.

THE CONTINUING SEARCH FOR NAVAL ADEQUACY

This brings us through to the present, and as we enter the eighties we see the Soviet Union embarking on yet another attempt to reshape its navy to meet changing requirements. The underlying theme, however, remains the same, and the allocation of resources to naval construction reflects Soviet perceptions of the threat of assault from the sea.

After World War II, we saw first the mass-construction programs designed to meet a misperceived threat, which was incorrectly inferred fom the capitalists' war-inflated navies and from a Marxist prognosis of history. This was followed by savage cuts in shipyard allocations when the likelihood of seaborne invasion was realized to be low. Then we have the heavy investment in nuclear submarine construction facilities, responding to the new and correctly-perceived threat from carrier-borne strike aircraft, and to the need to oppose them in Western-dominated waters. The 1961 period not only added Polaris to the immediate problem, but saw a more complex formulation of threat as the Soviets thought through the implications of war fighting with nuclear weapons and of sea-based systems being withheld from the initial intercontinental exchange. And then in 1968, it was decided to put the national nuclear reserve to sea, generating a qualitatively new requirement to ensure the integrity of home waters in the north and the Pacific.

THE CHINESE DIMENSION

These naval requirements all stemmed from the threat of war with the West, but by the end of the sixties there was the added concern about the growing possibility of war with China. In such an event it had to be assumed that the Trans-Siberian railway would be cut and that the Far Eastern Front would have to be supplied by ship, either via the Red Sea or out through the Persian Gulf. These shipments would require protection from the Chinese submarine force (the third largest in the world), and the threat of attack could reach back to the Arabian Sea. This increased the strategic significance of the Indian Ocean, more than compensating for the shift in emphasis away from developing the means to counter Polaris in the area.

PEACETIME EMPLOYMENT OF NAVAL FORCES

The navy's move forward in strategic defense brought with it political opportunities to exploit the presence of Soviet forces in distant waters, but even here, wartime concerns assumed importance. Underlying the pattern of Soviet naval diplomacy over the last fifteen to twenty years, we can infer four types of objectives, each involving a different level of risk and degree of political commitment. At the high end of the scale, we have the requirement "to establish a strategic infrastructure to support war-related missions," an objective which has provided the primary motive for a broad span of decisions ranging from promoting a coup in a client state, to acquiring base rights by barely concealed coercion. The pressure on Egypt from 1961–67 for naval support facilities provides a good example. Base rights in Somalia provide another. The latter were originally intended to support the development of a counter-Polaris capability, but by the early seventies, the concern had extended to protecting the sea line of communication and to securing the entrance to the Persian Gulf.

At the low end of the scale of political commitment we have "protecting Soviet lives and property," which has received relatively low priority. In between these extremes we have the general objective of "increasing Soviet prestige and influence," which encompasses a wide span of activity from showing the flag and port-clearance operations, to providing support for revolutionary elements or to regimes threatened by secessionist elements. The Soviets are prepared to commit significant resources to this objective, but while the propensity for risk-taking has risen steadily, the underlying political commitment remains strictly limited.

Overlapping this general influence-building objective is the more restricted one of "countering imperialist aggression." Despite much bombast in talking of this task, it appears that when it comes to major confrontation with the West, Soviet political commitment is low. After fifteen years we have no hard evidence of Soviet readiness actually to engage Western naval forces in order to prevent them from intervening against a Soviet client state, although they have sometimes positioned themselves as if to do so.

What we do see is progressively greater involvement by the Soviet navy in the provision of logistic support, both before and during Third World conflicts. However, as an instrument of overseas policy, the navy's role remains secondary. The primary instruments are arms supply; military advice and training; the transport of men, munitions, and equipment by merchant ship and long-range air; and direct participation by combat troops of revolutionary states such as Cuba and Vietnam. The main role of the navy is to provide protection against interference by local states, and to serve as an earnest of Soviet commitment.

THE SEA IN SOVIET FOREIGN POLICY

This brings us to the question of whether there is some grand Soviet design driving a coordinated ocean policy in support of overseas objectives. The short answer appears to be no, but here we must distinguish between the operational aspects and the setting of objectives. The military-style organization of the merchant, fishing, and research fleets means that they can be used in peacetime for naval support tasks such as replenishment, forward picketing, and intelligence gathering. There are also geostrategic advantages to be gained with respect to a worldwide maritime infrastructure, actual or potential.

But when we turn to objectives, we see that the long-term interests of the three main fleets often diverge. The buildup of the fishing fleet stemmed from decisions in the late forties that fisheries were a more cost-effective source of protein than farming. The buildup of the merchant fleet reflected the post-Stalin shift toward trade, aid, and arms supply in the middle fifties, and the consequential requirements to earn hard currency and avoid dependence on foreign bottoms. And the navy's shift to forward deployment reflected the new threat to the Soviet homeland from distant sea areas. Inevitably, there is some conflict among these different interests, as could be seen at the law of the sea negotiations.

Only the merchant fleet, which brings in military supplies, takes out local commodities such as bauxite and rubber, and is both a well-disciplined and a pacific instrument, consistently serves the more general foreign policy goals of increasing the Soviet Union's share of world influence. To that extent, it can be seen as the principal maritime instrument of Soviet overseas policy.

U.S. Maritime Policy

The development of U.S. maritime policy has followed a very different path from that of the Soviet Union. America was both the offspring and the inheritor of Western attitudes, experience, and traditions concerning use of the sea, and its geographical position ensured that its interests would be predominantly purposive. Since the end of the nineteenth century, the U.S. Navy has been an important instrument of U.S. foreign policy, and its potential was vastly increased by the Second World War, which ended with America as the world's paramount power and its Navy second to none.

POST-WAR DECADES

In the immediate postwar years, strategic land-based airpower came to be seen as a primary instrument of U.S. policy, and the Navy went into partial eclipse with the size of the active fleet falling well below 300 major combatants. However, war broke out in Korea, a conventional conflict where strategic air power could not be brought to bear, but where carriers showed they had an important role to play. Heightened perceptions of the Soviet threat prompted a buildup of naval forces, and between mid-1950 and mid-1953 the reactivation of reserve units almost doubled the number of major U.S. naval combatants.[3] Meanwhile, construction started on the Forrestal-class of attack carriers, and the United States found itself at the head of a Western maritime coalition, with a virtual monopoly of sea power, which was used to some effect.

The 1950s were good years for the aircraft carrier. A new one was authorized for the U.S. Navy in each of the seven years 1951–57, and the carrier was able to demonstrate its versatility in the Taiwan Straits, off Lebanon, and even (in the British and French navies) during the Suez operation. Furthermore, the development of a nuclear weapon which could be carried by a relatively small aircraft meant that the carrier could also assume the mission of strategic nuclear strike against the Soviet Union.

At the same time, the Navy was concerned with the threat to the Atlantic lines of communications from the Soviet submarine force, which was already some 500 strong in the mid-fifties, with reports that it was building up to a force of 1,200. This assessment was reflected in a 1957 projection of the shape of U.S. naval forces in the 1970s, where it was foreseen that there would be some 400 ASW units (including 9 carriers) in a fleet of 927 units. However, by 1960, the West had come to appreciate that the Soviet mass-production submarine program had been abruptly terminated some four years earlier. The submarine threat lost some of its urgency, and the tendency for the strike carrier to become the focus of the fleet was reinforced.

THE NAVY SINCE VIETNAM

Until the late sixties, the West enjoyed overwhelming preponderance at sea, and naval forces were used extensively as instruments of national policy by the United States and other Western powers, with the carrier being seen primarily as a means of projecting force ashore. The 1965–75 period, however, saw a number of developments, many of them unrelated, which combined to produce serious problems for the U.S. Navy. One of these was the Navy's involvement in the Vietnam War, which had adverse effects on its long-term operational readiness. It paid a heavy price in losses of pilots and aircraft; backlogs in repairs, modifications, maintenance, and training; and the sheer wear-and-tear of men and ships. Whether it was necessary for the Navy to be so deeply involved in a war involving negligible enemy naval forces and with air bases available on friendly territory is arguable; but the effects reached right back to the shipyards, where the pressure for operational repairs and modifications helped to push up costs.

At this same period, a significant part of the fleet was reaching block obsolescence, as the large World War II classes passed the twenty-five-year mark, and the cost of keeping these ships operational rose disproportionally. In order to release funds for new construction, the Navy decided it would be advantageous to retire most of these older units without direct replacement, ending up with a leaner but more effective fleet. In any event, the cutback in the size of the fleet was much more severe than foreseen. The reasons included the war-induced inflation on top of rising shipyard costs, the increase in pay rates which accompanied introduction of the all-volunteer force, the high cost of new technology, and the reluctance of Congress in the post-Vietnam period to appropriate adequate sums to restore the armed forces.

Meanwhile, the U.S. Navy was acquiring new commitments, while its operating environment was becoming steadily less benign. The major new commitment reflected U.S. growing dependence on Middle East oil, which unhappily coincided with British withdrawal from east of Suez, a situation which was subsequently worsened with the loss of Iran as the main U.S. ally in the area. This was to some extent offset by the rapprochement with China; but on balance, the Navy's liabilities increased significantly. The deterioration in the operational environment stemmed in part from the Soviet navy's shift to forward deployment, which became fairly effective by the early seventies and meant that U.S. naval commanders had to take account of the threat posed by Soviet units operating in company. But there was also the proliferation of sophisticated weapons systems among coastal states, a steadily increasing number of which owned missile-armed fast-attack craft, which could cause significant damage to a carrier. These same coastal states were extending their territorial seas to twelve miles and adopting a more exclusive approach to their contiguous waters.

Sea Power in the World Today

This brings us to the situation today. On the one hand we have the United States, a traditional maritime power, isolated from the rest of the world by 3,000 miles of ocean to the east and 5,000 miles to the west, the sea a primary means of access to friend and foe and to key raw materials. On the other hand we have the Soviet Union, a traditional land power and the epitome of Mackinder's heartland, extending across 170 degrees of longitude (a full 180 degrees if we include the Warsaw Pact) and thus looking down on half the globe. About 85 percent of the world's population lives within 3,000 miles of Soviet territory, while Western Europe, North Africa, the Middle East, and the Indian subcontinent are all within 2,000 miles (military airlift range) of the Soviet Union.

DIFFERENT NEEDS, DIFFERENT NAVIES

For the last eighty years or so, America has found it desirable to have a worldwide naval capability comprising powerful fleets supported by naval bases around the globe, in order to be able to project force ashore (latent or applied) in distant parts of the world. For the past 150 years,

Russia has found it essential to have a large navy (split between four fleet areas) in order to prevent the traditional maritime powers from dictating the outcome of events in its adjacent areas. For the last thirty years, the United States, as part of a maritime coalition of advanced industrial states, has found it expedient to rely on the other members to ship its trade, since they own about 85 percent of the world's tonnage. It can produce all the protein it needs from livestock, and fisheries are a local, not a national, activity. For the last twenty-five years, the Soviet Union has deemed it essential to have its own merchant fleet, so as to escape dependence on the capitalist powers and to earn foreign exchange; and it has had to develop a worldwide fishing industry in order to provide the protein its people needs.

Soviet naval requirements have been determined primarily by the need to protect the homeland against assaults from the sea, a threat which has grown steadily during the last twenty-five years in geographical scope and military significance. To this traditional mission has now been added the requirement to ensure the security of the sea-based element of the national nuclear reserve for the duration of any war. The capability for naval diplomacy in peacetime appears to have been seen as a fortuitous byproduct of these war-related requirements; so far this role does not appear to have had influence on fleet structure or the characteristics of warships.

The derivation of U.S. naval requirements is more complex, partly because America belongs to several maritime alliances, which allows for load-sharing and delegation of specific tasks to allies, and partly because of the Western tradition of using naval forces as an instrument of policy in peacetime. Ostensibly, the size and shape of the fleet has been tailored to meet the possibility of war with Russia; indeed, every component has a specific mission in such a war. But in practice, the requirement to bring timely force to bear in distant parts of the globe has had an important influence on force structure.

In the past, these fundamentally different requirements have produced two very different kinds of navy with very different concepts of operation. In the Soviet case, the primary arms of service are the submarine force and shore-based air, and the traditional emphasis on area defense has been increased by the need to ensure the security of the SSBN force. In the U.S. case, the emphasis on projecting force ashore in distant parts of the globe has favored the attack carrier and the amphibious assault group. The convoy escort role is shared with allies, while the nuclear submarine force operates as almost a separate branch of service. However, developments over the last ten years are tending to diminish the differences between the Soviet and American fleets.

A NEW TREND IN SOVIET NAVAL DEVELOPMENTS

On the Soviet side we have seen the sharp rise in the allocation of resources to surface warship construction, with a very marked increase in the size of different ship-types as well as in the number of distant-water units delivered annually. But, just as important as this impending increase in distant-water capability are the indications that the navy's influence within the Soviet defense establishment may have increased over the last ten years, and that a fundamental shift in the theoretical basis of Soviet naval policy may be under way.

Evidence for the latter is provided by reviews of the book *Seapower of the State*, published under Admiral Gorshkov's name in 1976. Authority to produce this book would seem to have been a byproduct of the argument about naval force requirements in the 1969–71 period, which spilled over into a wider debate on the navy's role in war and peace. While it restated much of the material published in the "Gorshkov series" of articles, the book was about three times as long; its scope was much broader and included an extensive discussion of the ocean and of the non-military aspects of seapower, a subject which was treated very cursorily in the articles.

The book was well-received, and the tenor of the reviews is exemplified by Marshal of the Soviet Union Bagramyan's comment in *Izvestiya* that "for the first time in Soviet literature, the author formulates the concept of sea power as a scientific category." This does not mean that all the ideas in the book have been fully accepted, but it does imply that the concept is now established in the mainstream of Soviet analytical discourse and (to quote Admiral of the Fleet Lobov) "the book will be an important source for developing a correct viewpoint of the sea power of the state." This is significant, because up to now Soviet theorists have had an ideological aversion to the concept of sea power, which they equated with Mahan, capitalism, and colonialism. Just as Keynes's "General Theory" legitimized the idea of deficit financing and induced a shift in Western national economic priorities, so may this "scientific formulation" engender a shift in Soviet perceptions of the navy's role in war and peace.

But the book is not just an exposé of the role of sea power in the contemporary world; it is part of a continuing argument about naval missions and the allocation of resources, one in which the navy has been notably successful. During the decade, the Soviet naval position has evolved from defensive advocacy, to a more rounded discussion of the importance of the ocean and of sea power in a broader sense, to challenging the primacy of the continental theaters of war. Evidence of the navy's increasing political clout is provided by the procedural trappings of the ongoing debate. The initial argument was deployed in the navy's "own" journal during 1972–73 in some 54,000 words. Three years later the argument had been extended in a book of 151,000 words; and within four years a second (and somewhat longer) edition of 60,000 copies had been published. The first edition was categorized as being for "military readers," while the second edition is for "admirals, generals, and officers of the Soviet Army and Navy"; three of the contributing authors were promoted between the first and second editions, two to vice admiral and one to rear admiral. There is a world of difference between the ill-conceived "cruise missile solution" imposed on the navy in the mid-fifties, and the successful argument about naval requirements in the mid-seventies.

Meanwhile, naval design-criteria have shifted from short-term survivability to sustaining combat operations for the duration of a war, and, for the first time, wartime requirements will generate a general-purpose navy with a true worldwide capability. This, combined with a strong naval voice in Moscow and the formulation of an acceptable theory of sea power, may lead to a change in Soviet assessments. While the requirement to defend the SSBN bastions will tend to work against continuous distant deployment, concern for the Chinese threat acts in the opposite direction, as do wartime interests in the Persian Gulf area. The Soviet navy is likely to be emboldened by increasing operational experience and, as the more capable warships begin to join the fleet, we may see a new Soviet willingness to use naval forces to counter the projection of Western military power in time of peace.

THE CHANGING UTILITY OF NAVAL POWER

While the unfolding of events may have provided a new impetus to the employment of Soviet naval forces in distant waters, other developments have tended to put in question traditional Western assumptions about the value of naval forces as an instrument of overseas policy in peacetime.

The most significant of these developments is the proliferation of nation-states and their membership in the United Nations, the corollary of which has been the progressive dismantling of the infrastructure of colonial occupation which played such an important role in bringing imperial retribution to bear.

There has also been a change in general attitudes toward the acceptability of coercive force. The circumstances in which long-range intervention is likely to be acceptable have been progressively circumscribed; in the last thirty-five years, large-scale coercive intervention by major powers has been successful only within their respective contiguous national security zones, where power gradients and political commitment are both high. Effective intervention overseas now requires an initial favorable balance of political forces in the "host" country, as well as sufficient weight of sustained response.

But even if attitudes had not changed, warships would no longer be able to serve as the autonomous wielders of graduated retribution. The specialized demands of modern warfare mean that naval units now lack the military flexibility of the prewar general-purpose cruiser, with its numerous guns and comfortably large ship's company. Meanwhile, the proliferation of sophisticated weapons systems means that no longer are warships necessarily invulnerable when lying offshore. Sensors may have to be manned continuously, weapons may have to be at standby alert, and it may be difficult to spare a landing party without hazarding one's ship. The modern equivalent of the cruiser with its landing party is the carrier task force and its marine battalion landing team. But while the political effects that each could achieve may be comparable, the political stake is obviously very different.

None of this means that military intervention by sea is no longer likely or possible. But it has placed constraints on the almost casual use of force which used to be the norm. And it does mean that the economic and political costs are likely to be very much higher, and the chances of a successful outcome are smaller. Attitudes about the use of coercive force by extra-regional powers have altered fundamentally, and the new states do not "respond" to the threat of violence in the formerly accepted fashion. This means that the utility of *coercive* intervention is increasingly in doubt, except for short, sharp, small-scale, rectifying operations, and possibly at the other end of the spectrum of violence, where the scale of operations changes "intervention" into "overseas war."

Supportive intervention has a better record, but the increasing costs and risks raise the question of whether navies are necessarily the most effective instrument for such purposes. Aircraft carriers have an unmatched capability for bringing flexible firepower to bear in distant areas, but their high political symbolism and their need for sea room places constraints on their unfettered use. Meanwhile, the Russians have shown what can be done with merchant ships and airlift, making use of facilities in the host country.

Many of the attributes that in former times were the monopoly of naval forces and gave them their special value as instruments of foreign policy have now been dissipated or are shared by other instruments. The international news media and satellite surveillance have removed knowledge of warship movements from the flag state's exclusive control, to be released (or not) as circumstances indicate. Naval units can no longer deploy the graduated range of violence that used to be at their disposal; the level of force needed to achieve comparable results is very much higher. Violence (punishment) at the high end of the spectrum can now be inflicted on nonadjacent areas by aircraft and missiles, as well as by ship. In fact, the air is often a viable, alternative means of gaining access to distant areas, and the response time is of quite a different order. Modern communications allow heads of state and other ministers to transmit their concerns, interests, and intentions to their opponents in carefully chosen language; this compares favorably with the crude signaling of naval deployments. And the explicit language can now be backed by latent force located on home territory.

As a further complication it appears that the areas where the United States is most likely to want to project military force in the years ahead will be in those regions that are directly adjacent to the Soviet Union, most notably in the Middle East. This will bring U.S. naval forces within range of Soviet land-based strike aircraft, which are seen as the most dangerous element of the antisurface threat.

LOOKING TO THE FUTURE

In other words, those halcyon days when Western fleets enjoyed unquestioned maritime supremacy in almost every corner of the globe are gone, and we have to think carefully before using the U.S. Navy to draw tight the circle of containment around the Soviet Union. This is not because the U.S. Navy is now weaker than it was at the beginning of the sixties; in aggregate terms it has a greater capability, although spread among fewer hulls. But power is a relative concept, and what we are faced with is the proliferation of countervailing naval capabilities around the world and the greatly increased effectiveness of land-based maritime weapons systems.

Does this mean that the United States should now strive to regain worldwide naval supremacy in order to protect its maritime interests? There are several reasons for answering no. First is the matter of practicality. In the early sixties the United States had close to a thousand units (including twenty-five carriers) and the British fleet was still a significant force with a worldwide capability. The Soviet navy, meanwhile, was relatively weak and confined to home waters, and the growth of lesser navies had yet to take off. The European powers still controlled colonies (and hence bases) in key parts of the world, and much of the rest was reassuringly tied up in anticommunist alliances. None of this pertains today, and to achieve a comparable degree of supremacy would require the United States to go on a war footing, with extreme austerity at home.

Second is the question of comparative advantage. The projection of force by sea used to be very cost-effective because of the disproportionate advantage held by the Western maritime powers in the key areas of mobility, weapons technology, administrative capability, and industrial capacity. This comparative advantage has been severely eroded, while the cost of providing any kind of projection capability has risen exponentially.

Third is the matter of national interests. Mahan's theories derived from a historical analysis of the years 1660–1783, the height of mercantilism and monopoly trade. He saw sea power as one of three interlocking circles, the other two being colonies and commerce; the process he described was the overseas plunder of largely defenseless territories, with the main conflicts taking place between the competing European maritime powers. That world no longer exists, and the change has been in progress for a century and a half. The Pax Britannica depended far more on Britain's industrial supremacy than on the ships of the Royal Navy, and the administrative infrastructure which grew up to support that phenomenal commercial development relied mainly on the Indian Army for its day-to-day security. Today, we live in a world of over 150 independent states, and we have to rely on commercial arrangements to gain access to their markets and resources. Seaborne trade is international, and the world's shipping is in hostage to each other. Mahan's historical analysis is not a useful guide to present-day affairs.

In a world where our comparative advantage in using force overseas is badly eroded, where the cost of such a capability is becoming prohibitive, and where the political utility of long-range military intervention is increasingly in doubt, worldwide naval supremacy would not solve our problems, not least because it implies an urge to coercive solutions, when the only hope for the future lies in attempts at cooperation. This is not to say that the United States does not need a powerful navy, able to secure the use of the sea for its own purposes and to prevent disadvantageous use, both in peace and in war. Rather, it argues for a clearer understanding of the country's long-term interests in this rapidly changing world, and the role that naval power can play in protecting and promoting them.

Looking ahead to the end of the 1980s, some of the present distinctions between the Soviet and U.S. navies will be blurred; but we will still be left with the inescapable fact that Russia is a continental power and America is a maritime one, which means that their interests and their priorities in the use of the sea will inevitably differ. Traditionally, Russia has seen its navy as an expensive necessity, whereas the Western maritime powers have seen theirs as preferred instruments of overseas policy. This basic divergence is likely to persist, even if the Soviets try to make greater use of their navy in the pursuit of overseas objectives. The United States, meanwhile, may find that the utility of naval power in peacetime is gradually diminishing.

NOTES

1. This is based on John McDonnell's analysis of the 1959–62 period.

2. The information on missiles in this paragraph draws on the analysis done by Robert Berman.

3. From 271 units to 534 units, the increment including 17 carriers, 180 destroyers and escorts, and 46 submarines, all from reserve. *Source:* Norman Polmar.

National Defense at Sea: The United States Navy

Richard T. Ackley

Title Ten of the United States Code defines the U.S. Navy's mission as: "To be prepared to conduct prompt and sustained combat operations at sea in support of U.S. national interests." The implication is clear: global interests require a global navy—a fact that appears less apparent to the United States today than in the past. Indeed, a recent advertisement by the Bath Iron Works Corporation illustrates the issue vividly by stating, "America needs a bigger navy. Or smaller oceans."[1] It follows that the major thesis developed by Admiral Alfred T. Mahan at the turn of the century has yet to be faulted, namely, command of the sea is the dominant form of political power and the decisive factor in the political relations of nation states.[2] The United States is not as capable a maritime power as Mahan envisaged.

The purpose of this essay is to assess the current status of the U.S. Navy. The subject is approached through the following questions: Why have a navy at all? Why did our momentum falter? What are the capabilities and limitations of the U.S. Navy today? And, looking to the future, how can we regain the momentum?

Why Have a Navy at All?

Historically, the U.S. Navy has been an important tool in the management of dynamic situations ranging from maintaining stability and deterring war to fighting when necessary. In order to satisfy these needs, one strategic and three general-purpose force missions have evolved:

- Strategic nuclear deterrence
- Sea control
- Power projection
- Peacetime presence

The Navy's contribution to the nation's strategic nuclear deterrent posture has consisted of some 656 submarine-launched ballistic missiles (SLBMs) in 41 nuclear-powered ballistic missile submarines (SSBNs). This mix of missiles and SSBNs will vary as the new 24-tube Trident SSBNs come on-line and older 16-tube Polaris missile-carrying SSBNs are converted to nuclear-powered attack submarines, or retired.[3] "Sea control," on the other hand, no longer implies control of the seas, but rather control of those portions of the ocean vital for the protection of friendly naval and merchant forces. And "power protection" is the use of sea-based forces for air or naval attacks, blockade, or amphibious landings to influence events ashore.[4] Finally, "peacetime presence" is no more than "showing the flag" overseas as a symbol of American power, influence, and advanced technology.

While the use of naval power in combat situations is self-evident, often the use of naval forces in support of political objectives is not. For example, throughout the post-World War II period the United States turned to the Navy more than to any other service when limited force or military show of force was desired. Naval units participated in 177 of the 215 recorded show of force or limited use of force incidents, or more than four out of every five. "In short, the Navy clearly has been the foremost instrument for the United States' political uses of the armed forces; at all times, in all places, and regardless of the specifics of the situation."[5] And within the naval service, carrier-based aircraft participated in 106 of these 215 incidents.[6]

PROTECTION OF OCEAN TRADE

In the decade of the 1980s, one word alone—*oil*—commands a strong global navy. In fact ". . . few Americans faced the fact that the U.S. loss of energy self-sufficiency had virtually extended our economic boundaries one-half way around the world."[7] American sea lines of communications (SLOC) for the movement of oil are worldwide, extending from the Persian Gulf across three oceans to the United States. Additionally, Alaskan oil must transit the Pacific Ocean, often continuing through the Panama Canal to Gulf Coast refineries; and Indonesian oil must be hauled across the entire Pacific basin. Without a modern global (three-ocean) navy, protection of these sea lanes becomes problematical if challenged. "So, the question is not: Can we afford a modern navy? The question is: Can we afford not to have one?"[8]

Insuring free and uninterrupted movement of oil over the world's sea lanes is perhaps the most apparent potential naval requirement today, but it is only one portion of a much larger economic maritime reality. For instance, there was a time when the United States produced more raw materials than it used—but not today. Of the seventy-one raw materials generally classified as "critical" for U.S. industrial, economic, and national defense needs, the United States must import sixty-eight in whole or in part.[9] Most of these materials are transported by sea. Overall, more than 90 percent of America's import and export trade is oceanborne. In a typical year, American seaports handle over 1.6 billion tons of cargo, in addition to some $30–40 billion worth of imported petroleum products. In fact, the United States is the world's largest ocean trader—a role that has expanded by 500 percent over the last thirty years.[10]

Without doubt, the Soviets are rapidly increasing their capability to interdict our SLOC with the growing surface, subsurface, and air elements of their naval service. This has been evidenced by their growing global naval presence and improved military posture relative to our oil routes, and in the Middle East petroleum producing areas.[11] In any future superpower conflict, the United States will not be afforded the time that was available during World War II to build or rebuild a navy. We will fight with what we have at the outset. As former Secretary of the Navy J. William Middendorf II said, "Our ability to control the sea is indispensible to deterrence. In the event deterrence fails, control of the seas is essential in preventing interdiction of sea lines of communications, and to secure areas from which to project power ashore."[12]

Why Did Our Momentum Falter?

As a major world power the United States maintained a navy second to none from World War II into the Vietnam era. In 1968, at the height of the Vietnam war, the U.S. Navy reached a peak of 976 ships in its active inventory. By May 1974 the number had declined to 522, and further dropped by January 1978 to a post-World War II low of only 459 ships, where it has leveled off for all intents and purposes.[13] (See Figure 1 and Tables 1 and 2.) Conversely, Soviet naval combatants increased from a force level of 1,586 to 1,651 in the same period of time.[14] Why, one must ask, did a maritime power, whose very existence depends upon the free use of the sea, allow its maritime forces to dwindle in numbers?

INADEQUATE FUNDING

Despite the fact the Navy had the largest budget of all services for eight consecutive years, it was underfunded throughout the Vietnam War. The underlying issue was a traditional one for democracies in time of war: guns or butter. The political decision was "both" and without placing the nation on a wartime footing. It follows, then, that normal naval construction for routine replacement, as well as major overhauls of existing ships, were postponed so that these funds could be diverted into expendables such as bombs, helicopters, fuel, and supplies. Not surprisingly, by 1970 the U.S. Navy was still large, but aging and wearing out.

Subsequently, new and more capable ships were built, but at a lesser rate than older ships were being retired. Funding was again a problem.

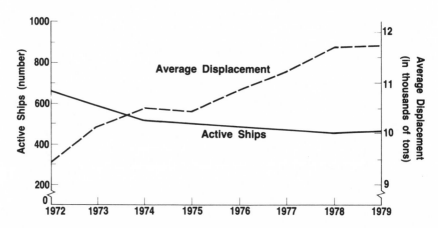

Fig. 1. Number of U.S. Navy Active Ships and Average Displacement, 1972-79

Source: U.S. Congress, Congressional Budget Office, *Shaping the General Purpose Navy of the Eighties: Issues for Fiscal Years 1981-85* (Washington, D.C.: Government Printing Office, Jan. 1980), p. 66.

For example, in 1960 the Navy budget was 2.5 percent of the gross national product (GNP). By 1980 the Navy's portion of the GNP had slipped to 1.5 percent (a 40 percent reduction).[15] The result is that today's Navy is basically new and highly capable, but low in number of ships.

The Carter Administration aggravated a deteriorating situation by placing its defense emphasis on the "Central Front" in NATO at the expense of naval ship construction. Even early in the Carter era naval strategists were arguing that the Central Front certainly is an important potential theater of operations, but probably the least likely combat situation the nation will face.[16]

CONTRACTUAL DISPUTES

To suggest that a lack of funding was the sole reason for our faltering naval momentum is both simplistic and not wholly accurate. Three other forces complicated the problem: contractual disputes, the attitude of Congress, and internal naval problems.

Shipbuilding disputes between the Department of the Navy and civilian construction yards have been divisive, both inside and outside of government. Not only are there traditional "pork barrel" concerns about "in whose district should the contract be placed," but cost overrun disputes seem to have become the order of the day. Unfortunately, because of a warship's extensive building time and high unit cost, inflation dramatizes the discrepancy between the initial contract price and the final delivery price some four to five years later. For instance, a 10 percent per year price increase of $1.00-a-gallon gasoline over a five-year period results in a cost of $1.61/gallon—something we learn to live with. The same 10 percent per year increase in the cost of an $800-million ship over a five-year building period prices out at a whopping $1.29 billion—a headline maker, to say the least.

What is less understood, however, is that during the multiyear period between letting a ship contract and its delivery, technology marches on. In other words, the Navy is driven continually to make design changes and updates in shipborne equipment as newer and more capable items reach maturity. This, of course, creates delays in the shipyard, resulting in "missed" delivery dates and additional cost overruns. Nevertheless, it is difficult to argue that the Navy should accept a new ship that is less capable than American state-of-the-art know-how can create.

Table 1: Naval Combatant Force Level Trends

Active Fleet	1969		1979	
Combatant Classification	**U.S.**	**USSR**	**U.S.**	**USSR**
Aircraft Carrier	22	0	13	2
Surface Combatant	279	220	178	269
Submarine	156	354	123	357
Command	2	0	0	0
Patrol Combatant	9	148	3	120
Amphibious Warfare	153	103	63	91
Mine Warfare	74	165	3	165
Auxiliary Ship Classification				
Mobile Logistics	112	56	59	150
Support	119	624	20	610
Total Status Active Fleet	**926**	**1670**	**462**	**1764**
Naval Reserve Force (NRF)***				
Combatant Classification				
Surface Combatant	35	*	20	*
Submarine	20	*	0	*
Patrol Combatant	6	*	0	*
Amphibious Warfare	1	*	3	*
Mine Warfare	14	*	22	*
Auxiliary Ship Classification				
Mobile Logistics	0	*	2	*
Support	1	*	6	*
Total Status NRF	**77**	*****	**53**	*****
Naval Fleet Auxiliary Force (NFAF)				
Auxiliary Ship Classification				
Mobile Logistics	0	**	12	**
Support	4	**	13	**
Total Status NFAF	**4**	******	**25**	******
Total Ship Operating Force	**1007**	*****	**540**	*****

*Not available.

**A daily average of six Soviet merchant ships, from a total fleet of over 1,700 ships, routinely support Soviet naval out-of-area operations.

***Soviet reserve combatants are not maintained in a status comparable to U.S. NRF combatants and are not included in the total operating force figure.

Table 2: U.S. and Soviet Naval Force Levels, January 1981

Active Fleet	United States	Soviet Union
Strategic Missile Submarines	36	62
Old Strategic Missile Submarines	—	25[a]
Submarines[b]	83	275
Aircraft Carriers	12[c]	3
Cruisers	27	~ 40[d]
Destroyers	81	~ 65
Frigates..............................	74	~160[e]
Command Ships	3	—
Amphibious Warfare Ships	58	~ 85
Patrol Combatants	3	~120
Mine Warfare Ships	3	~160
Auxiliary Ships........................ ~	80	~760
Naval Reserve Force (NRF)		
Destroyers	16	—[f]
Amphibious Warfare Ships	6	—[f]
Mine Warfare Ships	22	—[f]
Auxiliary Ships........................	8	—[f]
Naval Fleet Auxiliary Force (NFAF)		
Auxiliary Ships........................	25	—[f]
Naval Aircraft (Including Marine Corps)		
Tactical	1900	700
Antisubmarine	650	400
Transport-Training-Utility	2300	280

[a]"Hotel" SSBN and "Golf" SSB classes.
[b]Includes research, training, and special-purpose submarines.
[c]Plus *Saratoga* (CV-60) in three-year modernization.
[d]Includes two Moskva-class CHG helicopter carrier-missile ships.
[e]Includes approximately 28 Krivak-class frigates.
[f]Data not available.

Source: Norman Polmar, "The U.S. Navy, State of the Fleet," U.S. Naval Institute *Proceedings,* Feb. 1981, p. 105.

Source, Table 1, opposite page: Admiral Thomas B. Hayward, USN *CNO Report: Fiscal Year 1981* (Wash. D.C.: Dept. of the Navy, 1980), p. 35.

CONFLICTS WITH CONGRESS AND WITHIN NAVY

Congress, on the other hand, complains about the Navy's lack of consistency in shipbuilding requests, while interjecting its own ideas into shipbuilding plans. Naval ship construction policy seems to waver in the face of the growing Soviet and Third World naval threat. This, in turn, hinders formulation of a logical, defendable, and affordable long-range shipbuilding program. Additionally, Congress is concerned about what it considers the lax naval supervision of shipbuilding.[17]

Internal naval problems provide their share of detraction from a rigorous shipbuilding plan. For instance, as the former Chief of Naval Operations (CNO), Admiral Elmo R. Zumwalt, Jr., often stated, the Navy has three competing unions. By this he meant the ongoing struggle between advocates of surface ships, submarines, and naval aviation. This parochial infighting tends to skew a true "what's best for the Navy" outcome. Additionally, the new Secretary of the Navy, John F. Lehman, Jr., has expressed the view that shipbuilding plans "over the past decade" are evidence of "basically inconsistent" naval strategy.[18] Making this issue even more menacing is the cyclic change in Chief of Naval Operations every four years, and their key deputies more often.[19] As in many bureaucracies, the new "boss" makes a clean sweep of many of his predecessor's policies. This, of course, can play havoc with an existing five-year building program. Furthermore, it tends to make Congress skeptical of all naval programs.

Several years ago there appeared to be consensus that an 800-ship U.S. Navy was required to meet future contingencies. Today, however, this figure has dipped to about 600. For example, Congressman David F. Emery, a member of the Subcommittee on Sea Power and Critical and Strategic Materials of the House Committee on Armed Services, believes a firm goal of 600 naval ships by mid-1990 should be established.[20] Vice Admiral John Doyle, Jr., Deputy Chief of Naval Operations, has called for 25 more cruisers, destroyers, and frigates, bringing total naval combatants near the 600 mark.[21] And Secretary of Defense Caspar W. Weinberger listed attainment of a 600-ship U.S. Navy fleet among his "main goals."[22] As might be expected, the "mix" of ships composing the 600 is unsettled and indeed contentious. Nevertheless, it does appear we have a numerical target that is receiving general support. What is clear, however, is that the Navy can no longer fall back on U.S. quality offsetting Soviet quantity. Recent Soviet ship designs and production have rendered this rationalization marginally useful.

Today's Navy: Capabilities and Limitations

There is an old adage that goes: "The way to measure relative military power is to exercise it." True as that may be, it is preferable to assess the current status of the U.S. Navy intellectually, rather than emperically. Accordingly, a starting point is to determine, as best as possible, the principal responsibilities of the Navy for the 1980s, then assess the problems and prospects for meeting these responsibilities.

Admiral Thomas B. Hayward, Chief of Naval Operations, lists three principal responsibilities of the U.S. Navy for the 1980s:

- contribute to strategic deterrence;
- contribute to the deterrence of major Soviet aggression in Europe, the Middle East, and Asia by demonstrating that the United States, with its allies, has an undefeatable capability to reinforce and resupply forces opposing the Russians around the periphery of the Soviet Union; and
- protect U.S. interests in the Third World—whether these interests are threatened by the Soviets, by Soviet surrogates, or by local power.[23]

There is no question that the U.S. SSBN force is an essential contributor to the strategic "Triad" consisting of land-based intercontinental ballistic missiles (ICBMs), manned bombers, and submarine-launched ballistic missiles. At present, the SSBN force is the most survivable "leg" of the Triad, and this quality is expected to continue into the future. While the value of the SSBN force is not questioned, there is an ongoing debate as to the best (efficient, cost-effective, or useful) submarine type and missile system to support national strategic objectives. Additionally, a weak link identified in the SSBN system is assured communications between the launching submarine and national command authority during a nuclear exchange. Effective war fighting and retargeting depend on rapid, accurate communications. A hardened, extremely-low-frequency communications system has been proposed by past administrations, but to date it is not in existence. Nevertheless, the basic point for this discussion is: Yes, the U.S. SSBN force is an effective contributor to strategic deterrence.

The two general purpose responsibilities of deterring major Soviet aggression around the Soviet periphery and protecting U.S. interests in the Third World (sea control and power projection) involve questions of both quantity and quality. Historically, U.S. naval doctrine has preferred to take the fight to the enemy rather than risk damage to the United

States. Now faced with the USSR as a major adversary at sea, the American Navy initially may have to defend against a Soviet naval offense directed against the United States and/or its allies. The simple fact of having to react to another's offense adds additional uncertainty to naval planning. In other words, the absence of naval superiority over one's prime antagonist dictates conservative and, for the most part, defensive tactics—not the best of ways to win battles.

DECREASE IN FORCE LEVELS

Despite the fact the U.S. Navy is outnumbered by the Soviets and likely will remain so, there are areas of U.S. superiority that can be exploited. For example, carrier-based aviation, at-sea endurance, and certain weapons systems technologies clearly favor America. The foregoing notwithstanding, it is still important to understand that "quantity is a quality" in itself. Inasmuch as one ship, no matter how sophisticated, can be at only one place at one time, numbers are important.

In the annual Navy Net Assessment exercises, which are scenario driven, the international naval balance is estimated from analyzing campaigns, strategy, tactics, order of battle, and other relevant factors. Recent results were summarized in the CNO's report for fiscal year 1981 as follows:

> This (net assessment) process leads to the conclusion that today the Navy is marginally capable of carrying out its mission in support of national strategy. Although the war-fighting capability of individual U.S. Navy units has grown, the numerical size of the Navy has remained low. Qualitative unit capabilities cannot fully compensate for a lack of numbers.[24]

In the same context, the Congressional Budget Office has stated:

> The decrease in force levels has led observers to question whether the Navy can continue to carry out all of its missions worldwide. Indeed, statements by the former Chief of Naval Operations, Admiral Holloway, implied that, unless force levels were increased, the United States could only fulfill the sea control mission in the North Atlantic, leaving unprotected the sea lanes to its allies in other parts of the world.[25]

Concurring with the above, Vice Admiral Thomas J. Bigley, Commander of the Second Fleet, has written, "Even under the higher defense budgets expected from the Reagan Administration, the U.S. Navy will not be able to protect sea lanes to Europe, the Persian Gulf, and the Pacific at the same time."[26] And not to be outdone, former Chief of Naval Operations Admiral Arleigh Burke said the Navy is "drastically short of ships and aircraft, lacks sufficient weapons systems, and could not wage sustained action with its present level of munitions."[27]

On a more conservative note, the current Chief of Naval Operations, Admiral Hayward, sees the Navy improving every month across the board. He does, however, offer two cautionary notes: first, the high tempo of operations is hurting predeployment training; and second, our ability to maintain adequate numbers of properly trained people in our operating units is a problem.[28]

EFFECT OF INCREASED DEPLOYMENTS

American diplomats act upon the belief that there is a strong and causal relationship between regional stability and a naval force presence.[29] This was certainly demonstrated during the Carter Administration when naval forces were sent to the Caribbean following the "discovery" of a Soviet brigade in Cuba, and when a task force was sent to the Indian Ocean after the seizure of American diplomats in Iran.[30] These actions reemphasized the ability of the Navy to deploy on short notice with minimal base support to overseas areas and remain on station for prolonged periods of time. This type of response fosters new naval requirements. However, as Admiral Hayward noted, the Navy is stretched thinner today than at any time since the late 1940s. Increased demands are being met with a fleet roughly one-half the size it was a decade ago. "The simple fact is that today we are trying to meet a three-ocean requirement with a one-and-one-half-ocean navy."[31]

President Carter's deployment of a 21-ship naval task force to the Indian Ocean is a vivid example of the fact that current naval forces are stretched too thin to accept additional commitments without overtaxing men and equipment, and dropping or at least eroding other commitments. For example, the Navy's overall shortage of some 20,000 specialists and technicians forced seventy-hour work weeks on some key ratings in the Arabian Sea Task Force. Additionally, the force was assembled at the expense of the Pacific Fleet and our NATO commitment in the Mediterranean Sea. In other words, the new fleet was created by stripping two other fleets, and by maintaining many vessels—like the aircraft carrier *Kitty Hawk*—on station far beyond their normal rotational schedule, factors that hardly assist reenlistment rates.[32] Furthermore, there are those who claim the Indian Ocean Task Force has no substantial antisubmarine warfare (ASW) capability other than self-defense, thereby leaving tankers easy prey to Soviet submarines if attacked.[33]

Creation of the Indian Ocean Task Force also had repercussions for naval operations in the continental United States. For example, key operating personnel were drawn from ships operating in the Atlantic Fleet to the point that the oiler *Canisteo* (AO-99) and two Naval Reserve destroyers could not go to sea because of an inadequate number of specialists in critical ratings.[34]

To build another numbered fleet, an Indian Ocean Fleet, from the keel up takes time, men, equipment, and money. For instance, the probability exists that the freeing of the U.S. hostages from Iran will not signal a U.S. Navy abandonment of the Indian Ocean. America's increasing dependence on foreign oil and the unsettled political conditions in the Persian Gulf—not to mention the Soviet interest in the area—combine to create a need for a permanent U.S. naval presence. To do this would require a 30 percent overall increase in the fleet, including three aircraft carriers and associated naval aircraft. This amounts to an eight- to ten-year project costing an extra $10 billion a year. Allowing for inflation, the grand total would amount to about $100 billion extra over a five-year period.[35]

As former Secretary of Defense Harold Brown pointed out, since World War II we have had to cope with many crises, but usually one at a time. However, having witnessed developing problems in the Caribbean, Southeast Asia, Korea, Afghanistan, and Iran, it becomes apparent the United States needs a defense posture capable of coping with simultaneous demands well into the future.[36] A reality is that the heart of our fighting forces are the twelve carrier-battle-groups with their tactical air wings. These groups have been stretched to a maximum. In fact, it will take about eighteen new ships per year to modernize the fleet at an acceptable rate to support these battle groups while maintaining current force levels.[37] The U.S. Navy presently is operating at the margin. In fact, Colonel John M. Collins, a senior defense analyst at the Library of Congress, believes "America's Navy is marginally capable of carrying out its mission in support of national strategy. . . . The future U.S. Navy faces reduced options and reinforced risks."[38]

The Carrier-Battle-Group

As suggested above, carrier-battle-groups are the key members of our naval offensive force. Each group consists of an aircraft carrier with embarked fighter, attack, and ASW aircraft. The carrier is escorted by surface and submarine units that provide antiair, antimissile, antiship, and ASW protection. Without doubt, carrier-battle-groups provide the greatest naval power that can be assembled to counter all threats at sea.[39]

With all the inherent advantages of carrier-battle-groups riding on twelve carriers, the United States has limits to the number of groups that can be maintained on station at a given time. This is particularly true in view of the fact we have committed two carriers to be positioned in the Mediterranean Sea in order to please our NATO allies.[40] Moreover, the "dead" time involved in overhaul and upkeep, and the transit time to and from overseas deployment, added to the possible wartime loss of even one or two carriers, can produce a significant decrease in U.S. naval offensive capability. The point is that the existence of twelve carriers does not imply all of them can be deployed and maintained on station overseas at one time.

PERSONNEL RETENTION

The Navy is short some 20,000 senior petty officers. These are the "old salts" who have the talent and experience to make the Navy run. Moreover, the Navy is experiencing the highest personnel turnover it has seen in years. The second "hitch" reenlistment rate has fallen from 77 percent in 1971 to 53 percent today. Most certainly, low pay is a major factor.[41] For instance, the commanding officer of the U.S.S. *Belknap*, Captain Ross Hatch, reports that he has two petty officers giving advice on how to apply for food stamps and other public aid. He notes that "a guy who works eighty hours a week here is paid the same as a kid at McDonald's. . . . To have Navy people on food stamps is wrong."[42] Preliminary figures following the October 1980 across-the-board pay raise suggest an improvement in the reenlistment rate, but indications are that the "pay problem" is not solved.[43]

Officer retention, according to the Chief of Naval Operations, fell to 40 percent for unrestricted line officers when 60 percent was required. As a result of these severe shortfalls, the Navy faces a combined shortage of about 2,300 unrestricted line officers in the mid-grades.[44] Without doubt, competition with industry and business for high-quality young people is increasing. Additionally, the pool of recruitable-age youth will decrease in the next decade. The likely but unfortunate result foreseen by Admiral Hayward in his fiscal year 1981 CNO Posture Statement is that ". . . we are approaching the point where we may have no realistic alternative but to consider standing down some ships and aviation units."[45] And indeed, this has come to pass.

The naval "can do" tradition, as admirable as it is, perhaps must give way to the reality of personnel shortages when they exist. A cheery "I'd like to do it, but I simply do not have the qualified manpower" may become a more often heard statement.

SHIPS AND EQUIPMENT

Sea-Based Strategic Forces. Of the original 41 Polaris/Poseidon SSBNs, the oldest 10—equipped with Polaris A-3 missiles—are reaching the end of their service life. Accordingly, they are being decommissioned or converted from SSBNs to nuclear-powered attack submarines (SSNs). This represents a decrease in deployed SLBMs from 656 to 496. The 31 newer SSBNs, carrying either MIRVed Poseidon or Trident I missiles, will probably last some twenty-five to thirty years with the last ship retiring about 1996.[46] This means that in order to keep 656 SLBM tubes in the force, the Navy will need 27 Trident-class SSBNs by 1996. To do this requires nearly double the production rate of the first 8 Tridents already programmed.[47] (See Table 3.)

Table 3:   Proposed Navy Shipbuilding, Fiscal Years 1982-86
(Outgoing Carter Administration)

Newbuildings	FY'82	FY'83	FY'84	FY'85	FY'86	Total
TRIDENT	1	1	1	2	1	6
SSN-688	1	1	1	1	2	6
FA-SSN	—	—	—	1	—	1
CG-47	2	2	4	4	4	16
DDGX	—	—	—	—	1	1
FFG-7	1	—	—	—	—	1
FFX	—	—	1	2	3	6
MCM	1	—	4	4	4	13
ARS	2	1	1	—	—	4
T-AGOS	4	3	3	—	—	10
T-AKX	1	1	2	2	2	8
T-AO	1	—	2	2	2	7
T-ARC	—	—	—	—	1	1

Source: Shipyard Weekly, Jan. 22, 1981, p. 1.

Despite the fact the first Trident-class SSBN, the U.S.S. *Ohio*, was to deploy in the Pacific in 1981 armed with Trident I missiles, contract disputes between the Navy and the Electric Boat Division of General Dynamics Corporation of Groton, Connecticut, delayed delivery of the *Ohio* until mid-1981.[48] Fortunately, the Trident submarine and missile provide a qualitative and quantitative advantage over the older Polaris/Poseidon systems. Therefore, although the reduction of SLBM tubes in the force during the Polaris/Poseidon-Trident transition period remains undesirable, it is not as serious as the numbers indicate.

Attack Submarines. In terms of general purpose forces, U.S. nuclear-powered attack submarines still retain an advantage over similar Soviet submarines in the very important area of quietness. U.S. efforts in sound isolation and overall quieting are of long standing, and the results are most satisfying. Submarine noise reduction is important in two respects: first, it allows the submarine's own sonar greater detection ranges of other ships; and second, it makes the detection of one's own ship difficult for enemy sonar operators.

The Navy has been consistent in its position that 90 SSNs are required. Currently, however, the Navy has 74 SSNs and 5 diesel attack submarines (SSs). Considering the normal twenty-five-year life cycle of an SSN, the 90-ship level cannot be reached within the final proposed Carter fiscal year 1982 five-year shipbuilding plan (Table 3). The plan calls for construction of one SSN each year through 1985, and two in 1986. The 90-unit force level can be reached only with a construction rate of 3.5 SSNs per year. Current projections indicate a 90-SSN force will occur briefly in the mid-1980s, then decrease to 70 SSN's by the year 2000 if a 1-per-year building rate is maintained.[49]

Carrier-Battle-Groups. As suggested earlier, the Navy's offensive punch rests with the aircraft carrier-battle-group concept. The carrier vulnerability issue still persists. That is, conventional wisdom is that large surface ships—carriers in particular—will become more and more vulnerable to antiship cruise missiles. The rebuttal to this belief is as follows:

- Ships are mobile and in a conventional war are able to tolerate a small number of hits.
- Vertical and short takeoff and landing (V/STOL) aircraft can improve the capability of any carrier to conduct flight operations even after suffering damage.
- The number of hostile missiles able to penetrate a battle-group

will be reduced as the new antimissile systems deploy, that is, the Phalanx close-in-weapons system, and the Aegis area air defense system.

- The F-14 interceptor and E-2C early warning aircraft provide good capability against hostile aircraft launching antiship missiles. Additionally, hostile surface ships can be engaged by carrier-based aircraft and shipborne surface-to-surface missiles (Harpoon) as these systems are deployed.[50]

Despite the Navy's dependence on carrier-based air power, it has been cut in half since 1965 when 25 carriers (exclusive of helicopter platforms) were in active service. With 25 carriers, the United States had a two-ocean capability and truly first-rate flexibility.[51] Even with the 12-aircraft carrier force today, there is a shortage of tactical aircraft to replace those that wear out. According to Vice Admiral Wesley L. McDonald, Deputy Chief of Naval Operations for Air Warfare, the Navy needs 330 new tactical aircraft a year for replacements. For the past five years Congress has appropriated funds for an average of 159 planes per year,[52] and it is allowing only 104 aircraft in fiscal year 1981.[53] Even over the past ten years, the Navy has averaged only 247 new aircraft a year.[54] What this means is that aircraft force levels can be maintained only through extending the lives of older planes by major modifications and overhauls.[55]

Fleet Force Levels. Vice Admiral M. Staser Holcomb, Director of Navy Program Planning, advises that the fleet itself, with about 500 ships—300 of them warships—is the smallest it has been since 1939 and is about one-half the size of the fleet of the late 1950s and 1960s.[56] Additionally, fleet force levels are expected to drop sharply during the late 1980s and early 1990s because of expected ship retirements. (See Figure 2.)

Perhaps the most significant shortfalls in these years will be the Aegis ships—the units with advanced weapons systems using the phased-array Spy-1 radar for rapid target detection and weapon control.[57] The Navy looks forward to the deployment of one, and preferably two, Aegis ships with each carrier-battle-group. At a cost of about $930 million per copy, a force of twenty-four is indeed expensive. At present rates, the Navy will have one Aegis ship operational in 1981, but has sixteen proposed for construction through fiscal year 1986.

Amphibious Forces. In terms of amphibious capability, Vice Admiral Holcomb complains that the Navy has enough amphibious ships to land only one of the Marine Corps' three divisions. Since the ships are divided

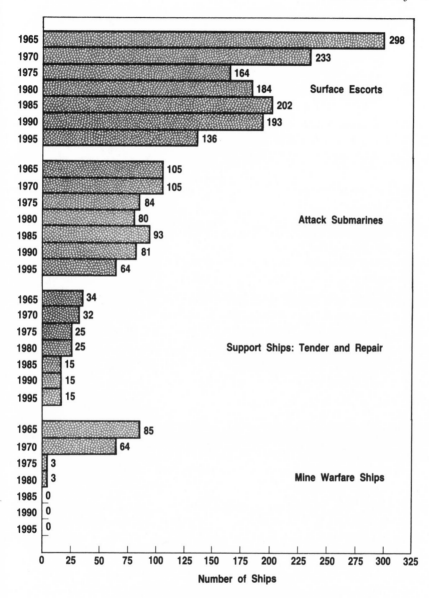

Fig. 2. Recent and Projected Active Force Levels,
Selected Ship Types, 1965-95

Source: U.S. Congress, Congressional Budget Office, *Shaping the General Purpose Navy of the Eighties: Issues for Fiscal Years 1981-85* (Washington, D.C.: Government Printing Office, Jan. 1980), p. 2.

between the Atlantic and Pacific Fleets, a one-division assault in either ocean cannot be done without time-consuming interfleet ship transfers.[58]

Weapons and Sensors. Standoff weapons systems for submarines and surface ships—that is, the Harpoon and Tomahawk surface-to-surface missile (SSM) systems—will upgrade fleet defense considerably; however, at present almost every Soviet warship is equipped with SSMs. In the area of antisubmarine warfare, the United States has a qualitative advantage in technology of submarine systems, ASW sensors, and airborne ASW platforms. Yet, the edge is fragile.[59]

ALLIED NAVAL SUPPORT

With the current low level of U.S. naval ships, the question arises: Can our allies compensate for the U.S. shortfall in warships? The answer is, clearly, no. The Congressional Budget Office advises that unless NATO shipbuilding rates are increased, there could be a decline in both the overall level of allied escorts in the 1990s and in the contribution of the NATO allies to sea-lane defense in the North Atlantic.[60] A similar decline is possible in allied submarines, inasmuch as by 1989 more than ninety allied diesel-electric submarines will be at least twenty years old; and only twelve diesel-electric and ten nuclear submarines are under construction.[61] What must be remembered also is that our NATO allies are not likely to assist the United States in anything short of an East-West conflict involving NATO and the Warsaw Pact.

In the Pacific, United States allies have relatively small naval forces. Most of the ships are for local defense, with limited endurance and equipped with obsolete weapons. Japan is the major exception.[62] In the case of Japan, probability is high that in any conflict involving the USSR, Japanese naval forces would be dedicated to protecting their own SLOC and not be available for Pacific escort duties.[63]

Despite the fact the United States, more often than not, thinks of a conflict at sea as one that would include our allies, the very concept of the rapid deployment force (RDF) acknowledges the United States is preparing to move quickly and without allies, even if the USSR is involved directly.[64] Substantial naval assistance from our traditional allies is not self-evident.

SMALLER NAVY REQUIRES FAVORABLE ATTRITION RATIOS

"The U.S. Navy is clearly outnumbered in most ship categories by our principal adversary and is likely to remain so for the foreseeable future."[65]

Prudent naval planning accepts the possibility that some initial battle losses be recognized. This, in turn, mandates that naval commanders seek out engagement opportunities that likely will produce attrition ratios favoring the United States. In other words, battles must be selected carefully, and marginal situations of combat must be avoided. This is the only realistic formula for aiming to defeat a larger navy in the worldwide war at sea. When outnumbered, a one-for-one exchange ratio represents ultimate defeat.[66]

NET ASSESSMENT

The Soviet navy outnumbers the U.S. Navy by about three to one, some of which are older ships and small craft; but on the other hand, many are armed with modern surface-to-surface cruise missiles that give them a potent "kill probability." The United States is superior in aircraft carriers, while the USSR has about 80 more principal surface combatants, 235 more submarines, six times as many auxiliaries, and a large land-based naval air strike force.[67]

While the size of the U.S. fleet will expand in the mid-1980s, the trend is projected to reverse thereafter. (See Figure 2.) At the same time, demands for additional forward deployments are expected to grow. Personnel manning will continue to be a problem without a clear-cut near-term solution. Additionally, allied naval forces are not expected to accept a larger share of the naval burden.

American maritime responsibilities exceed our present capabilities. As Admiral Hayward said, "In spite of the fact that we're going to increase by thirty or forty ships, that's not enough to give us the three-ocean capability, simultaneously. It just isn't there. We will still be a one-and-one-half-ocean navy, basically."[68]

What is to be done?

How Can We Regain the Momentum?

The normative solution to America's naval problem is simple: Spend more money, build more ships, increase pay, increase funds for research and development. Pragmatically, however, the problem is more complex and vexing. Fiscal and political realities require naval appropriations to compete with other programs for limited federal dollars. For instance, while the priority list of the Chief of Naval Operations for correcting the Navy's ills is correct, it is not funded. That is, Admiral Hayward clearly and simply states his needs in three categories of decreasing importance:

people, aircraft, and ships.[69] In order to fund these priorities a cohesive naval strategy must demonstrate convincingly both present and future naval needs in terms of national defense.

STRATEGY AND FORCE PLANNING

Threat assessment probably is the most pertinent, yet the most elusive, element of strategy and force planning. Although the Soviet Union is America's principal adversary, the fleets of these nations have not engaged in combat. Some would argue the U.S. Navy should continue a strategy of deterrence rather than looking toward war-fighting scenarios. On the other hand, the U.S. Navy has periodically engaged in confrontations in the Third World, for example, in Korea, Cuba, Lebanon, and the Persian Gulf.[70] How then, does one develop a naval strategy for the future?

Ships, it seems, are designed in response to certain scenarios such as a contemporary battle at sea between U.S. and Soviet naval and land-based forces. However, naval ships have a life cycle of twenty-five to thirty years, meaning they will outlive the scenarios. The "hard" question becomes: Who can see far enough ahead to design the proper ships for the forthcoming mission? Who, for instance, was able to see at the end of World War II that the Soviet Union would develop into a formidable sea power that would challenge American use of the sea? And who was able to foresee that U.S. support of Iran would lead to the requirement for a U.S. naval task force to be stationed in the Persian Gulf? More important, who can estimate the nature of future threats and what equipment will best be able to cope with them? The most one can do, perhaps, is to "have military capabilities that will deter other nations, whether large or small, from pursuing policies that threaten our vital interests."[71]

Since naval ships are expensive and long-term investments, certain requirements might be applied to each ship to insure future utility, namely:

- Naval ships should be designed to accommodate change and modernization readily. (Carriers can do this by changing aircraft types.)
- Small surface combatants should be designed to take some aircraft.
- Ships should be designed in such a way that changes can be

made readily in sensor and weapons suits, for example, in modules.[72]

The point is, not all naval ships need to be highly capable and expensive to fulfill missions short of the all-out war at sea with the USSR. The problem of personnel enters in here also; that is, today's navy is having recruiting and retention problems, which a larger navy will magnify.

MANPOWER

This "sexist" term immediately brings to mind better utilization of women in the naval service. The Navy has been and is active in promoting the assignment of women to both shore and sea billets. Federal law, however, precludes assigning females to combat ships. If and when the country is ready to make a drastic change in this law, then all armed services can increase the use of females accordingly.

Other avenues for increasing manpower pools include reinstitution of the draft and increasing the enlistment age to accommodate unemployed skilled and semiskilled workers who want to work. The draft issue is beyond the scope of this paper; however, increasing the enlistment age for selected skills would seem to merit serious consideration. Most certainly, incentives must be increased for both recruiting and retention. Foremost consideration should be given reinstatement of the G.I. Bill as proposed by Senator William Armstrong (R-Colo.) in the 96th Congress. "By giving the individual a stake in his future—via college education— more quality high school graduates can be attracted to serve in the military."[73]

Servicemen on active duty who have a G.I. Bill eligibility earned prior to its termination on January 1, 1977, will be faced with the decision to leave the service prior to December 31, 1989, or lose their G.I. Bill benefits. This is a prospect that should not be imposed upon career-minded servicemen.[74]

Military pay is another major issue for both recruiting and retention. In July 1980 Admiral Holcomb said a 25 percent pay increase was needed to retain skilled seamen.[75] In October 1980 the military pay raise was 11.7 percent plus a variable housing allowance, and a 5.3 percent raise was proposed for fall 1981. These help, but do not solve the pay problem. Military service is not price competitive with civilian industry. In the view of the American Enterprise Institute, the first and most immediate requirement is to increase military pay by 3 percent per year over the cost of living between now and fiscal year 1986 and to maintain the current value of benefits and bonuses.[76] Certainly, more military housing is needed to preclude the impact of the inflated housing market on married servicemen ordered by the Navy from one ship or station to another.

SIZING THE FLEET: HOW MUCH IS ENOUGH?

Since 1977 the U.S. five-year naval shipbuilding plan has had no consistency and appears to lack direction. The plan has varied between 67 and 157 ships, with former President Carter's fiscal year 1982 budget, sent to Capitol Hill on January 15, 1981, showing a cut from 97 to 80 newbuildings.[77] (See Table 3.) What seems certain is a 600-ship three-ocean navy, but the timetable and mix of ships is in doubt. For instance, Secretary of Defense Caspar Weinberger plans to seek an expanded 600-ship navy emphasizing large ships such as aircraft carriers, as well as amphibious assault craft.[78]

The argument over high-low mix or quantity vs. quality continues. Depending upon the scenario one chooses, either fewer sophisticated ships or more less-capable ships can be defended. Since a carrier, for instance, authorized in the next year or two can spend over half its service life in the twenty-first century, and with future naval requirements in doubt, the answer is probably a compromise—some of each in a balanced fleet.

The Heritage Foundation suggests a 600-ship three-ocean navy, claiming the necessity to increase shipbuilding from a current rate of 17 per year to 28–30 per year. Heritage believes that an additional nuclear-powered carrier should be authorized in fiscal year 1982 for the prospect of a continued naval presence in the Indian Ocean. They also call for at least four CG-47 cruisers and six FFG-7 frigates in fiscal year 1982 to complete the nuclear-powered aircraft carrier (CVN) task group. And, for sea control, Heritage sees a need for three to five SSN-688 attack submarines each year throughout the next five fiscal years.[79] The Heritage Foundation recommendation is close to the recommendations of Melvin Laird and Lawrence Korb. (See Table 4.)

What is clear is that, to ensure by the year 2000 even the same size and type of fleet that we have today, shipbuilding requests will have to be 30 percent higher than for fiscal year 1980. "The longer we wait, the less likely [it is that] such increases will occur."[80]

Strategic Naval Systems. Perhaps the single most important item in the

Table 4: Laird-Korb Shipbuilding Program, Fiscal Years 1982-86

Ship Type	1982	1983	1984	1985	1986	Total
Trident	2	1	2	1	2	8
SSN-688	3	2	3	2	3	13
CVN	1	0	1	0	1	3
DDGX	0	0	0	1	1	2
CG-47	3	3	4	4	4	18
FFG-7	6	6	6	6	6	30
FFX	0	1	0	4	4	9
LSD-41	1	1	1	1	1	5
MCM	1	2	4	4	4	15
T-AGOS	4	0	0	0	0	4
T-AO	2	2	2	2	2	10
T-AKX	3	3	3	3	3	15
ARS	2	1	0	0	0	3
Total New Ships	28	22	26	28	31	135

CODE—Trident: nuclear-powered ballistic missile submarine; SSN-688: Los Angeles-class nuclear-powered attack submarine; CVN: Nimitz-class nuclear-powered aircraft carrier; DDGX: new class of guided missile destroyers; CG-47: Ticonderoga-class "Aegis" fleet air defense guided missile cruiser; FFG-7: Oliver Hazard Perry-class guided missile frigate; FFX: new class of frigates; LSD-41: new class of amphibious ships; MCM: mine counter-measures ship; T-AGOS: ocean surveillance ship equipped with SURTAS towed arrays; T-AO: civilian-manned oiler; T-AKX: commercial roll-on/roll-off (RO/RO) ship; ARS: salvage ship. The Reagan Administration is believed also to favor conversion of a number of other ships now in the active inventory as well as reactivation of the carrier *Oriskany* and the four Iowa-class battleships (which would be upgraded and modernized to carry several helicopters and both Harpoon anti-ship missiles and Tomahawk all-purpose cruise missiles).

Source: Adapted from Melvin R. Laird and Lawrence J. Korb's American Enterprise Institute study cited in James D. Hessman, "Redressing the Balance," *Sea Power,* Jan. 1981, p. 18.

strategic submarine field is the construction of an extremely-low-frequency communications system for the SSBN fleet in hardened sites. A major concern with the sea-based leg of the Triad today is reliable communications during a nuclear exchange. This item should receive top strategic priority.

The retrofitting of Trident I (C-4) missiles into 21 Poseidon submarines is well underway. In fact, the U.S.S. *Francis Scott Key* (SSBN 657) was the first conversion and has completed an operational patrol with 16 Trident I missiles.

As Trident submarines become operational along with the phasing out of Polaris, the number of SSBNs in the near-term will decline, but force capability overall will increase.[81] Both the Heritage Foundation and American Enterprise Institute recommend that the Trident SSBN building rate be increased from one per year to the original schedule of three every two years. (See Table 4.) Heritage also recommends the fitting of sea-launched cruise missiles (SLCMs) on the Polaris SSBNs that revert from a strategic to an attack submarine role.[82]

Probably the major contender with Trident for the sea-based leg of the Triad is the SUM concept. This idea (small sub underwater mobile) was advocated by Sidney Drell of Stanford University and Richard Garwin of Harvard as a substitute for the Air Force's proposed MX system. Their idea calls for 55 diesel-electric (eventually fuel cell) propelled highly automated submarines of 1,400 to 1,800 tons each—about one-twelfth the Trident's size. Each submarine would have two encapsulated MX missiles outside its pressure hull, and would cruise at low speeds within 600 miles of U.S. shores.

The claim is that the SUM would be harder to detect than Trident, would not act as a lightning rod on U.S. soil for Soviet missiles, would cost roughly $10 billion less than the fully deployed MX system, and can be initially deployed by 1988 and fully deployed by 1992.[83] The obvious disadvantage of SUM is that it removes the land-based missile targeting problem for the Soviets, while at the same time inherits any and all disadvantages associated with sea-based systems..

Attack Submarines. The U.S. Navy has set a requirement for 90 nuclear-powered attack submarines, and the Department of Defense has supported this requirement. To reach and maintain this level, an average of three SSNs must be authorized each year. Currently, the SSN-688 class is the only SSN in production, costing about $500 million a copy.

Recently the Navy conducted a major review of the SSN situation, called the Navy Submarine Alternatives Study, concluding that less expensive attack submarines could indeed be built but with correspondingly reduced operational capabilities. Former Secretary of Defense Harold Brown favored a smaller nuclear-powered submarine which might cost about $350 million, and included it is his final shipbuilding program for fiscal year 1983.

Still another promising option is a combination of SSNs and advanced technology diesel-electric submarines. Missions suitable for conventional submarines could include ASW barrier patrol, antishipping, mining, surveillance, and support of clandestine operations.[84] The SSN-688/ conventional submarine combination is favored by many analysts as an optimum and cost-effective mix.

Aircraft Carriers and Surface-Action-Groups. The CVN is large, costly, controversial, and the most capable warship afloat today. It can operate 75–90 aircraft in forward areas for long periods of time with minimal base support.[85] The CVN costs over $2 billion; understandably, with this price tag the ship's survivability in combat is an issue.

One option to the high cost CVN is the conventionally powered carrier. Another even less less costly possibility is the V/STOL ship. These ships carry fewer and less capable aircraft than the CVN, but are indeed mission-capable in the areas of ASW, airborne early warning (AEW), and over-the-horizon targeting for cruise missiles.[86] The V/STOL ship can provide air defense for other ships, which resurrects the idea of surface-action-groups. Soviet obsession with missiles for offense led to adoption of the carrier-battle-group as the most survivable and mission-effective force we could field; technology now permits additional choices.

Conceivably there are and will be future naval missions that will not require carrier aircraft, such as ASW, naval blockades, limited actions in the Third World, and simply a show of force. With a V/STOL ship combined with an Aegis antiair warfare (AAW) ship, a surface-action-group becomes feasible. Aegis is basic to this concept.

Aegis is an integrated, computer-controlled air defense system employing a network of radars for tracking and targeting enemy projectiles and missiles. The standard SM-2 missile is guided by sample-data command until the final phase of its intercept, when it receives continuous semi-active illumination. In other words, Aegis is a complete "area" defense system capable of protecting a naval task force from missile and air attack.[87] Priced at $930 million each, the CG-47 class Aegis ship is not a bargain basement special. Perhaps a goal of 24 Aegis ships for the 1990s would be optimum, considering their use both with carrier-battle-groups and with surface-action-groups. For the ASW threat to the surface-action-group, towed array sonars on surface combatants and one or two SSNs in company should provide adequate protection.[88] The offensive punch of such a force would be provided by cruise missiles on surface ships. The Reagan Administration's proposal to reactivate and refit the World War II battleships *New Jersey* and *Iowa* with cruise missiles is a step in this direction.

Certainly, with timely and accurate target location data, the Harpoon antiship cruise missile with a range of about 60 nautical miles, combined with the Tomahawk missile with a range of about 300 nautical miles, together produce an effective "smart" weapon combat capability for surface-action-groups.[89] And new technologies that are within reach will enhance surface-action-groups of the future. For instance, the new hull design called SWATH (small waterplane area twin hull) will permit smaller ships to launch aircraft even in rough waters. New vertical missile launch systems also will improve offensive and defensive capabilities of small ships.

Mines and Mine Warfare. Mine warfare is an effective and inexpensive military capability. Mines not only can destroy enemy merchant and naval ships at low cost, but the threat of mines can paralyze harbors and shipping routes. Mines can give an inferior naval power an ability to limit the dominant powers' free use of the seas.[90] These advantages are not overlooked by the USSR, a naval power that possesses an extensive capability in this area.

The United States used mines effectively in World War II and as recently as the mining of Haiphong harbor in the 1970s. Today, American mines reflect technology of the 1950s, and our capacity to sow them lies in aircraft and attack submarines. As for minesweeping, since 1970 the United States has decommissioned 60 of 63 ships. Granted, mines can be swept by aerial platforms, but ships are superior in many situations.[91]

Present-day technology adds innovative aspects to mine warfare that were unthinkable in past decades. For instance, new influence firing mechanisms are available that make a mine sensitive, selective as to target, and difficult to sweep. Also, deepwater capabilities are available that can pose threats to submarines along their transit routes. And modern moored mines can launch a torpedo-like vehicle to attack its selected target.[92]

There is little doubt that U.S. offensive mine operations are in need of updating, particularly since the technology is available. Additionally, production of the Navy's proposed new class of mine countermeasure ships (MCMs), 13 of which are in the five-year shipbuilding plan through fiscal year 1986, should be accelerated. These ships will be equipped with new hardware, including improved minehunting sonar and precision navigation equipment. Accurate navigation, of course, is basic to efficient minesweeping and minehunting.[93]

OTHER MEANS OF SELF-HELP

Arapaho. There are assets within the U.S. government that can assist greatly in increasing our maritime capability in terms of both speed and economy. For instance, the "Arapaho" concept, that has been bandied about in the design stage far too long, should be implemented forthwith.

Arapaho calls for placing an ASW force on commercial container ships during a national emergency. The idea is to use standard 20 ft. × 40 ft. prefabricated containers as modules for living and ASW operational support facilities. The concept calls for loading three to five containers with the latest ASW electronic listening gear and positioning them in various North Atlantic commercial ports or setting them aside on designated ships. Perhaps every tenth container ship traveling in convoy would have an Arapaho package. Additionally, each convoy would have six to eight helicopters (VTOL aircraft) capable of conducting ASW operations.

A complement of about sixty officers and enlisted personnel would be required for each Arapaho unit. Planners say it is a mission readily assignable to Naval Reserves. The overall effect would be a reduction of two cruiser/destroyer escorts for every Arapaho convoy.[94] Perhaps the Navy itself has been the major stumbling block to this program because of fear of compromises on the purchase of other first-line ships and aircraft.

Use of Merchant Marine. Another easy assist to naval operations is available in our existing U.S.-flag merchant marine. The Soviet navy routinely refuels its warships from Soviet-flag merchant oilers. The same applies to other logistic support during underway replenishments. The United States has generally resisted this concept despite the proven *Erna Elizabeth* tests in 1972 involving refueling and replenishing deployed navy units. This type of capability could have been useful for support of the recent Indian Ocean operations which tended to exceed purely naval capabilities for protracted operations.[95]

T-AGOS Program. Another program of potential value in ASW is the civilian-manned T-AGOS program. These Navy-owned, civilian-manned ships will carry the surveillance towed array sonar (SURTAS), the effective new passive sonar array. Ten of the ships are in the proposed fiscal year 1982 five-year shipbuilding budget, but their production should be accelerated in order to supplement the existing seafloor submarine detection systems.[96]

Civilian Helicopters. To increase the available inventory of ASW helicopters for wartime, Captain Gerald G. O'Rourke says that by 1985 there will be "a thousand or more" helicopters in civilian use "big enough, rugged enough, and capable enough to perform adequately in naval service."[97] What would be required is to identify the helicopters, pay a modest subsidy to the civilian operators for minor design modifications to hold the ASW equipment, then stockpile the equipment. The civilian ASW helos could be operated by Naval Reserve pilots. As with the civilian helicopters, U.S. Coast Guard assets could be upgraded with state-of-the-art ASW equipment and weapons systems and exercised on a regular basis with USN units.[98]

SAC Bombers. Strategic Air Command bombers have the capability to sweep the world's seas for hostile surface ships within a matter of hours. With minimal costs, SAC bombers could be equipped with both radar transponders and ASW "smart" weapons, and their crews trained in sea surveillance and attack missions. (Some SAC B-52Gs were equipped and trained for electronic intelligence missions in 1976.)[99] It seems that current policy and funding restraints for collateral missions by the service assigned such missions is the limiting factor today. This certainly is a solvable problem, along with the understanding that ocean surveillance would not detract from SAC's strategic mission and alert posture. Additionally, the bomber aircraft would remain under the operational control of SAC with, perhaps, a few USN air intelligence, operational and communications personnel assigned to SAC's numbered air force command centers as advisors.

MORE ASSISTANCE FROM THE ALLIES?

Our NATO allies possess some 200 ships applicable to a NATO maritime effort. However, all but 60 or 70 are likely to be required for missions in local European waters. Transatlantic convoy protection will again fall on American shoulders.[100] Additionally, in any contingency outside of a Warsaw Pact-NATO conflict, it is highly unlikely that our European allies would be willing to contribute any maritime support at all.

NATO, perhaps, could be convinced to increase its fleet, thereby helping share peacetime naval mission requirements. Vice Admiral Thomas J.

Bigley, for instance, thinks NATO partners should build an aircraft carrier on their own simply because the United States will not have enough carriers to cover all the hotspots for the foreseeable future.[101] This is certainly an alternative that should be pursued, even if the probability for success is marginal. It should be remembered that in 1968 President Lyndon Johnson had a choice of three strategies for protecting U.S. interests in the Persian Gulf. He could subsidize a continued British presence; he could put a small U.S. force in to replace the British as they pulled out; or he could use the cooperation of the Shah of Iran.[102] Despite the fact he opted for supporting the Shah, the Royal Navy departed, and the chore of protecting the oil pipeline to the West will surely become an American burden. The stark reality seems to be that our allies' naval contribution to the Western alliance is not likely to increase.

DIVERT MORE DEPARTMENT OF DEFENSE FUNDS TO THE NAVY?

If traditional national defense responsibilities and protection of our international import-export trade—including our vital oil and mineral life lines—are both necessary but beyond our ability to pay, and if new money is not forthcoming, an alternative is to "rob Peter to pay Paul." At the risk of suggesting another unproductive bomber-vs.-carrier interservice feud, another possibility will be tabled for consideration.

The Center for Defense Information argues that throughout history the principal roles of ground forces have been to defend the territory of the United States or to invade and capture foreign territory. However, nearly one million U.S. soldiers and marines have neither role. Instead, U.S. ground forces are trained and equipped primarily to support and defend our allies overseas. In 1978 over 30 percent of the U.S. Army and 16 percent of the Marine Corps were based permanently outside the United States, primarily in West Germany, Japan, and South Korea.[103]

Since Western forces have been limited by economic constraints, their security concepts seem preoccupied with defense on land rather than at sea. The belief seems to be that by strengthening ground forces in Europe, the use of nuclear weapons will become less likely. However, as Admiral Worth H. Bagley, USN (Ret.), so eloquently argues, as this process develops, the role of sea power in helping to resupply and reinforce Europe across the North Atlantic declines, and a nuclear response on land becomes the only option open to NATO,[104] short of surrender.

The suggestion, then, is based on the fact that more than 50 percent of the Department of Defense annual budget is earmarked for personnel expenses. And, with the limited prospect of having to defend the continental United States with expensive heavy armor divisions, and the near-term political improbability of having to fight another overseas war like Korea or Vietnam, a reduction of armored and mechanized divisions might be a sensible tradeoff for the increased national security of a three-ocean modern navy—if there is no other way. In other words, an application of the Nixon Doctrine to NATO is a possibility. In no way would the United States consider NATO less important; it would provide naval, air, and logistic assistance to its allies. In turn, it would expect NATO to raise the ground forces necessary for European defense. The "trip-wire" of American uniformed troops in the route of a possible Soviet advance can be provided by independent U.S. nuclear-capable artillery and missile elements attached to NATO armies.

The Center for Defense Information calculated that from 1978 through 1983, about $11 billion could be saved by pruning five divisions from the Army.[105] To repeat, such a suggestion is a last-resort measure in the event naval forces cannot be procured in sufficient quantity with new money or in some other way. The Soviets are probably correct in their notion that "more is better." The United States will have to make some hard decisions in the next few budget years if its national security is to be assured.

Conclusion

Naval requirements range from maintaining stability and deterring war, to protecting sea lanes of commerce, to war fighting. Throughout the last decade, U.S. naval requirements have increased to include an Indian Ocean presence and an increased emphasis on the protection of ocean "oil routes." Meanwhile the number of U.S. ships has fallen from almost 1,000 to fewer than 500. At the same time, our Soviet adversary has increased its naval strength to more than 1,600 vessels.

Recruiting and retention of trained officer and enlisted personnel continue to be serious problems. At the same time there seems to be general agreement that the Navy must be built up to at least 600 warships.

To arrive at and maintain a 600-ship navy will require about a 90 percent increase in recent shipbuilding rates, that is, from about 17 ships per year to 28–30 ships per year. This takes time (perhaps a decade or more) and money, for shipbuilding yards have closed and their trained workers are gone. Additionally, since 40–60 percent of the cost of a ship is in materials purchased by the shipyard—steel, pipe, valves, pumps, etc.—and the subcontractors involved have cut back because of a lack of business, it will take three to five years before there can be a realistic increase in the number of ships under construction. Concurrently, incentives for personnel recruiting and retention, such as pay raises, more government housing, and the G.I. Bill are required if the present and proposed ships are to be manned adequately.

To obtain maximum effectiveness from funds expended, the Navy should: look to the resurrection of the surface-action-group; build new carriers for an Indian Ocean presence; increase mine-warfare capabilities; accelerate wartime contingency planning by developing and employing the U.S. merchant marine for underway replenishment; put the Arapaho ASW convoy protection systems in place; identify and pre-position ASW equipment for use in civilian helicopters; and work with the USAF's Strategic Air Command and the U.S. Coast Guard for cooperation in strengthening national maritime missions.

Today's and tomorrow's naval requirements are expensive. However, they directly affect the security of the United States. If these needs cannot be met from new funds, then serious consideration must be given to diverting money earmarked to the protection of our allies, such as the U.S. Army in Europe, to our own self-help.

"The true strength of a sea power can only be measured in terms of its ability to use the sea in the furtherance of its national objectives despite any atmosphere created by rivals or competitors."[106] Without doubt, this ability is in jeopardy and might be lost if our relative naval strength continues to falter. The simple reality is that to maintain the current inadequate Navy force levels, increased funding will be required. And even if the Navy gets all the money it wants (which is highly unlikely) it will be many years before present problems can be resolved. Meantime, the burden continues to fall on the shoulders of the sailors who man the fleet today.[107]

Naval analysts Polmar and Bessette have stated, "If more ships and aircraft cannot be provided to make the Navy's strength a better match for its commitments, an alternative is to reduce commitments."[108] That is, the two-carrier force in the Mediterranean Sea, the two carriers in the Western Pacific, and so on, may have to stand down to one carrier. (See Figure 3.) This would indeed be dangerous for U.S. national security as well as a temptation to aggression by our adversaries.

It should be recalled that contemporary U.S. naval strategy sees the oceans as barriers for defense of the continental United States, as well as

Fig. 3. United States

Source: John M. Collins, *U.S.-Soviet Military Balance: Concepts and*

necessary trade routes for international commerce essential to the sustained industrial health of the United States and its allies.[109] The very existence of our society depends upon being able to protect our vital interests at sea. To do this into the future requires heavy expenditures now. The question is: Will America meet the challenge?

NOTES

1. Bath Iron Works Corp. advertisement in *Sea Power*, Dec. 1980, p. 5.

2. Harold and Margaret Sprout, *Foundations of International Politics* (Princeton, N.J.: D. Van Nostrand, 1962), p. 320.

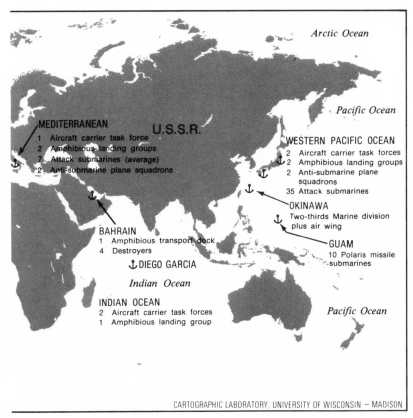

MEDITERRANEAN U.S.S.R.
1 Aircraft carrier task force
2 Amphibious landing groups
7 Attack submarines (average)
2 Anti-submarine plane squadrons

Arctic Ocean

Pacific Ocean

WESTERN PACIFIC OCEAN
2 Aircraft carrier task forces
2 Amphibious landing groups
2 Anti-submarine plane
   squadrons
35 Attack submarines

OKINAWA
   Two-thirds Marine division
   plus air wing

BAHRAIN
1 Amphibious transport dock
4 Destroyers

GUAM
10 Polaris missile
   submarines

DIEGO GARCIA

Indian Ocean

INDIAN OCEAN
2 Aircraft carrier task forces
1 Amphibious landing group

Pacific Ocean

CARTOGRAPHIC LABORATORY, UNIVERSITY OF WISCONSIN – MADISON

Naval Deployment
Capabilities 1960-80 (New York: McGraw-Hill, 1980), p. 247

3. By Sept. 22, 1961, all 41 of the current U.S. Polaris/Poseidon SSBNs were authorized. The mix consists of the five original George Washington-class, followed by five Ethan Allen-class and finally 31 Lafayette-class SSBNs. Each class was slightly larger and more capable than its predecessor. Four generations of solid-propellant missiles were in turn developed for this fleet of submarines. The 1,200-nm range Polaris A-1 was quickly followed by Polaris A-2, which extended the range by some 300 nm's. An advanced Polaris, the 2,500-nm range A-3, followed in 1964. Polaris missiles were followed by the Poseidon (C-3) missile. This weapon is three feet longer than the 31-foot Polaris and 1.5 feet larger in diameter. Poseidon was followed by the new long-range Trident I (C-4). Basically, this involved mounting a new third stage on Poseidon's second stage to achieve a design range exceeding 4,000 nm's.

The Trident submarine displaces approximately 18,000 tons, or twice as much as the Polaris SSBN. It carries 24 missiles rather than the 16 carried by Polaris. Additionally, it is quieter, faster, more maneuverable, and has improved sonar capabilities. The submarine is designed to be simpler to maintain and overhaul and should be able to spend far more time at sea than its predecessors. A Trident II or (D-5) missile is under consideration for the future. This missile will have an extended range up to about 6,000 nm's.

4. Norman Polmar and Ray Bessette, "General Purpose Forces: Navy and Marine Corps," in *Arms, Men, and Military Budgets: Issues for Fiscal Year 1981,* by Francis P. Hoeber et al (New Brunswick, N.J.: Transaction Books, 1980), p. 91.

5. Barry M. Blechman and Stephen S. Kaplan, *Force Without War* (Wash. D.C.: The Brookings Institution, 1978), p. 39.

6. *Ibid.,* p. 41.

7. Ann Hughey, "The Age of Aircraft Carrier Diplomacy," *Forbes,* July 21, 1980, p. 61.

8. *Ibid.,* p. 62.

9. *U.S. Life Lines,* OpNav-09D-PIA (Wash. D.C.: Government Printing Office, Jan. 1978), p. 3; and James D. Hessman and Ellen D. Bottiny, "U.S. Life Lines: Data and Statistics, Observation and Conclusions," *Sea Power,* Sept. 1978, p. 31.

10. Richard T. and Steven T. Ackley, "Missing Strategic Link: A Strong U.S. Merchant Marine," *Strategic Review,* Winter 1980, p. 52.

11. Admiral Thomas B. Hayward, USN, *CNO Report: Fiscal Year 1981* (Wash. D.C.: Dept. of the Navy, 1980), p. 11.

12. J. William Middendorf II, "National Naval Policy," *The Retired Officer,* Nov. 1976, p. 28.

13. James D. Hessman, "The U.S. Navy in the Eighties," *The Retired Officer,* Feb. 1980, p. 19.

14. *Ibid.,* p. 20.

15. F. J. West, Jr., "A Fleet for the Year 2000: Future Force Structure," U.S. Naval Institute *Proceedings,* May 1980, pp. 68–69.

16. Hessman, "The U.S. Navy in the Eighties," p. 18.

17. Polmar and Bessette, p. 74.

18. *Shipyard Weekly,* Feb. 5, 1981, p. 1.

19. Polmar and Bessette, p. 74.

20. *Shipyard Weekly,* Jan. 1, 1981, p. 3.

21. "Navy Needs 203 New Vessels to Meet Minimum Requirements," *Coordinated Action,* Dec. 1980, p. 2.

22. *Shipyard Weekly,* Jan. 8, 1981, p. 3.

23. Hayward, pp. 9, 10.

24. *Ibid.,* p. 41.

25. U.S. Congress, Congressional Budget Office, *Shaping the General Purpose Navy of the Eighties: Issues for FY-1981-1985* (Wash. D.C.: Government Printing Office, Jan. 1980), pp. 65–66.

26. George C. Wilson, "Admiral Urges NATO Allies to Build Carrier," *The Washington Post,* Nov. 15, 1980, p. A-15.

27. Stephen Webbe, "Chorus of Retired Admirals and Generals: 'Make U.S. Forces Battle-Ready,' " *Christian Science Monitor,* Dec. 31, 1980, p. 6.

28. Hayward, p. 14.

29. West, p. 73.

30. *Ibid.*

31. Hayward, p. 3.

32. Jack Anderson, "Severe Naval Shortage," *The Sun* (San Bernardino, Calif.), Mar. 16, 1980, p. B-12.

33. Andrew C. A. Jampoler, "America's Vital Interests," U.S. Naval Institute *Proceedings,* Jan. 1981, p. 32.

34. John D. Alden, "Tomorrow's Fleet," U.S. Naval Institute *Proceedings,* Jan. 1981, p. 112.

35. Anderson, p. B-12.

36. Hayward, p. 2.

37. *Ibid.,* p. 28.

38. John M. Collins, *U.S.-Soviet Military Balance: Concepts and Capabilities 1960–1980* (New York: McGraw-Hill, 1980), p. 267.

39. *CHINFO Fact File* NAVSO P-3002-1, 6th ed., rev. 8-80 (Wash. D.C.: Dept. of the Navy, 1980), p. 10.

40. West, p. 74.
41. Orr Kelly, "A Firsthand Look at What Ails the Navy," *U.S. News and World Report,* Sept. 22, 1980, p. 38.
42. *Ibid.*
43. John J. Spittler, "People Power Revisited," *Sea Power,* Feb. 1981, p. 4.
44. Hayward, p. 20.
45. *CHINFO,* p. 92.
46. Polmar and Bessette, p. 95.
47. *Ibid.*
48. *Shipyard Weekly,* Jan. 1, 1981, p. 4.
49. Polmar and Bessette, p. 97.
50. R. James Woolsey, "Planning a Navy: The Risks of Conventional Wisdom," *International Security,* Summer 1978, pp. 19–20.
51. Collins, p. 251.
52. "Cost of Navy Fighter Soars," *The Sun* (San Bernardino, Calif.), July 17, 1980, p. A-20.
53. *CHINFO,* pp. 81–82.
54. Jim Bencivenga, "Rigging U.S. Container Ships to Defend Themselves in Time of War," *Christian Science Monitor,* Jan. 6, 1981, p. 3.
55. Polmar and Bessette, p. 108.
56. Hughey, p. 59.
57. Polmar and Bessette, p. 103.
58. Hughey, p. 61.
59. Hayward, p. 38.
60. *Shaping the General Purpose Navy . . . ,* p. 60.
61. *Ibid.*
62. *Ibid.,* p. 61.
63. *Ibid.*
64. West, p. 74.
65. *CHINFO,* p. 8.
66. Hayward, p. 7.
67. *Ibid.,* p. 34.
68. John K. Cooley, "Navy's Task: Three-Ocean Strength," *Christian Science Monitor,* Apr. 29, 1980, p. 6.
69. *Ibid.*
70. Polmar and Bessette, p. 90.
71. Worth H. Bagley, "Sea Power and Western Security: The Next Decade," *Adelphi Papers,* No. 139, p. 1.
72. Woolsey, p. 23.
73. "Defense Policy and Program Planning in the Reagan Administration," *National Security Record* (The Heritage Foundation), No. 28, Dec. 1980, p. 3.
74. "GI Bill Extension," *Shift Colors,* Vol. XXVI, Winter 1980, pp. 10–11.
75. Hughey, p. 61.
76. James D. Hessman, "Redressing the Balance," *Sea Power,* Jan. 1981, p. 20.
77. *Shipyard Weekly,* Jan. 22, 1981, p. 2.
78. "Who Are These People — and What do They Stand For?" *U.S. News and World Report,* Jan. 19, 1981, p. 19.
79. "Defense Policy and Program Planning. . . " p. 2.
80. West, p. 69.
81. Hayward, p. 28.
82. "Defense Policy and Program Planning . . ." p. 2.
83. Patrick O'Driscoll, "Put MX missiles in small subs?" *The Sun* (San Bernardino, Calif.), Dec. 17, 1980, p. A-3.
84. *Shaping the General Purpose Navy . . . ,* pp. xviii, xix, 94.
85. Polmar and Bessette, p. 99.

86. *Ibid.* p. 102.
87. *Shaping the General Purpose Navy* . . . , pp. 15n, 88, 69–70.
88. West, p. 74.
89. *Shaping the General Purpose Navy* . . . , p. 69.
90. *Ibid.*, p. 78.
91. Collins, p. 265.
92. *Shaping the General Purpose Navy* . . . , pp. 78–79.
93. *Ibid.*, p. 98.
94. Bencivenga, p. 3.
95. Ernest L. Schwab, "A Need For Speed," *Sea Power*, Jan. 1981, p. 16.
96. Polmar and Bessette, p. 111.
97. Gerald G. O'Rourke cited in "Scoop & Scuttle," *Sea Power*, Dec. 1980, p. 7.
98. Schwab, p. 15.
99. See "Washington Whispers," *U.S. News and World Report*, Aug. 30, 1976, p. 11, and "Notebook," U.S. Naval Institute *Proceedings*, Oct. 1976, p. 143.
100. *Shaping the General Purpose Navy*. . . . , p. xvii.
101. Wilson, p. A-15.
102. Joseph C. Harsch, "Hostage Release—New Oil Policy," *Christian Science Monitor*, Jan. 23, 1981, p. 1.
103. "U.S. Ground Forces: Inappropriate Objectives, Unacceptable Costs," *The Defense Monitor*, Vol. VII, No. 9, Nov. 1978, p. 1.
104. Bagley, p. 1.
105. "U.S. Ground Forces: . . . ," p. 1.
106. CHINFO, p. iv.
107. Kelly, p. 38.
108. Polmar and Bessette, p. 115.
109. Collins, p. 246.

Marine Transportation: Moving the World's Trade

Herbert Brand

In any discussion of uses of the oceans for military or commercial advantage, one does well first to take note of a trend in basic U.S. industry toward "going overseas." In many cases, the conglomerates that operate outside the country find it quite advantageous to export their factories completely, using the home base solely as a sales market. In doing so, they give no consideration to the effect of business policy on national strategy.

To me, this trend is an indication of where the United States is headed politically in an increasingly hostile world—one in which America has more to lose than any other nation. As an American citizen, I am concerned about what I perceive as a decline in the position of the United States as a world power. Neither industrially nor in military strength—the two areas that together make a nation great, give it inspiration for leadership, and command respect—is our country the power that concluded World War II. Observation of the voting in the United Nations makes apparent our lack of influence. Other nations and people, adjusting to changing conditions and moving with them, are passing us by. Perhaps the United States has reached its zenith without having done what is necessary to preserve or enhance its strength to go beyond. If this were not so, perhaps sea power would not present the problems that it does today nor so deeply concern the specialists who are here discussing it. For what is being discussed is nothing less than the security of the United States.

An essential element of that security is the maritime industry.

A Small but Vital Industry

Marine transportation is a small industry in this country. Fewer than 600 active deep-sea American ships remain under U.S. registry. Of these, some 200 vessels operate in what are known as liner trades, that is, they have regular runs between specific ports throughout the world. Another 275 are the bulk carriers, which will go anywhere in the world although their trade is mostly to and from the United States. They are of two varieties, differentiated by cargo: the liquid bulk carriers, or tankers, and the dry bulk carriers.

Of the 578 ship total, about 150, a relatively small percentage, are subsidized. Contrary to what one hears about this being a heavily subsidized industry, the sum provided in the current federal budget is no more than about $400 million, and that includes the subsidies for building as well as operating these 150 vessels supported by that allocation.

The subsidy is intended to provide some offset differential for the shipbuilder and the operator to help them meet foreign competition in labor and other costs that are elevated by higher American standards. The subsidy rationale is based on the premise that the American merchant marine is essential to U.S. national security. And regardless of how poorly the American merchant marine may have been treated by any national administration by way of appropriations, nobody has ever successfully defended the contention that a merchant marine capability is not vital to national defense.

Approximately 22,000 seamen are employed on American ships; about 19,000 have jobs aboard vessels in the private sector, and another 2,000 or so work for the United States Navy in civil service capacity on ships carrying matériel for the military services. The merchant fleet has been dwindling steadily, and very few ships are under construction at the present time; the book is virtually blank for the shipbuilder. Nobody is building ships in the United States today except those who are required by the conditions of their subsidy contracts to replace vessels that are overage; and even in those cases, extended use is sometimes taken as an alternative to replacement.

Moving the World's Trade

The United States maritime industry moves very little of the world's trade. Of the 3 billion 415 million metric tons of world commerce that is transported annually over the oceans, U.S. vessels carry virtually nothing. What is more shocking is that we depend on foreign vessels for 98 percent of the carriage of our own dry bulk, 97 percent of our liquid bulk trade, and 75 percent of our general liner cargo. In short, we carry only 4.4 percent of our own foreign commerce in American-flag ships.

On the other hand, the United Kingdom carries 34 percent of its foreign commerce; France carries 33 percent of its; the Norwegians carry 30 percent of theirs; the Japanese, 44 percent of theirs; and the Soviet Union carries 55 percent of Soviet Union foreign commerce. Furthermore, a number of countries do even better than we do ourselves in carrying our foreign commerce: Canada and the United Kingdom, for example, each carries slightly over 5 percent of U.S. foreign commerce, and Greece carries 12 percent.

Those figures explain one major function of the National Maritime Council, to which reference is made later—namely, the promotion of use of American-flag ships by American companies

DECLINE OF THE MERCHANT MARINE

Several factors have contributed to decline of the U.S.-flag merchant marine. These include: (1) the lack of national attention to the gradual erosion of American maritime capability; (2) a lack of recognition that the programs used by the United States to bolster its maritime industry have been no match for the more aggressive and realistic programs of other maritime countries; (3) an ideological commitment on the part of the U.S. government to principles of free trade that are totally out of step with shipping practices in the rest of the world; (4) dependence of U.S. defense planners on a new "maginot line" that relies primarily on massive weapons systems as a deterrent, and undervalues less dramatic factors, such as American sealift capability, as essential to national defense.

Periodically the maritime industry has been criticized by the press and others who advocate the use of foreign-flag vessels, with the argument that if it is cheaper to use a Liberian- or Panamanian-flag ship (or any other) than American, why not do it? That is the classical economist's point of view, and it is widely held in some U.S. government agencies. In the Office of Management and Budget, in the Treasury Department, people ask repeatedly, "Why have an American merchant marine? Why is it needed?" They say that the United States is not competitive; and singling out the higher cost of American labor as a major cause, they contend that it never can be. We in marine transportation must counter that position every working day.

Of course the American merchant marine cannot compete in a free market. Undeniably it cannot compete against a vessel that is built in a Korean shipyard and manned by a Pakistani or mixed crew with a Greek captain—not if it uses ships built in American yards and manned by American seamen. But in our opinion, a free market does not exist for the merchant marine. Free trade no longer exists. This is a totally different world from that described by Professor Craig Symonds of the Naval Academy elsewhere in this volume. And even in that earlier world, he points out, in 1890 the United States was reduced to carrying only 12 percent of its foreign commerce in its own ships. Except for artificial periods of war, the grade has been downward ever since. The cycle of "off and on" referred to by Dr. Athelstan Spilhaus (in his introduction to this book) as characteristic of all aspects of American sea power is particularly applicable to our merchant marine; in the industry it is called "feast or famine." In modern times, there has never been an American merchant marine of a size and quality consistent with the position of this nation as a world power, a merchant marine appropriate to a country that is conscious of the demands upon it as a world leader and its responsibilities to its citizens and to its allies. Instead, as a general rule the United States has "floated" along with a kind of motley merchant marine, carrying a small percentage of U.S. commerce, always behind in upgrading its fleet until confronted with a war situation.

This was the case in World War I when, fortunately, our allies were holding off the enemy in Europe while we built ships and weapons and sent them across the Atlantic. We had some lead time. And again in World War II we had lead time to effect this great miracle by which the U.S. industrial machine could eventually provide all the ships and matériel essential to victory. But after the conflicts came the reversion to status quo—the drop back in our sea power standing. In getting rid of the five thousand ships that we had after World War II, we went from one end of the spectrum to the other. We sold our fleet to all buyers. Most of the ships we sold in quantities to our allies, and at the same time we began helping the Japanese and West Germans to build shipyards which were eventually to be used to the exclusion of our own.

SHIPYARD CAPABILITY ESSENTIAL

It is important that we understand that without a shipyard capability a country will be deficient as a power and its defenses will be seriously jeopardized. Some people feel that the United States can never be competitive with foreign shipyards. So long as there are differences in national shipping policies and in living standards, that is true. But pure competition in a free market is absent in world shipping and shipbuilding. Other countries do not build ships nor attempt to sell them on the basis of cost alone. The Japanese do not do it; the British, the Koreans do not do it. Where they feel that it is in the national interest to maintain jobs, they build a ship for whatever they can get for it. The Japanese, of course, have a society quite different from ours, a paternalistic society with values and loyalties that do not exist here. They do not have the problems we have. If their shipyard business is a little slow, they do not let that work force drift away; they move it to some other area of the economy to return when it is again needed. They preserve the skills and the capability. The fact is that they build ships in the national interest, not for the benefit of a single shipyard alone. And the Japanese use their own ships for their overseas commerce because they are moved strongly by overall national interest.

Let me illustrate with personal experience. When the National Maritime Council was organized in 1970 (with very substantial assistance from the Nixon Administration, which believed the United States needed a strong merchant marine) and began to address the problems of the industry, it was found that virtually all cars imported to this country from Japan were coming here in Japanese vessels. Through the Office of Market Development in the Department of Commerce, where there was a strong assistant secretary for maritime affairs, and with full backing of the White House, steps were taken to alter that situation. Government people went to Japan and insisted that some of those cars be transported on U.S. vessels. There was resistance, but the threat of unfavorable tariffs persuaded the Japanese to comply, and for a while at least, a portion of imported Japanese cars arrived on American-flag ships. Unfortunately, we Americans do not have what was called, in the days of the '20s, "stick-to-it-ive-ness;" we do not stick to that kind of practice as a matter of policy. So, when the pressure was off, the purpose was no longer there.

In contrast, while the Japanese do not have a single cargo preference law, everyone involved understands what is meant when the Japanese trade ministry stresses the need to move cargoes aboard their own ships to keep their fleet active. Regardless of problems—and there are problems, of course—the orders are given: Japanese shippers are to use Japanese ships. There may be disagreements behind closed doors, but in the final analysis, they move their cargo on Japanese ships. (Incidentally, I might point out that Japanese seamen are rather well paid; I think they are not far, if at all, behind American seamen, and their wages are increasing more rapidly.)

MARITIME UNIONS

I have referred to the function of the National Maritime Council in promoting use of American-flag shipping. The Council has also provided a forum for labor and management where the problems of the industry are laid out and discussed. It might be well to point out that a considerably different situation exists today in the maritime industry from that existing years back. At one time there was much more fragmentation; some union and company mergers have taken place. Even so, considering the small size of the industry, with only 578 ships and some 22,000 people making their livelihoods in marine transportation, there are more individual unions and less unity than one would expect. However, on one fundamental basis, all industry segments work together. Everyone understands that without a ship there can be no cargo; and without cargo, there can be no work.

The maritime unions are generally regarded as being strong and very active. That some are licensed and some unlicensed militates against uniform approaches and cohesive policy, but the situation is improving. The industry is almost totally organized for both dry cargo and liquid cargo ships, with the exception of the major oil companies' American-flag ships. On these, the companies maintain what they call "non-aligned unions;" the seamen call them "company unions." Management has no problem working with the unions, because the approach to industry problems is no longer based on the particular needs of each. Realizing that one cannot exist without the other, and that the industry's weakened condition demands the combined efforts of both, labor and management have aligned themselves and work together as a cohesive force on an industrial basis. Both are active politically, labor to a somewhat larger degree than management, but neither to the extent that the press would sometimes seem to indicate. They take advantage of the political process because that is the way a democracy works. However, the few thousand dollars that the maritime industry contributes to campaigns of all the various candidates for Congress does not insure that constructive laws or policies result. Where there is a rational approach, where industry representatives have the necessary facts and can get an audience to convince, they may succeed. If the occasional cartoon depiction of the maritime industry as a fat lobbyist with a big cigar, buying influence and favors, were accurate, the U.S. merchant marine would not be in the position it is today.

MARITIME MANAGEMENT

The problem of America's inability to maintain a fleet cannot, as some would suggest, be laid at the door of management. American maritime management is as good as that in any business. It has changed from the old days when shipping was maintained by single entrepreneurs—the example comes to mind of the longtime sea captain who developed a fleet of vessels. In many if not most cases, American shipping up until World War II was owned by American shipping families who took great pride in their enterprises and who were extremely successful "Yankee traders." In today's more impersonal business world, a number of the best operated shipping firms are owned by conglomerates whose chief interests may be in hotels or food or some other apparently unrelated area. Many are managed by bright young graduates of Harvard's business school or similar institutions. All in all, one has to conclude that American management in shipping is as knowledgeable and expert as any in the world.

Furthermore, it is as innovative. Innovation has been a hallmark of American shipping enterprise. The container ship is an American innovation, as is the so-called sea-bee vessel and the LASH—lighter aboard ship—concept. Virtually all the new and ingenious types of vessels in the postwar period have been American in origin, and they have been copied by the rest of world shipping.

American seamen, too, are as good as any in the world, and they are constantly being trained; unions and management jointly maintain schools to upgrade their people. When the ships of the El Paso Natural Gas Company and those of others engaged in the transport of liquid natural gases were put into the water, special training was needed for their highly specialized operations; the unions and management developed training programs at their jointly operated schools. These are constantly maintained—and not at government expense, it should be noted.

No Coherent U.S. Maritime Program

What, then, is the reason for the poor state of our U.S. merchant marine? I personally believe—and this opinion is shared by many people in the industry and in certain parts of government and in Congress—that a coherent maritime program has been lacking in this country. We lack a sea power concept that can be worked on from day to day, based on the realities of current conditions in the world. For example, our competition is no longer the private enterprises of the old British or Dutch shipping companies. We are now facing a proliferation of state-owned fleets. We now have to compete, for example, against Russian ships where the profit factor is not a consideration at all.

An illustration: in 1974–1975 or thereabouts, the Department of Transportation had some articulated buses built in Germany for shipment to eleven cities in the United States under a grant program, as a pilot project to determine their feasibility for municipal transportation. American shipping companies bid for carrying these across the ocean. One of the companies, Lykes Brothers of New Orleans, made the low bid and believed it had the contract. Then came the word that the Russians had undercut them by about a thousand dollars per bus. Lykes Brothers lowered their rate. The Russians again lowered theirs, and that ended the bidding. The cargo was awarded to the Soviet ships. Meanwhile, the National Maritime Council protested, with help from the Department of Commerce's Maritime Administration, to the Department of Transportation, on grounds that the laws of this country say that at least 50 percent of U.S. government-generated cargoes, which the buses were, must be carried on American-flag vessels. The Department of Transportation was unmoved. Its legal department interpreted the purchase as not being government-generated cargo within the purview of Public Law 664, the applicable statute. The Council's objections precipitated a hearing in the Congress, which became very upset and angry over this disregard of its law and national policy. The Department of Transportation then backed down, and subsequently the rest of the shipment was awarded to vessels of other countries, including the United States.

When I testified at the Congressional hearings, I stated that—aside from the fact that the Department of Transportation was performing an illegal act in having the Soviets carry this cargo—even if they were eligible—it was a dastardly thing to do. It would certainly be preferable to give it to the Swedes, or to the Norwegians, or to the Italians or the French or the British.

SOVIET COMPETITION

That incident illustrates only one facet of a new Soviet encroachment upon our shipping trades. They began building container ships and getting involved in the carriage of goods between the United States and our trading partners and caused considerable damage to American shipping companies on the Pacific Coast. The demise of one of those companies might have been influenced somewhat by Russian incursion into our trades. By 1978, on the East and West Coasts, the Soviets carried approximately 7 percent of our commerce. And again, the American shipping industry got little or no support from its government. In that respect, it is well to mention that, while the government might like to see a cohesive, aggressive sea power policy, including a strong maritime policy that will sustain the shipping industry, the involved agencies are in complete disarray and incapable of following what the law calls for at the very minimum.

For example, in the early days of the Carter Administration, it was felt that the activity of the American merchant marine should be encouraged, and the President established a maritime task force to investigate what could be done for the industry. Some twelve or fourteen agencies were involved. Invariably, when it came to doing anything to benefit the merchant marine, the voting would run about 12–2, with only the Departments of Commerce and Labor supporting the concept of a U.S. maritime industry. Every one of the other agencies would vote with the Office of Management and Budget or the Treasury Department against any positive support of U.S. shipping interests and policy. One Treasury representative asked at a meeting, "Why do we need an American merchant marine?" He was not convinced.

U.S. GOVERNMENT/MARITIME INDUSTRY RELATIONS

I should like to give a few examples of what the maritime industry is contending with in its relations with the U.S. government. Among the federal bodies with which it has constant problems is the State Department. The Russians do not become members of shipping conferences unless they absolutely must in order to get business. When they entered our shipping trades they did it by means of predatory rate setting; they kept cutting and cutting to attract cargoes. This, of course, impacted on the other nations whose vessels were engaged in carriage of our foreign commerce. All the traditional "allied" shipping nations of the world felt that this undercutting was an outrage and that something should be done about it. But none would take the initiative; they looked to the United States to deal with the problem.

A bill was introduced under sponsorship of Senator Daniel Inouye of Hawaii that would have required the Russians to file their rates with the Federal Maritime Commission, the U.S. regulatory agency, and to demonstrate that these rates were compensatory. Naturally the Russians opposed such requirements. Surprisingly, when Congressional hearings were held, there was also opposition from our State Department. Eventually the bill was passed and became law, but the State Department had not helped; in fact, it had been an impediment much of the way. The Russians have since gone from the trade; they chose not to compete under regulation.

I have already told how the Department of Transportation balked at complying with existing law that at least 50 percent of government-generated cargo for import must be carried in American-flag ships. The Treasury Department constantly poses problems on the basis of its theory that the U.S. merchant marine is not competitive and the subsidy is an excessive burden. The Office of Management and Budget takes the identical position. And the Department of Justice continues to pursue antitrust proceedings against American-flag companies, even though under the Shipping Act of 1916 the maritime industry was excluded from antitrust laws by virtue of the character of international shipping.

An illustration of how the Justice Department in effect deters the U.S.

maritime industry in competition with foreign companies is its method of prosecuting rebate cases. It is a common practice among foreign shipping nations to carry on a system of rebating—a term with an ugly connotation in the United States but accepted business practice overseas. After a shipper has used a certain company's vessels for a regular period of time, the company will give a rebate, a sort of discount, for a certain added use of their vessels. This is not allowed in the United States, so American shipping companies are handicapped in competing with foreign firms. In fact, a few years ago, a number of American shipping companies conceded that some of their overseas offices, which are often manned by nationals of the country in which they are located, gave rebates. Consequently they were fined hundreds of millions of dollars. One major operator alone was fined fifty million dollars.

The military, of course, uses American-flag shipping as the law requires, but the Navy chooses to compete with the private shipping sector by operating cargo ships itself, adding unnecessarily to the woes and problems of the industry and posing a contradiction to our free enterprise system. I think it is important, also, from a policy standpoint to remember that one of our secretaries of defense, Mr. McNamara, while in office made the charge that the United States did not need shipping; everything could go by air. Of course he was solidly contradicted in the course of the Vietnam conflict, when it was demonstrated that 95 percent of all logistical support had to move on American ships.

What to Do About the Merchant Marine

What about all of this? Where do we go? Is there something that is "do-able" about the sad state of the merchant marine? We in the industry think there is, but we also think there must be a full and thorough orchestration of whatever efforts are made to promote American-flag shipping, and that there will be no change until there is recognition by the nation's leadership, until the President himself understands what is involved. The two major pieces of shipping legislation that the United States has enacted—the Merchant Marine Acts of 1936 and 1970—were the result of presidential initiatives, coordinated with the Congress and the industry. President Franklin Roosevelt hoped that America would carry at least half its foreign commerce itself, and the 1936 legislation he promoted set up a system of subsidies to provide for differentials in foreign costs of building and operating ships. This formula is no longer completely effective because whenever an attempt is made to advance the interests of our merchant marine by whatever means, our competition comes up with some device of their own as an offset. The final answer, in our opinion, is that cargo is "the name of the game." Unless a means can be found to "crank in" cargo, and to some extent to integrate cargo and use of U.S. ships as a national policy, there will be no assured American capability on the seas.

POSITION OF REAGAN ADMINISTRATION

President Reagan was very supportive of the maritime industry in his campaign, and although thus far he shows every sign of sticking by his statements, it remains to be seen what the results will be. His director of the Office of Management and Budget, David Stockman, wanted to kill the subsidy program—which would have destroyed the merchant marine at that precise moment. I do not think the industry is irrevocably hung up on subsidy. It is in place now; without it—or something to substitute for it—the industry could not survive. But those in the industry feel that the subject should be examined, to learn whether there are other ways and means to assure a viable fleet. It is unfortunate that the government does not go sufficiently beyond the payment of subsidies to maintain a balanced shipping fleet. It provides for the distribution of the differential funds, but shows no further responsibility nor further interest in perfecting the method of reaching the overall objective.

Briefly, this is what President Reagan said he felt necessary for improvement of the U.S. merchant marine's standing: a unified direction for all government agencies that affect maritime interests; preservation of our vital shipbuilding base; increased utilization of our commercial fleet in support of auxiliary functions of the military; a new recognition of the challenges created by the cargo policies of other nations; the restoration of competitiveness in U.S.-flag operations; revitalization of our domestic water transportation; and a reduction in the severe regulatory environment which inhibits the ability of American-flag operators to compete effectively in world trade. I think there is hope. I think the President has a sincere desire. We shall see whether he, as others before have tried, can overcome the advice of economists and others who do not understand the use of the oceans or sea power, and do not care strongly enough about it to listen to those who do.

THE INDUSTRY VIEW

The Number One thing that could be done to improve the competitive position of the American merchant marine, in my view, is in the area of bilateral shipping arrangements with our shipping partners—that is, with England, France, Japan, West Germany, Israel, the Scandinavian and South American countries, and the many others. We are the world's largest shipping nation, but we carry only 4.4 percent of our own trade. Our trading partners carry a very substantial share, as do ships of other nations, such as Panama. Bilateral possibilities should be explored thoroughly. With the help of the Commerce Department, the industry has worked out one or two in South America that are highly workable and effective.

Next, there should be improved relations with the United States Navy. We think that the Navy should be required to maximize its use of the private shipping sectors. I am not referring to that part of the Navy that is engaged in the operation of combat vessels. I refer to the "United Parcel Service" part of the Navy—the part engaged in the transport of goods and effects—the Military Sealift Command. This function can be performed by the maritime industry. But for this to happen would require a relationship with the Navy that we do not now have.

During the Carter Administration, the industry recommended to the President the establishment in the White House of a maritime advisor, someone with a broad understanding of ocean use who could keep him informed. The idea was sabotaged by people in the Department of Commerce and the Navy who felt such an advisor "unnecessary"—that it duplicated already existing channels. Our position is that it still would be wise to have such a maritime advisor to the President; in fact, I personally am leaning toward the desirability of a "maritime department" with cabinet rank, so that someone who had an understanding of the oceans in all its aspects would sit in White House councils to speak for and of sea power to the President of the United States. It seems a far better solution than having maritime policy fragmented in agencies and departments all across the government.

As a minimum, however, we need absolute adherence to existing laws of the country by all agencies, so that maritime policy enacted by the Congress and signed by the President will be carried out. I refer particularly to those laws calling for the use of American-owned ships under

U.S. registry whenever government-impelled cargoes are shipped. With that kind of beginning, solutions to the problems are possible. But for that to happen, there must be some kind of dialogue. We suggested to Mr. Reagan's people during the campaign that the best thing he could do, if elected, would be to call an immediate conference between representatives of the industry and the concerned government agencies so the slow, arduous process of working out the problems could begin. Some meetings are being set up; but there are priorities, and the merchant marine does not seem to be one of them.

National Interests at Stake

At one time the Congress was very kindly disposed to the merchant marine. Congressmen understood it. Committee members with a sea power interest had longevity in the House and Senate in those days, and they understood armed services, they understood maritime, and they understood U.S. sea power. The character of the Congress has changed radically, however. Every two years the members get younger and less ocean-oriented, and the job of directing attention to sea power becomes more difficult and complicated. It would seem the new congressmen do not have the same concerns over national security that members had in past years. At the risk of seeming paranoid on the subject, I would remind one and all that the Russians are a permanent adversary, and the Soviet Union grows bigger and stronger in influence every day. With that kind of opposition, it is imperative that we maintain vigilance in every way we can. One way is to strengthen our sea power, which is so badly deficient. And that includes building an American merchant marine component consistent with the demands and responsibilities on us as a world leader.

The realities are that this country's friends are diminishing. Those who remain are increasingly timid when it comes to support for our positions in the world community. The United Nations is dominated by unfriendly, non-democratic nations. They are waiting, in effect, for us to tumble.

The point is, there is a question here of self-interest and self-preservation. The events of the past year and a half in the Indian Ocean area have dramatically illustrated our dependence on having our own sealift to carry and sustain the armed forces of the United States where our vital interests are at stake. In addition, there is growing understanding of the need to ensure the flow of raw materials for our industry and to be able to deliver the products of our farms, factories, and mines.

The realization that we had neither the required sealift assets nor the naval forces, already spread paper-thin, to guarantee their safety was part of the fallout from the hostage crisis of Iran and the Soviet aggression in Afghanistan. Even more sobering will be the realization that the rebuilding of an effective merchant marine and a navy capable of controlling the sea lanes will be a slow and costly process.

Meanwhile, America is in danger from hostile acts from small as well as powerful nations who challenge our leadership of the free world. Our safety and well-being will continue to remain in jeopardy unless our policy makers act promptly and decisively to rebuild the U.S.-flag merchant marine to the point where it can provide the logistical capability necessary to support American armed forces and a secure lifeline for the flow of critical raw materials needed to maintain the United States economy in peace and war.

America's Seaports—
Gateways for World Trade

Harry C. Brockel

"Whosoever commands the sea commands the trade; whosoever commands the trade of the world commands the riches of the world, and consequently, the world itself."

Sir Walter Raleigh

Admiral Alfred Thayer Mahan, in his monumental work "The Influence of Sea Power Upon History," makes frequent reference to the strategic and economic importance of ocean trade routes, and suggests that navies exist, not as an extension of military might per se, but for the critical necessity for maritime nations to protect ocean trade routes, on which their existence depends. A nation's economy functions by the importation of that which it lacks, and the export of that which it can best produce and sell abroad. Raw materials, such as minerals, are drawn from many parts of the globe, processed by industrial nations, and reexported. The iron ore of Australia and the coal of the United States meet at some Japanese industrial center to emerge as efficient automobiles, trucks, or television sets, which penetrate world markets and provide sustenance for an island almost bare of raw materials but skilled at making and marketing.

Thus the world's minerals, foodstuffs, and manufactured goods flow over scores of ocean trade routes to fill stomachs, to fuel furnaces, to supply luxuries; the whole spectrum of global resources, human wants, and industrial skills is reflected in the vast flow of world trade over these routes and through the world's port gateways. These gateways in our time are about 2,000 in number. They are located on ocean shores, in deep sheltered bays, in river estuaries, on inland rivers, on the Great Lakes, in the remote Arctic, and wherever navigable water exists and climatic conditions permit men to survive and ships to operate.

Global Demand for Port Capacity

The best available estimates indicate global ocean commerce to be about three billion tons annually. This vast flow of goods is shifted about the globe by fleets of ocean carriers, of great variety. Including only ships over 1,000 tons, the 1981 *World Almanac* reports a 1978 count of 24,641 vessels totaling 380,312,000 gross tons. Of total world trade, almost 99 percent is by ships, a little over 1 percent by air.

With a few exceptions, almost all this vast flow of cargo has a port of origin and a port of destination (exceptions are fisheries from the open sea, minerals extracted from seabeds, sand and gravel dredging in open water, and the like). Therefore, a global commerce of three billion tons must be doubled in terms of its effect upon ports and port capacity. The global port system therefore must be presumed to have a yearly capacity of about six billion tons. There are estimates that by 2040 global cargo movement could rise to twenty billion tons as populations grow and resources are exploited. The demand for port capacity at these levels would be staggering.

Although the United States has diminished as a maritime power and only 5 percent of our world trade moves in American-flag vessels, we are by far the largest trading nation of the world. Our waterborne trade flow for 1978 (the latest year for which figures are available) is reported by the U.S. Corps of Engineers to have been in excess of 2.021 billion tons, of which just under a billion tons was foreign trade, and just over a billion was domestic trade on our own waterways (946,057,889 net tons foreign; 1,075,291,865 net tons domestic; total 2,021,349,754 net tons). Half is petroleum; about 40 percent, other bulks; general commerce, 10 to 12 percent.

In the thirty years from 1949 to 1978, the waterborne trade of the United

States has approximately tripled, from 740 million tons to the two-billion-ton-plus figure just cited. The response of the port industry has had to be substantial.

U.S. Port Resources

World maps list some 2,000 ports, but only about 200 of these handle more than a million tons per year. The American sea coasts are speckled with ports, large and small, of which 110 are considered of importance and 75 are of major commercial consequence. There are nearly 150 ports, large and small, on the U.S. side of the Great Lakes; and several score more on our many navigable rivers and canals.

A harbor has been defined as a natural shelter for ships; a port as a harbor plus terminal facilities. Typical major seaports have certain physical attributes in common. There is a protected haven or harbor, which can be natural, man-made, or typically a combination of both. There are, of necessity, approach channels and localized channels giving access to all areas of the port. There is a complex of wharves and terminal facilities suited to the commerce of the port and its vessel traffic. These in turn are supported, usually, by warehouse and distribution facilities, access highways, railroad tracks and terminals, cranes, storage areas, and the like. Human resources are the labor force, the service specialists, the port administration, fire and police, and the intricate maritime family which provides the essential service to load or unload the ship, service the vessel, and safeguard its cargo as it moves through the stream of commerce.

If the port is a typical commercial port, it will serve not only local population and industry but a hinterland of some magnitude, which will fill its needs through the port gateway and will generate commerce outward bound also.

Every seaport of the United States and of the world is unique from all others, by reason of its geography, topography, climate, resources, economic structure, and other variables. Ports also vary widely in their development, methods of administration, degrees of political influence, labor productivity, and similar human factors. Some are so strategically located that they have an inherent force or advantage that permits them to flourish despite adverse man-made factors.

A port can spring into prominence as a result of a major new force, such as the Alaska oil pipeline. Valdez, an obscure fishing village ten years ago, is now the fifth ranking port of the United States, with a 1978 commerce of 55.5 million tons. Baton Rouge obscurely slumbered for many years in the shadow of nearby New Orleans, but in 1978 was the fourth ranking port, with almost 75 million tons of cargo, as a result of industrial and agricultural developments. Ports can rise or fall precipitously as a result of resource development, changing transport technology, new industrial developments, or other forces for change, such as a foreign policy decision by a government. The U.S. embargo of grain to Russia was decisive in reducing the export flow of grain through U.S. ports, as well as in the consequent effect on shipping patterns, port tonnage, and shoreside employment.

TYPES OF PORTS

There are many kinds of ports in the United States and elsewhere. These include:

- Raw material ports, specializing in the shipment of major localized resources, such as iron ore, limestone, coal, petroleum, phosphates, nitrates, and other large volume items. These tend to be single-purpose ports.
- Special purpose ports, such as steel centers or petro-chemical complexes on the coast of the Gulf of Mexico. A new development is the appearance of local ports to serve the special needs of offshore oil and gas drilling areas.
- Historically, a number of major ports were built around naval bases, such as Norfolk, San Diego, and Singapore. Interestingly, these have later developed into diversified, strong commercial ports, but retain their historic naval base function, except for Singapore, a trade center par excellence with no military ambitions.
- Population center ports (New York, London, Chicago, Tokyo). Such ports combine good geographic location with a concentration of people, industry, hinterland, and distribution function. In the New York metropolitan area are twenty million bodies to be fed, clothed, and sustained, and whose product must go to market. Chicago is the westerly terminus of the Great Lakes-Seaway system; is the continental transport hub; is a vast distribution center; meets the Ohio-Mississippi River systems; is the grain trade center of the world. As a shipping

executive recently remarked, "Chicago is a problem port, but it
cannot be ignored."

- Strategic geographic location ports (New Orleans at the mouth
of the Mississippi, Montreal, Rotterdam, and again Singapore).
The facts of geography and of shipping economics gave birth to
these ports. They flourish, both from strategic geography and
from the economic growth of their trade areas.
- Fisheries ports.
- Recreational ports.
- A goodly number of U.S. ports cannot be categorized rigidly by
these classifications, and represent simply a favorable combination of population, industry, agriculture, rail and highway
access, hinterland, and other elements, all found at a useful
location on navigable water, and serving a particular region
according to its needs.

U.S. Port Administration

Just as U.S. ports are diverse in geography and function, they are
varied in their administrative structure. There is a general tendency to
involve the public and governmental authority by the commission form.
A number of states favor a state port authority with policy direction over
all ports of the state—a form found in the South Atlantic states primarily.
There are bi-state port agencies, such as the Port Authority of New
York/New Jersey, and the Delaware River Port Authority. Texas favors
"navigation districts" or county bodies. There have been multiple port
bodies in a single port area (Chicago, New York, Portland).

The most typical public port in the United States is municipal in nature.
Some have been broadened to reflect a metropolitan area concept. Some
combine seaport and airport functions; in a few cases, the so-called port
authority is a broad-based transport authority, such as the Port Authority
of New York/New Jersey.

Time and space do not permit an exhaustive discussion of port administration, but it must be emphasized that the public port authority is a
bridge between government and the business world. The port is essentially a business enterprise that needs the authority and sanction of
government in its financing, planning, building, managing, and regulation. A degree of autonomy is considered essential for the best achievement of these goals. Elective port commissions have generally been

disasters in U.S. port history; fortunately very few ports have been so structured.

Port managers and key staff can be selected by the civil service process; occasionally by political patronage process; by various other recruitment methods. In some cases, port managers are now retained for a term of years, under a contract, or they may serve at the pleasure of the appointing body.

Successful port managers tend to be strong personalities, skilled in the arts of government, public persuasion, and acceptance in the business and shipping community. A typical public port management embraces challenges such as land use, planning, engineering design, maintenance, operation, pricing, marketing, personnel management, industrial development, port finance, economic analysis, international relations, labor negotiation, legislative rapport, media interaction, environmental challenge, and other problem areas. He or she must be a man or a woman for all seasons.

There have been occasional disasters in port management, but the profession has been fortunate in developing or finding people of great force and of great capacity for the unique demands of a unique profession. A good port executive will get the business, maintain the port, expand prudently, meet the competition, and keep up with technology and world changes.

Challenges to Ports

A phenomenon of the past fifteen years is that the technology of the ship outran the technology and capacity of most ports and of the great interoceanic canals. Shipping, traditionally a most conservative industry, exploded with innovation and new technology. The ship left the shore far behind. The shipping revolution brought the container ship, the LASH concept, supersize tankers and bulk carriers, cryogenics, and a great variety of special purpose ships. Early in 1981 a Chinese shipping line took delivery of an enormous tanker, the world's largest ship, *Seawise Giant*. This particular giant is 1,489 feet long; 224 feet in beam; has a draft of 97 feet; and has a deadweight of 564,763 tons. (The *Santa Maria* is estimated to have been about 90 tons.)

These developments on the water have brought compelling demands on the ports, such as:

- Need for much deeper channels
- More and longer berths

- Expanded anchorages and maneuver areas
- Road and rail interchange capacity for intermodal methods
- New mechanical handling concepts
- Automation of records and procedures
- Expansion to meet increasing volumes
- Vessel traffic control guidance systems
- Potential electronic docking systems
- Financing port expansion, with rising construction and interest costs.

Under time pressures and financial constraints, United States ports have responded fairly rapidly and well to this era of change. It is to be noted, however, that with 180 deepwater ports around the world, it was not until the spring of 1981 that we achieved our first so-called superport in United States waters. It is designated LOOP for "Louisiana Offshore Oil Port." As in the case of the Louisiana port, projected deepwater ports in Texas waters have been beset by problems of finance, organization, jurisdiction, environmental challenges, and state/federal approval requirements. Except for the new LOOP, all our petroleum still comes in medium-size tankers, on available local drafts, usually forty-five feet or less. We have thus belatedly and in a very limited way embraced the new technologies of the petroleum age and of the supership.

World population growth foretells rising demand for American grains, which flow through U.S. ports to world markets. Coal will move in world commerce in rising volumes and will be a major factor in American exports; major ports on all coasts are actively planning large-scale investment and large construction programs for storage and modern handling systems for export coal, both steam and metallurgical.

CONTAINERIZATION

Container traffic through world ports reached a record 29,569,763 TEU's (20-foot equivalent units) in 1979, up 11.2 percent over 1978. Two hundred world ports served container shipping in 1979, twenty-five more than in 1978. Containerization is concentrated in Japan, Australia, Northern Europe and North America, but is gaining in Africa and the Middle East.

This concept, originating on a large scale only fifteen years ago, is now handling an estimated 60 percent of world general cargo. It is forecast that by the turn of the century, it will serve 80 percent or more of this valuable cargo.

In 1979, U.S. ports handled 24 percent of world container shipping. Twelve U.S. ports rank in the first fifty of the principal container ports of the world. New York is the leading port of the world in this field. Other ranking U.S. ports include:

Oakland	Honolulu
Seattle	Charleston
Los Angeles	Houston
Long Beach	New Orleans
Hampton Roads	Philadelphia
Baltimore	Savannah

(Container traffic is negligible at Great Lakes ports.)

SOCIAL AND REGULATORY CHALLENGES

Today's ports, especially the larger ones, are in the arena of social and environmental problems: problems of water pollution, hazardous cargoes, oil spill control, vessel sanitation. There are demands for recreational or residential use of strategic waterfronts. Freeways are thrust through port areas.

Add in port security problems, unemployment programs, civil rights issues, equal employment criteria, militant unionism, and conservationists who are convinced that wetlands are for ducks, not for ships and cargoes.

A fairly substantial port can come under the purview of up to forty federal bodies—the Coast Guard; U.S. Customs and Immigration; U.S. Corps of Engineers, on dredging and permitting procedures; transport regulation bodies like the Interstate Commerce Commission, the Federal Maritime Commission, the Department of Transportation, and the U.S. Maritime Administration (MARAD) in the Department of Commerce; the Occupational Safety and Health Administration (OSHA) and others on safety; Environmental Protection Agency (EPA), Coastal Zone Management (CZM), the Department of Interior on environmental concerns; and others, ad infinitum.

THE ENVIRONMENTAL CHALLENGE

It is in the coastal waters that man and nature collide. The bays and river estuaries are often centers for natural ecological systems, but they are also the necessary and desired locations for ports, power plants, steel mills, and other uses, sometimes harmonious, often conflicting. These are the waters sought for shipping, recreation, waste disposal, fisheries, industry, and other urgent needs. These are lands and waters most visible to the public, most sensitive in planning, and where conflicts of interest seem to be inevitable.

In this era of environmental concern, ports—whose mission is primarily economic—are enmeshed in environmental challenges. Some have been forced to add entire staffs and attorneys to cope with environmental issues, to prepare costly environmental impact statements for every projected expansion, and to deal with conservation authorities, EPA, CZM, Interior, and other zealous regulators.

For most of the past ten years, ordinary dredging for maintenance or for improvement of the port, has been a horrendous and costly issue. Early in the 1970s, ocean dumping or Great Lakes disposal of silt was prohibited in most ports. Alternate methods of disposal in land fills or in diked reservoirs presented stupendous costs. Dredging, after years of paralysis, is being resumed under rigid environmental control and at staggering cost both to ports and the federal budget.

As ports began at great cost to solve their environmental crises, they ran full tilt into the energy crisis, which affects not only the ports themselves but the ships that ply the water, and the industry of the port area. Here, too, there are no easy solutions—only new problems and new cost factors to overcome.

PORT FINANCE

Traditionally, there has been a well-understood division of responsibility as to building the ports of this country.

Through the U.S. Corps of Engineers, the federal purse funded channels, anchorages, often breakwaters and the basic navigation system. The U.S. Coast Guard built and operated aids to navigation and marine rescue services. The locality (i.e., the port authority) funded wharves, piers, terminals, and all the appurtenances of an operating port, including the dredging which was considered part of the proprietary venture as distinct from the federal channels.

Now galloping inflation brings the cost of a single crane to the $3 million level—a sum which would have built a major port facility twenty years ago. Capital costs for marine construction, of dredging, of all port structures, have risen to such high levels as to present a triple challenge—economic return on prohibitive first costs; prohibitive interest rates and bond flotation problems; and intense competition for the tax dollar, whether it be local, state, or federal. Federally mandated requirements have caused new budget problems.

To prove economic necessity, to project revenue expectations, to raise the funds, and to build within budget—these are challenges indeed for the public ports. In the current conservative federal budget environment, there are hints or forecasts for more matching funds, for user fees, for permit charges. It is even speculated that the U.S. Coast Guard may have its services put on a fee basis, with charges scaled for rescuing an overturned sailboat vs. the assistance to a 100,000-ton tanker in a catastrophe situation. Times have changed!

"Enterprise, Perseverance, Industry"

About 1500 B.C. the Phoenicians took to the sea, and launched trade by water for the first time. Global trade by water now employs a world fleet of 24,600 vessels, hauls three billion tons of cargo, and utilizes 2,000 world ports, large and small. As author George Rawlinson said in his *History of Phoenicia*, "They surpassed all other peoples of antiquity in enterprise, perseverance and industry."

The Yankee Mariner may no longer dominate the sea lanes, as he did in our fabulous clipper ship era, but Yankee ports handle more commerce than those of any other nation on earth.

The mariners and port officials of this troubled generation must similarly be enterprising, persevering and industrious—but also highly innovative, and responsive to fast-changing marine technology, new political climate, and difficult economic challenges to their mission.

Energy from the Oceans: Its Development and Delivery

L. Donald Maus

Although the first offshore oil well was drilled from a pier in the surf of southern California in 1897, it was not until the late 1940s that the U.S. oil industry began inching out of the bayous, bays, and marshes of Louisiana and Texas into the waters of the Gulf of Mexico. These efforts were largely aimed at exploring and producing offshore extensions of known onshore oil fields.

Today, we have a better idea of what might—with emphasis on the word "might"—await us offshore.

Offshore hydrocarbons are associated primarily with the margins that surround the continents and constitute 25 percent of the total ocean area. Extending from shore to the deep ocean floor, the margin consists of three units—shelf, slope, and rise. Figure 1 is a section across the continental margin that shows the nature of these major physiographic elements. The continental shelf extends generally out to a water depth of about 200 meters, the steeper continental slope to 2,500 meters, and the continental rise to oceanic depths of about 4,500 meters.

Because of their thick sediments (commonly, several thousand meters), the margins have much greater petroleum potential than the deep ocean floor, which has only a thin sediment cover.

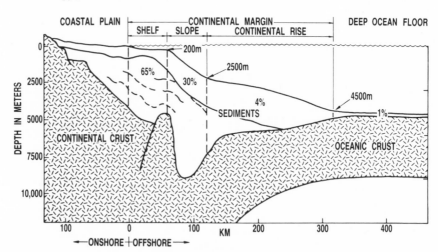

Fig. 1. Geologic section across typical continental margin. Estimated percentages of the oceans' potentially recoverable hydrocarbons are shown for the shelf, slope, rise, and deep ocean floor.

While prediction of petroleum potential is highly speculative, it has been estimated that the continental margins contain 99 percent of the oceans' potentially recoverable hydrocarbons, and that the deep ocean sediments contain only 1 percent. Further, it has been estimated that 65 percent of these hydrocarbons will be found at water depths less than 200 meters, 30 percent from 200 to 2,500 meters, and only 5 percent at greater water depths.

The accuracy of these estimates will be known only after the continental margins have been thoroughly explored, and this will take many years. However, this present understanding of hydrocarbon potential is one of the basic reasons that industry is currently developing the technology for exploring and producing from the continental shelves and slopes and is not actively considering the deeper parts of the continental margins or the deep ocean.

Exploration

As a first step in the exploration for offshore oil and gas, geological and geophysical reconnaissance techniques are used to define the most favorable areas for hydrocarbon accumulations. These techniques include study of sea floor bathymetry, knowledge of sedimentation patterns, gravity and magnetic surveys, and analysis of rock samples from outcrops and wells. The recent understanding of plate tectonics and the nature of seafloor spreading has provided very valuable insights as to where to look for oil and gas.

Detailed geophysical surveys, using the reflection seismic method illustrated in Figure 2, are next employed to define hydrocarbon prospects. Sound impulses, generated by a powerful energy source, are reflected from subbottom rock layers and picked up by detectors spaced along a cable towed by a vessel. The resulting records are then processed by computer and displayed to yield a picture of the subsurface sediments and of possible oil and gas traps.

At present, our ability to determine the presence of hydrocarbons directly from seismic surveys is limited to very special cases. It is still true that only by drilling into the prospective formation can we confirm the presence of oil or gas.

If oil or gas is discovered, additional wells must be drilled to determine the reservoir's extent, obtain an engineering description of its properties, and assess the commerciality of the discovery. Typically, only 15 to 20 percent of the wells drilled in new fields in the United States discover hydrocarbons, and, of these, only 2 to 3 percent prove productive.

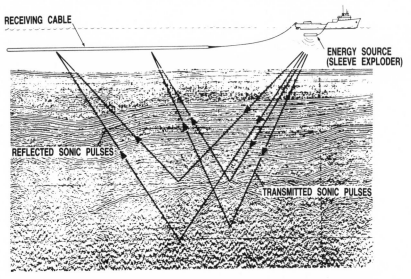

Fig. 2. Offshore reflection seismic method for conducting geophysical surveys

EXPLORATION DRILLING

Figure 3 illustrates several types of mobile offshore drilling units in use today for exploration drilling and their approximate water depth capabilities.

Submersible drilling platforms, introduced in the Gulf of Mexico in 1949, were the first mobile offshore rigs built. They evolved from the inland drilling barges that were being used in protected bays and marshes. These platforms are designed to be towed to the drilling site and ballasted with seawater to rest on the bottom. Once the exploratory well has been plugged and abandoned, the unit is refloated and towed to the next location. Submersibles generally operate in less than 25 meters of water.

Jack-up platforms provide a cost-effective drilling capability in water depths to about 100 meters. A jack-up is basically a barge with extendable legs. It is towed to the drilling location, where the legs are lowered to the bottom and the hull jacked up until the platform is well above the water. Once elevated, a jack-up provides a stable base for drilling operations. These units operate mainly in calm-weather areas such as the Gulf of Mexico, the Arabian Gulf, and Malaysia.

Floating drilling units were developed in the early 1950s to provide greater mobility and water depth capability than could be obtained with

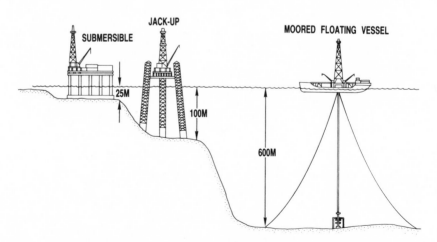

Fig. 3. Types of mobile drilling platforms used for offshore exploration drilling. Water depths shown indicate the approximate maximum depths of application.

submersibles or jack-ups. Floating units include barges, ships, and semisubmersibles.

Barges are used primarily in mild environmental conditions such as Lake Maracaibo, Venezuela.

Self-propelled drillships provide better motion characteristics and mobility than barges. Drillships have been used essentially worldwide but have a limited drilling season in very rough weather areas.

Semisubmersible vessels such as shown in Figure 4 were developed to

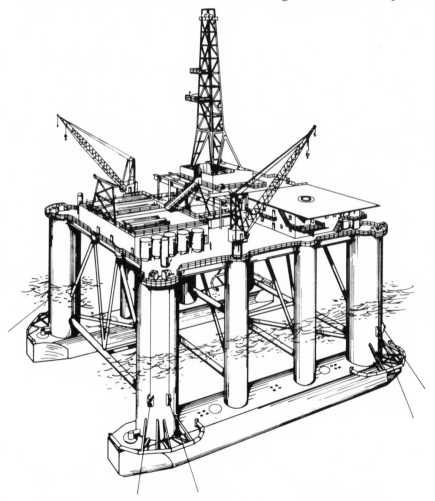

Fig. 4. Semisubmersible drilling vessel shown in drilling position

withstand severe weather environments. In the drilling position, the pontoons that provide most of the buoyancy for a semisubmersible are below the water surface, and only the columns supporting the deck pierce the waterline. Motions due to waves are thereby reduced compared with those of a ship or a barge. Semisubmersibles have operated in some of the world's most severe environmental conditions, including the North Sea and the Gulf of Alaska.

Floating drilling operations have prompted the development of a number of new drilling-related systems and procedures. Figure 5 illustrates some of the major systems:

- A vessel is needed to house the drilling equipment, support equipment, and personnel. Although most drilling barges and some of the drillships were converted from other vessels, most modern drillships and all semisubmersibles have been designed from the keel up for their special role.
- A special mooring system, consisting of an array of as many as

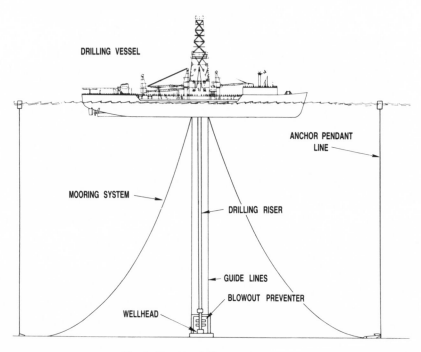

Fig. 5. Floating drilling system

twelve anchors with their wire rope or chain anchor lines, is required to hold the vessel over the wellhead. Since the vessel cannot deploy these anchors itself, special anchor handling boats are used to set and retrieve the anchors. This is done via buoyed pendant lines attached to the anchors.

- The drilling riser is a steel pipe that contains the drillpipe and circulates drilling fluids and rock cuttings back to the surface. It is highly tensioned to prevent buckling and has a telescoping section at the top to accommodate the heave motions of the vessel.

- A subsea blowout preventer is mounted on the seafloor wellhead to seal the well in the event of a well control problem. It is an assembly of special valves that can seal around drillpipe or an open hole, and can even shear drillpipe in two. It is controlled hydraulically from the vessel.

- Tensioned guidelines are used to guide much of this equipment as it is lowered to or retrieved from the seafloor.

In water depths beyond 600 to 900 meters, conventional mooring systems become impractical to deploy and ineffective in holding the vessel over the well. Thus, in deeper water, industry has drilled using dynamically positioned vessels similar to that illustrated in Figure 6. Computer-controlled thrusters respond to acoustic positioning information from seafloor beacons to hold the vessel on station. Deepwater operations also require guidelineless systems to reenter the well, electrohydraulic control systems for subsea blowout preventers, and special deepwater well control procedures.

Earlier, the offshore movement of the industry was characterized as "inching." From 1949 to 1965, the record water depth for drilling reached only 180 meters, or 600 feet. Since then, the pace of deepwater exploration has accelerated, as shown in Figure 7. The record currently stands at 1,486 meters or slightly over 4,870 feet. Industry has drilled roughly 600 wells in water depths greater than 200 meters.

The current water depth capability of exploratory drilling units is about 1,800 meters, or approximately 6,000 feet. This is limited more by the storage space for the drilling riser than by technological constraints. Existing equipment could probably be extended for service in waters out to about 2,000 meters. It remains to be seen whether incentives exist to push these limits further.

The equipment described above is quite expensive. The total cost to drill a single offshore well can vary from $500,000 for a shallow-water well near a supply base to more than $30 million for a deepwater well in a remote location.

Production Systems

Production operations moved into the open water of the offshore along with mobile drilling rigs. Since then, there has been a steady growth in the size of the platforms and in the water depths in which they are installed. Other challenges have been dealt with, such as the harsh operating environment of the North Sea. These activities have prompted the development of a large body of structural engineering technology needed to design, fabricate, transport, and install offshore structures. Costs for Gulf of Mexico platforms, including equipment and wells, range from $40 million for a shallow-water platform to more than $800 million for platforms in 300-meter water depths. North Sea production platforms have cost more than $2 billion.

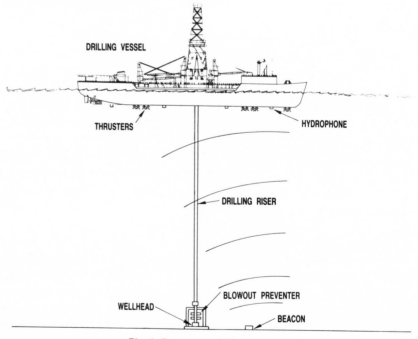

Fig. 6. Deepwater drilling system

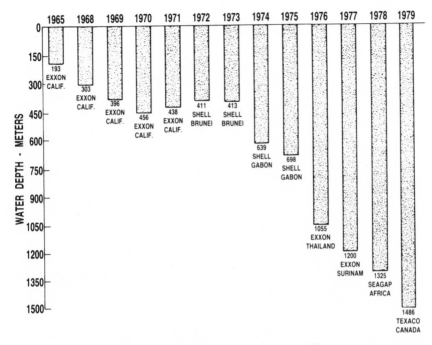

Fig. 7. Deepwater drilling records since 1965

FIXED STRUCTURES

Fixed, bottom-founded steel structures such as illustrated in Figure 8 have been the primary facility used for offshore production. These structures are anchored to the ocean floor with piling. Depth records for platform installations in the 1970s reached 259 meters in the Santa Barbara Channel of California and 313 meters in the Gulf of Mexico. Steel weights for these platforms are 17,000 and 47,800 metric tons, respectively, in contrast with steel weights of about 2,000 metric tons for a structure in 30-meter water depths in a similar environment.

The concrete gravity platforms of the North Sea are by far the largest structures installed offshore. Figure 9 illustrates a typical gravity platform. These structures contain around 300,000 metric tons of reinforced concrete, which is roughly eight to ten times the weight for the largest steel structure. Concrete platforms rest on a large base approximately 100 meters in diameter. They are held in place by their own massive weight instead of by piling and hence are called "gravity structures."

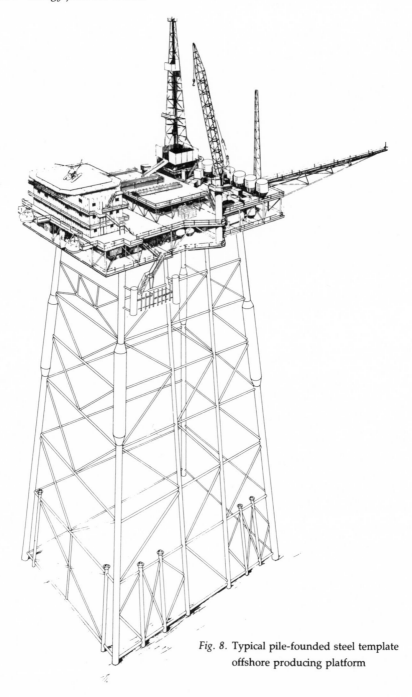

Fig. 8. Typical pile-founded steel template
offshore producing platform

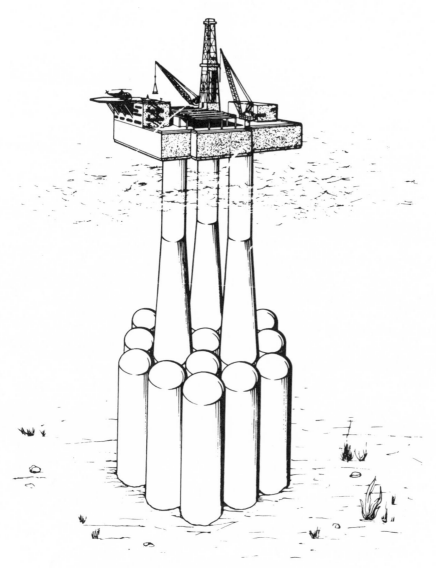

Fig. 9. Concrete gravity structure typical of the North Sea

Concrete gravity structures were developed in Europe in response to the particularly harsh conditions for producing oil from the North Sea. To date, their use has been limited to that area. However, American oil companies are heavily involved in North Sea operations and are quite familiar with this technology. As will be shown later, there are potential applications for this know-how in U.S. waters in the future.

As water depth increases, technical and economic constraints become more severe for offshore structures. Typically, platform structures are fabricated, transported, launched, and uprighted as a single unit. However, for deepwater platforms, special fabrication and water-phase construction procedures are required. The Hondo platform, in 259 meters of water in the Santa Barbara Channel, was built in two sections that were individually towed to an in-the-water assembly site where they were joined together. These sections were joined and welded with the structure floating horizontally. The structure was then towed to the nearby production site, upended, and installed.

The Cognac platform, in 313 meters of water in the Gulf of Mexico, was built in three sections that were stacked on top of each other at the field site. Steel dowels were inserted through the legs of the structure and cemented into place to form the structural connection.

The amount of steel required to resist the design loads increases at an ever greater rate as water depth increases. Figure 10 illustrates the problem. Because the environmental loads act farther from the base, large overturning moments are created. To resist these moments, a fixed platform in deep water must have a wide structural cross section at the mudline, more piles, and additional steel within the framework. Also, as the structure becomes long and slender, storm waves begin to cause some dynamic amplification of the stresses in the structural members.

In this business, stating a limit to the applicability of any particular concept is hazardous, since it seems to challenge some very good engineers to prove that one is wrong. However, it is currently felt that the economic limit of applicability of fixed structures is on the order of 200 meters in harsh environments like the North Sea and about 350 meters in mild environments.

COMPLIANT STRUCTURES

For deeper waters, the industry is turning to structures that are called "compliant" as contrasted with the "fixed" structures discussed to this point.

Compliant structures are designed to deflect under the action of environmental forces to reduce the effect of these loads. An example is the guyed tower shown in Figure 11. Guyed towers are held upright by an

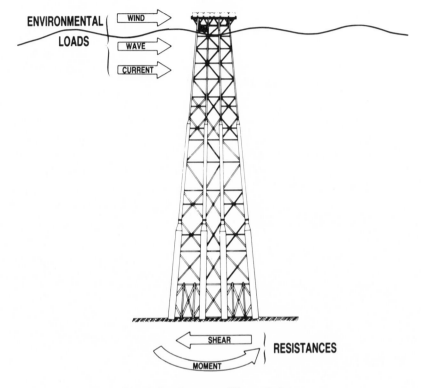

Fig. 10. Loads on an offshore platform

array of guylines radiating from the structure at a depth of about thirty meters below the sea surface. As shown in Figure 12, the guylines extend a distance of about twice the water depth to heavy, articulated clump weights on the sea floor. From the clump weights, the guylines extend to anchor piles embedded in the sea floor. Under all but the most extreme environmental conditions, the clump weights remain on the ocean floor and the tower is virtually stationary. However, during a severe storm, the weights lift off the bottom, permitting the tower to sway and avoid excessive loads. The motion of the tower is small enough to permit standard platform drilling and production operations.

Economic depths for guyed tower applications range from about 200 meters to beyond 600 meters depending on environmental conditions and deck loads. The guyed tower concept has been tested offshore with a one-fifth scale model of a structure designed for 450 meters of water and

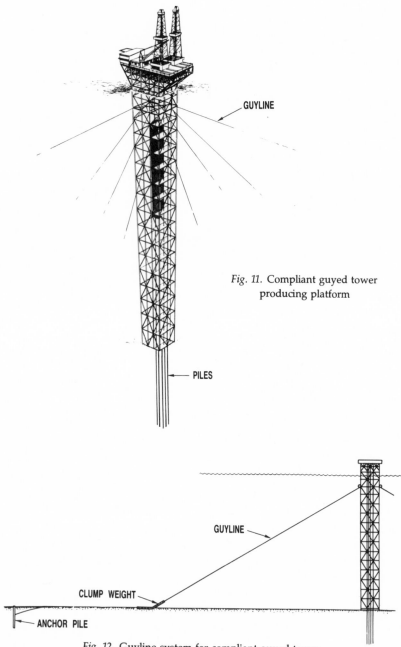

GUYLINE

Fig. 11. Compliant guyed tower
producing platform

PILES

GUYLINE

CLUMP WEIGHT

ANCHOR PILE

Fig. 12. Guyline system for compliant guyed tower

North Sea environmental conditions. The test was carried out success-fully in a water depth of 90 meters in the Gulf of Mexico. Plans have been announced for installation of a drilling and production guyed tower in 305 meters of water in the Gulf of Mexico in 1983.

The tension-leg platform, or TLP, is another form of compliant struc-ture that is approaching the stage of first application. It is illustrated in Figure 13. The TLP is basically a semisubmersible vessel with a vertical mooring system that holds it below floating draft. The vertical tethers or legs remain under tension, even in the most severe seastates, and largely eliminate the heave, pitch, and roll motions of the platform. These are the motions that significantly restrict operations on a conventionally moored semisubmersible in heavy seastates.

Plans to install a TLP as a drilling and production facility in the North Sea have been announced. This installation will be in a water depth of about 150 meters and should provide an in-service demonstration of the TLP as a production facility and as a forerunner to deeper water applications.

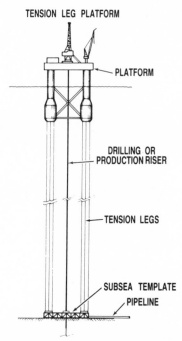

TENSION LEG PLATFORM

PLATFORM

DRILLING OR PRODUCTION RISER

TENSION LEGS

SUBSEA TEMPLATE

PIPELINE

Fig. 13. Compliant tension-leg platform

This TLP will use tubular steel structural members as the tension elements. Well conductors will extend from the deck to the ocean floor and conventional platform drilling and production operations will take place from this facility. Water depth capabilities for the TLP are expected to extend to around 600 meters or greater.

SUBSEA PRODUCTION SYSTEMS

In waters deeper than about 600 meters, the costs and technical difficulties associated with platforms that support the wellheads above the water grow rapidly in magnitude. For these deeper waters, depending on reservoir and environmental conditions, a subsea production system may prove more economical. In this type of system, the wellheads and a number of other components that normally are mounted above water are placed on the ocean floor.

Systems of this type will probably require on the order of ten years to develop fully. However, many of the concepts have already found application, such as shown in Figures 14a and 14b, in shallower waters in conjunction with conventional production systems.

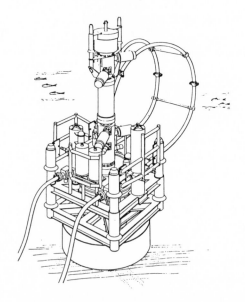

Fig. 14a. Wet subsea production system. Wellhead components are exposed to seawater.

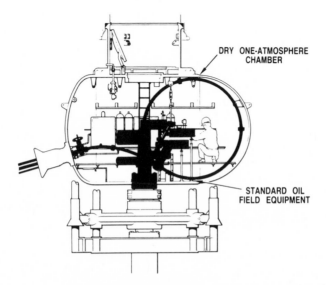

Fig. 14b. Dry subsea production system. Wellhead components are enclosed in a one-atmosphere chamber.

In mid-1980 more than 100 commercial subsea wells were active, and another 60 to 70 are planned for the next few years. These commercial wells are in water depths less than 150 meters and generally produce to a platform.

Figure 15 illustrates how the subsea wellheads can be grouped together on a seafloor template or installed as individual satellite wells connected by pipelines to a central gathering point. In some instances, oil flows to a floating production system for processing.

Seafloor systems will probably find increased utility in improving oil and gas recovery from existing offshore fields. This experience will also provide technical and operating know-how that will be useful in future deepwater applications.

In deepwater subsea systems, highly reliable components and techniques must be used throughout to minimize equipment malfunctions. The seafloor equipment is modularized so that maintenance is reduced to replacement operations by a remotely operated manipulator. Producing operations are controlled remotely from a nearby surface facility.

The development of submerged production system technology is well

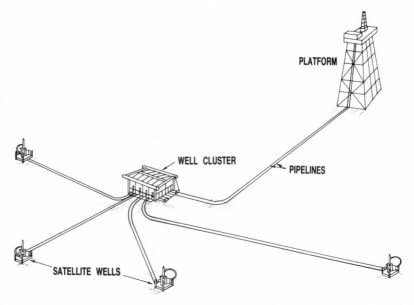

Fig. 15. Subsea wellheads, template, and producing platform

advanced for several deepwater system configurations. One possible system, illustrated in Figure 16, consists of:

- a subsea production template supporting a number of wellheads;
- flowlines to transport the oil;
- a deepwater production riser and loading terminal;
- a floating vessel for processing, storage, and offloading.

Wells are drilled from a deepwater drillship. Maintenance is performed remotely by a maintenance manipulator deployed from a surface vessel. A three-well version of this system was pilot tested in a Gulf of Mexico oil field in the 1970s.

Transportation Facilities

Subsea pipelines are the most common method of transporting oil and gas to markets, especially in highly developed areas like the Gulf of Mexico. These pipelines are laid on the seafloor by specially designed barges called lay barges, illustrated in Figure 17. Sections of pipe are welded together on the barge to form the pipeline which is lowered to the

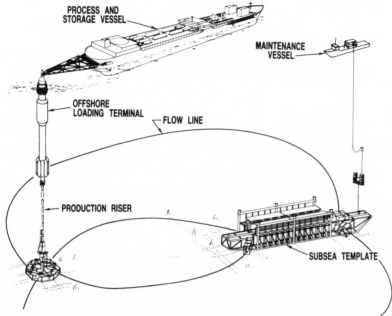

Fig. 16. Deepwater submerged production system

seafloor over a "stinger" designed to limit the bending of the pipe and prevent its collapse. The pipeline is maintained in tension by special gripping devices on the barge and by the tension in the forward mooring lines.

Pipelaying activities are strongly affected by water depth and environment. Semisubmersible technology, developed for exploration drilling, has been utilized in the design of present-day lay barges (Figure 18) to

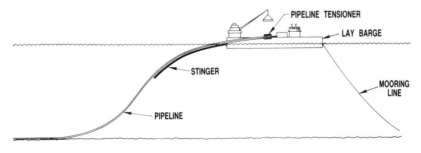

Fig. 17. Offshore pipelaying operation

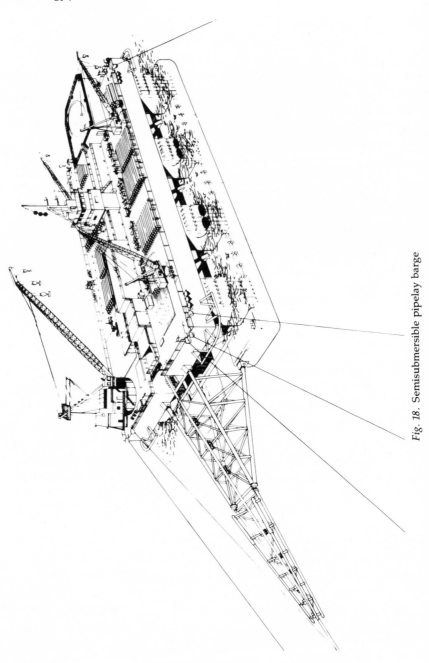

Fig. 18. Semisubmersible pipelay barge

provide rough-weather capability. With such barges, large diameter (36-inch) pipelines have been installed in 150-meter depths in the North Sea. The record length for such a pipeline is the 450-kilometer line from the Brent field in the North Sea to the United Kingdom. Existing equipment is capable of installing large-diameter pipelines in water depths to about 300 meters. Smaller diameter lines (20 inches) have been installed with lay barge techniques in water depths to 600 meters.

Typical costs for 36-inch diameter lines installed in mild weather areas range from $1.5 million to $3.0 million per mile. In harsh environments, costs are nearly double those amounts.

Offshore Production Terminals

Offshore production terminals represent an alternative to subsea pipelines for transporting offshore oil. The terminal shown in Figure 16 is typical of one type of installation. Offshore terminals are particularly attractive for locations remote from markets or for fields too small to justify the cost of a pipeline. They are also useful if production must begin sooner than a pipeline can be laid. Terminals have been installed in water depths to 150 meters. Some configurations can be extended to 1,500-meter water depths and possibly beyond.

An unmanned terminal with no storage capacity can be installed at a mild, shallow-water site for about $5 million. Manned deepwater terminals with storage capacity can cost up to $100 million in rough-weather areas.

Ocean Environment

Knowledge of the ocean environment and its effect on marine operations, equipment, and permanent structures is required to carry out offshore exploration, drilling, and production activities. This knowledge is acquired from many scientific fields, such as meteorology, oceanography, geology, and seismology, and is supplemented by site specific data that characterize conditions in an area of interest. While there have been many enhancements to offshore environmental knowledge through academic, institutional, and government research programs, the bulk of site-specific data has been acquired through the efforts of the international petroleum industry. Following are a few examples of industry activity in this area.

WAVE DATA

Long-term statistics on offshore wave and swell heights, periods, and directions are important to predict the dynamic behavior of floating and compliant structures and to assess the possible fatigue damage of fixed structures. Long-term measurements are available only in a few areas of the world, such as the Gulf of Mexico and the North Sea, where industry has operated for many years. In frontier areas, estimates must be made based on a combination of available meteorological data and air/sea interaction theories. These estimates are adequate for planning and preliminary design studies, but final equipment selection and design for remote areas can be performed more reliably if measured oceanographic data are available. The offshore industry has pioneered the acquisition of offshore wave data in such remote areas as the Gulf of Alaska, and is presently designing a comprehensive oceanographic measurement program for the Bering Sea.

WAVE AND CURRENT FORCES

The forces exerted by waves and currents on structures in the ocean have been the subject of extensive theoretical and laboratory research. Cooperative field projects, like the Ocean Test Structure program, lend strong support to the procedures used to design conventional steel frame structures. The objectives of the Ocean Test Structure were:

- to measure directly real storm-wave forces on a three-dimensional model platform;
- to evaluate wave force calculational procedures used in platform design; and
- to provide a basis for improving these design procedures.

The structure was installed in twenty meters of water in the Gulf of Mexico in December 1976, and the experimental program was completed in June 1978. Data were collected on waves and wave forces for over 200 large, rare-event waves that simulate design conditions for typical offshore structures. The results provided a basis for scientific advances in the understanding of properties of storm waves and forces. They also verified the accuracy of engineering approximations of the complex, nonlinear phenomena occurring in a three-dimensional, storm-generated sea.

EARTHQUAKE RESPONSE

In seismically active areas, the motion of the seabed caused by earthquakes must be accounted for in offshore structural design. Data generally exist on the type of ground motion that can be expected on land in earthquake-prone areas. However, the properties of the sea floor will modify the ground motion relative to adjacent land areas, and there are no data on strong ground motion available for the sea floor. A measurement program off the Alaska shore has been initiated in cooperation with the University of Texas. The objective of the program is to collect earthquake records from the ocean bottom. During a two-year period, a network of 10-15 seismometers will be operated on the floor of the Gulf of Alaska just south of the Aleutian islands and up into the Bering Sea.

Sea Ice Areas

To this point, this paper has been concerned with offshore operations in areas where sea ice is not a factor. However, substantial oil and gas potential exists in arctic and subarctic areas where the possibility of sea ice must be anticipated. Figure 19 identifies the major sea ice provinces in the northern hemisphere. Annual or first-year ice prevails in subarctic regions such as the Bering Sea. Multiyear ice is a major component of the perennial pack ice in the Arctic Ocean. These two ice provinces are separated by an intermediate region where annual ice and multiyear ice occur in varying proportions. The main environmental factors affecting offshore operations in these areas are the type of ice, the water depth, and the duration of the open-water season.

Substantial efforts have been under way for a decade to develop the scientific field of ice mechanics. Laboratory experiments, field tests, and analytical modeling all play a part in this field of expanding technical knowledge. Americans and Canadians have pioneered these areas.

EXPLORATION DRILLING SYSTEMS FOR ICE AREAS

The occurrence of sea ice presents unique problems in the development of offshore drilling and production systems. The solutions to these problems require specialized technology and operating techniques. The cost of offshore developments in the remote arctic and subarctic regions of Alaska is expected to be high.

Man-made gravel or sand islands appear to be the most generally

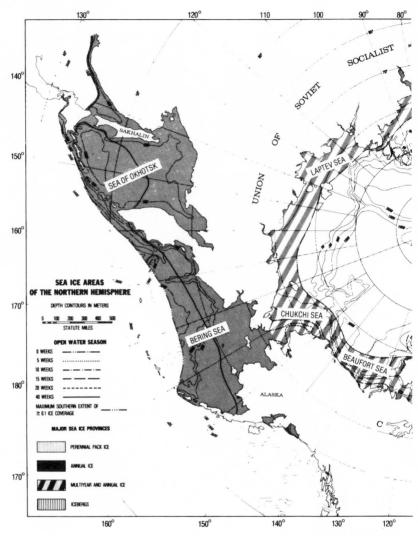

Fig. 19. Sea ice areas of

applicable exploration drilling platform in shallow arctic waters up to ten or twenty meters deep. These islands can be converted to production islands by enlarging them and providing permanent protection against wave erosion. Man-made islands have been used in the Canadian

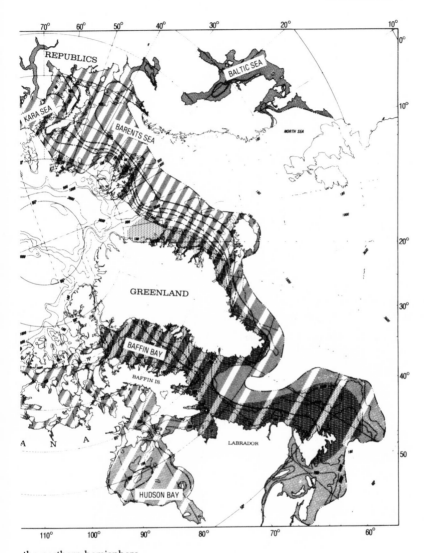

the northern hemisphere

Beaufort Sea since 1972. More than twenty exploration wells have been drilled by this method in water depths up to nineteen meters.

Special drillships strengthened against ice have been used in the Canadian Beaufort Sea where the open-water season is only about ten weeks. Ice-breaking workboats were used to extend the drilling season by diverting drift ice in the summer and by breaking up new ice cover around the drillship in early winter.

Other exploration drilling methods that involve ice thickening or the building of ice islands have been used in shallow arctic waters with some success.

In the deeper-water arctic regions (beyond twenty meters), additional technology is needed. Several companies are conducting programs to develop exploration drilling methods for these areas.

In subarctic regions such as the Bering Sea, with significant open-water seasons, more or less conventional floating drilling methods can be used.

PRODUCTION SYSTEMS FOR ICE AREAS

As stated earlier, production in the shallow arctic waters of twenty meters or less will likely be from man-made islands. For deeper arctic waters, cone-shaped gravity structures seem to have promise. The conical shape causes the ice to ride up the sloping surface and break up due to bending rather than crush against the side of the structure. This significantly reduces the loads on the platform. Extensive model studies have been conducted to determine the ice loads that are developed on cones with different slopes.

For production operations in subarctic areas, platforms must be designed for relatively deep water. In the moderate ice conditions of the seismically active Bering Sea, platforms may resemble those used in the Cook Inlet. These production operations date back to the mid-1960s. The platforms are characterized by large caisson-like legs and an absence of bracing between the legs in the vicinity of the water level. Wells are drilled through the legs, eliminating external well conductors.

Ice-strengthened concrete gravity structures, similar to North Sea platforms, with ice-breaking cones at the waterline, may also have application in several areas of the Bering Sea.

Offshore Oil in America's Future

The offshore oil industry had its beginnings in United States waters and was for many years dominated by U.S. companies. Although it is now a truly international industry, American companies and individuals are still highly influential in this vital use of the sea.

When compared with many other facets of American sea power, the U.S. offshore oil industry is seen to be in relatively good health. It is fortunate that many American oil companies operate internationally. This has given these companies broader opportunities and incentives to develop new technology. Much of this technology has been or likely will be used in exploring for and producing much-needed oil and gas from the U.S. frontier offshore areas.

Ocean Mining and Minerals from the Sea

John E. Flipse

In the late 1950s and early 1960s the International Nickel Company, which had long enjoyed a unique position in the nickel business, was faced with the problem of future sources of nickel ore, a choice that quickly narrowed to terrestrial laterite deposits in a belt centered on the equator, or manganese nodule deposits on the deep sea bed. Symptomatic of its desire to diversify its product line while utilizing its industrial skills, INCO's investigations stimulated the Newport News Shipbuilding and Dry Dock Company to mount a research program, leading to the later formation of Deepsea Ventures, the first ocean mining company. These pioneers were joined, after an exquisite selection/elimination process, by many U.S., international, and foreign corporations of two major types:

- metal companies or feed-stock seekers such as U.S. Steel, Kennecott Copper, Amoco Minerals, Metallgesellschaft, Preussag, Sumitomo Metals, Billiton, Nippon Steel, and many others;
- technology suppliers such as Deepsea Ventures, SEDCO, Lockheed, Lurgi, Bos Kalis Westminister Group, and many others.

The prospecting, research and development, pilot plant and small scale system tests, and the economic evaluation efforts of the resulting four major consortia/joint ventures were frequently obfuscated and always complicated by two major United Nations undertakings. The first, the U.N. Conference on Trade and Development, enjoys such worthy objectives as reduction of starvation, improving world health standards, elevating the gross national product and the average income of developing nations, developing markets for our manufactured goods, expanding trade, and so on. The product is the "New World Economic Order." The harsh translation of this euphemism is the "redistribution of the world's wealth," yours and mine. The deliberations are rich with lofty phrases but short on terms such as hard work, thrift, and self-sacrifice. The overtone, most disturbing to an industrial entrepreneur, suggests nationalization, expropriation, cartels, insecurity, and revolution. The deliberations have had severe impact on the development of ocean mining for two reasons: (1) the United States failed miserably to protest effectively or counter the thrust of the U.N. Conference on Trade and Development, thereby implying approval and encouraging the participants (the "other side" in the law of the sea debate); and (2) the United States delegates to the conference continued the apologetic stance taken so frequently by our nation in international negotiations.

In the opinion of many, the United States also made a serious strategic blunder by agreeing to couple the issues of navigation, research and environment, and resources (minerals and fisheries) in the second major debate, the United Nations Conference on the Law of the Sea (UNCLOS). The regression of our expectations in the process clearly indicates its "progress" over a decade of frustration. The United States was forced to readjust its goals, sequentially, to:

- a good treaty with guaranteed access to the resources of the seabed and fair regulations governing its exploitation, both operational and financial;
- effective control of the "Authority" (the governing bureaucracy) through the organization/administration and/or voting process;
- "justice" through a reasonable procedure for settlement of disputes;
- renegotiation at the obligatory "twenty-five-year review";
- renunciation of the treaty if it should prove too burdensome.

There is no doubt that the well-publicized U.N. debates referred to above adversely influenced the financial and moral support provided to the ocean-mining consortia by the boards of directors of the sponsoring corporations. The resultant delay, coupled with the high rate of inflation and the increased cost of energy, has, over the past decade, more than tripled the estimated capital and operating costs of a modest commercial program. However, a great deal of good science and engineering was performed during the decade, with important results.

The Resource: Manganese Nodules

Manganese nodules, the blue-black round to potato-shaped lumps found on the bottom of all oceans and many lakes, were first discovered and reported by the scientists aboard the British research ship *Challenger* more than a century ago. However, although many "finds" were noted over the ensuing years, little attention was given to these scientific curiosities until the late 1950s. The 1960s showed a marked increase in activity, with industry interest stimulating academic investigations, frequently with government support. And the development of an ocean-mining industry with the attendant law of the sea debate in the 1970s resulted in an explosion of papers, meetings, symposia, reports, and books describing this promising resource. There is still much to learn, but the quantity of information available now is impressive, raising the usual concerns about its quality.

There is no "accepted" theory of how manganese nodules form on the ocean floor but we do know:

- Manganese nodules contain 20 percent or more manganese, 5 to 8 percent iron, 0.5 to 2 percent nickel and copper, 0.1 to 0.5 percent cobalt, and smaller amounts of as many as thirty other elements. These are average assay ranges for resource grade nodules, with very wide variations recorded and worldwide nodule assay "averages" appreciably lower.
- There are micro-nodules (a fraction of an inch in the major dimension) and monster nodules (several feet across), but most resource grade nodules are one to four inches in major dimension, with the average size nodules contributing a high percentage of the metal values.
- Nodules form very slowly. A two-inch nodule may be two to seven *million* years old, with most deposits consisting of nodules about the same age. Where are the "baby and teenage" nodules?

- Most nodules form about a nucleus (a grain of sand, shark's tooth, and so forth) with many layers. The process is called agglomeration, and there is strong evidence that it is an electrochemical process with biological assistance.
- Nodules are found on the ocean floor in areas where the sedimentation rate is very low (buried nodules do not grow, they often go back into solution), or where currents sweep away the sediments. An interesting deposit is off the coast of Georgia and Florida where several rivers discharge large amounts of sediment but the fast-flowing Gulf Stream keeps the bottom clean.
- Nodule deposits that are "downstream" from volcanoes or the earth's crust fractures seem to be "richer" in metal content.
- Nodule abundance over an area may be highly variable—from 70 percent of the bottom covered to no nodules at all.
- Metal content seems to be related to sediment type, but there are exceptions to the rule.

Any trained scientist can produce "evidence" that demonstrates one or all of the above statements are wrong in specific cases. However, industry practice suggests that these data are useful in prospecting for and evaluating "commercial" deposits. To date, the most promising deposits identified lie within the major oceanic circulation systems, in deep water, with the "best" located between the Clarion and Clipperton fractures in the north tropical Pacific Ocean. Early reports of "limitless" nodules have proven to be exaggerated, while the case for the existence of "only tens" of mine sites worldwide is also false—an argument advanced by those who plan to control development of this resource for selfish reasons or to further the "New World Economic Order."

The above description of this interesting and promising future source of several important metals is grossly incomplete. As noted earlier, the literature is extensive and often controversial—it certainly is fascinating and raises many unanswered questions. The purpose of describing the nodules at all is to make the following description of ocean mining technology more understandable.

Ocean Mining Technology

The first technical problem facing the ocean miner is the location, definition, mapping, and evaluation of a seabed deposit of manganese nodules. The literature explosion has tremendously simplified the first part of the problem—prospecting or finding a deposit on the ocean floor. The rapid improvement of oceanographic tools over the past decade has also been very helpful, but the high rate of inflation and the increased cost of energy have resulted in a financial burden which encourages even more sophisticated exploration techniques in a search for cost-effectiveness. No one questions the potential value of sophisticated electronics and the computer, but the application of more complex hardware in the unforgiving marine environment has yet to be proven cost-effective.

EXPLORATION

In fact, most of the techniques used today for the determination of the quantity and quality of a manganese nodule deposit are rather state-of-the-art, while some are truly antique. A first requirement is a ship to provide a working platform, hotel, and transportation to and from the area to be explored. Small (100–150 feet long), high endurance (30-plus days), diesel-propelled, seaworthy, slow vessels are the norm. A ship under 300 measurement-tons avoids stringent manning and operating regulations but can prove unseaworthy; some have been lost. Photography, television, and sampling by grabs, box corers, or dredges provide data on nodule coverage and population, as well as samples for later analysis and assay. The box cores may also provide soil/sediment data for scientific correlation and mining equipment design. Position keeping is done by careful use of thrusters and main propulsion, while buoys and celestial, loran, or satellite navigation help locate the ship on the wide, empty ocean. Normal oceanographic data for scientific or engineering purposes are obtained by standard equipment. The dearth of synoptic current or wave data suggests that reliable, accurate, and long-lived equipment is the exception rather than the rule.

Deploying an oceanographic or sampling package on the ocean floor in deep water takes many hours, as the descent speed is always limited and the recovery speed is frequently reduced below maximum winch speed to protect the equipment and/or the sample. Even free-fall or boomerang samplers have their limitations, although their use does improve ship time utilization. And before a deposit can be judged "mineable," the seabed topography and the presence of obstacles must also be determined. Measurement of topographic relief of the seabed from the sea surface is inherently inaccurate because of the limitations of the acoustic techniques employed. Towing a transducer near the ocean floor to supply accurate micro-topographic information slows the process severely, due to cable drag and "flying" of the transducer vehicle. Hence good data are expensive, as excellent equipment, skills, personnel, and much time are required for their acquisition.

The severe requirements described above have resulted in several research programs of great promise. Deep-ocean vehicles capable of high speed, equipped with precise depth-sounders, side-search sonar for locating obstacles, soil and nodule samplers, and *in situ* assay equipment are under investigation. Taking advantage of military R&D (sometimes called technology transfer), the industry, given a profit motive, is expected to support these academic/government R&D undertakings. A word of caution: searchers have not yet found the *Titanic*, a far less demanding endeavor than locating and quantifying manganese nodules. In summary, finding, mapping, and evaluating a mineable deposit of manganese nodules is certainly feasible and has been done, but at great cost in time and money.

MINING

The most promising deep-ocean mining systems now under development consist of the following key components: (1) a seabed *collector*, to pick up the nodules from the seabed and deliver them to (2) the *dredge pipe* extending from the collector to a surface ship; (3) a *pumping system* to move the nodules and water continuously from the seabed to the surface; (4) a *mining ship* to serve as a hotel, working platform, power plant, a temporary nodule holding vehicle, and a warehouse for equipment, stores, and fuel; (5) a *slurry-transfer system* to move the nodules from the mining ship to (6) the *ore transports* that periodically will carry the nodules to shore for processing. A brief description of each component for a commercial mining system follows.

The collector must move across the ocean floor, separating the nodules from the sediments and delivering them to the dredge pipe inlet. This most proprietary element of the system can slice, pick, wash or ingeniously levitate the nodules onto ramps, conveyors, or ducts to clean the nodules of the clinging sediments, while delivering them to the dredge pipe. It must be able to negotiate small obstacles (three-foot boulders) while avoiding major obstacles (cliffs, trenches, wrecks) and picking up nodules over a wide swath because of its slow speed of advance. A "smart" collector will temporarily "store" excess nodules (to compensate for bare patches) while it meters into the dredge pipe the correct quantity to assure high productivity without overloading the pipe. It should function for weeks (it is hoped, months) without requiring repair or recovery from the bottom—a very time-consuming process.

The dredge pipe, connected to the collector by a hose or other "soft" means (to prevent incidental pipe motions from becoming collector motions) must transfer the nodules from the seabed to the sea surface, a distance of three to four miles. The pipe must be manufactured in sections of high strength steel with easily assembled and disassembled "joints" of great strength. It must be stowed aboard the mining ship and assembled at sea, a tedious process at best. In addition, it must be protected (coatings and fairing), and used as a "route" for power and control cables from the ship to the collector with several station connections in between. While performing its primary function, it must safely withstand severe pressure differences, support its own weight, and, very likely, tow the collector across the ocean floor. Commercial dredge pipes are likely to be one to two feet in diameter with wall thicknesses of one-half to two-plus inches.

A commercial mining system will probably pump the nodules up the dredge pipe using **mixed-flow in-line pumps** spaced at intervals along the pipe, or an **"air-lift" system** with widely spaced air injection points. The "staging," or separation of the pumping units along the pipe, limits the pressure difference across the dredge pipe while increasing the efficiency of the system and facilitating its deployment. Although in-line pumps have been used in many commercial applications, pumps of this size and power are not "off-the-shelf" items, and while efficient, they are very expensive. Supplying electric power in large amounts to deeply submerged motor-driven pumps also creates problems. On the other hand, air-lift pumps, while simple, are notoriously inefficient, with systems of this power and capacity far exceeding present practice. The air-lift depends on air or gas bubbles expanding as they rise up the pipe, creating a pressure difference and continued upward motion. A home aquarium cleaner is a simple air-lift system. Both systems work but have problems, making a challenging tradeoff study.

The mining ship or vehicle will most likely resemble a large oil field drillship, performing many of the same functions, such as hotel, power plant, working platform, and storehouse for equipment, fuel, and food. It will perform several other functions peculiar to ocean mining, such as towing the collector and dredge pipe for about fifty to seventy-five miles per day (measured over the bottom), holding "buffer tonnage" of nodules, and transferring these large quantities of ore to transport ships. A ship form appears to meet these diverse requirements well, while providing moderate platform motions and efficient transit. Special equipment will be required to navigate and propel the ship in a manner that assures positive collector control and efficient nodule collection.

A **slurry-transfer system** is required to move the nodules from the mining ship to transport ships for delivery ashore to a processing plant. The transports can be brought alongside the mining ship (with proper protection), maneuvered alongside, or towed behind the mining ship with the reslurried nodules pumped from the mining ship's holds to a dewatering and distribution system on each transport. It is also likely that while the ore is being transferred to the transport, fuel oil will be pumped from the transport to the mining ship. Several ore and coal slurry-transfer systems are in use worldwide, which suggests that these systems can be adapted to ocean mining service.

The last component of the ocean mining system is the **transport ship** (ore carrier) itself. Refinement of the ship's maneuvering capability, installation of cable and hose handling equipment, fitting of an ore distribution and hold dewatering system, and careful selection of operating personnel would qualify most modern ore carriers for the task. The port facility, including piers, unloading gear, storage areas, stacking gear and so on, is usually considered part of this function. These ships and facilities are complicated and expensive and, if we consider the potential permitting problem, can be the source of serious program delays. They are, however, within the state-of-the-art and do not require extensive engineering development.

METAL WINNING

The purpose of ocean mining is to produce useful and valuable metals. The processing of this unique ore poses some serious problems while providing some exciting opportunities. The slow accumulation of the metals, as metal oxide molecules in a mineral lattice, suggests that normal gravitational or size separation techniques will fail. Perhaps smelting, roasting, or heating the nodules will eliminate some constituents (certainly the water trapped within the nodules), but it appears that it will be essential to put the nodules back into solution to separate the metals efficiently. Fortunately the nodules readily dissolve in most acids and in certain ammonia-base liquids.

The consortia investigating the feasibility of commercial ocean mining approach the winning of the metal values from two divergent points of view. In one approach, the operation would be vertically integrated with *one company* doing the whole job: exploration, mining, transporting, processing, and selling the metal products. The alternate approach is to ship nodules, or some intermediate product such as roasted nodules, to each consortium member, who could then process the material by his choice of techniques, perhaps in existing plants. Even where vertical integration is the objective, there is a strong incentive to use proven (often expensive and proprietary) technology rather than accept the risks incumbent in the development of new technology. This tendency is regrettable if it leads to excess energy consumption and environment-threatening wastes, or if it precludes the investigation of innovative techniques that take advantage of the unique characteristics of this ore.

In summary, we may conclude that the location, dredging, and processing of manganese nodules has been demonstrated to be technically feasible. Some research, much engineering development, and extensive system testing must be done before a commercial system can be put into service. The economic feasibility has not been demonstrated, and that may present greater obstacles to commercialization than the technical problems.

Ocean Mining Economics

Unfortunately, Mother Nature did not endow the nodules with metal values consistent with our current industrial needs. A good commercial nodule deposit might have the following metal content on a dry weight basis: manganese 30 percent, nickel 1.3 percent, copper 1.1 percent, and cobalt 0.25 percent. If mined at a rate of 1.5 million short tons per year yielding 1 million tons of dry ore (as mined, nodules are about one third water), an efficient process would produce approximately the following metal: 260,000 tons of manganese, 12,000 tons of nickel, 11,000 tons of copper, and 1,700 tons of cobalt. For a copper company or a nickel company this is an inadequate metal production level; consequently there were two cases of corporate and consortium planning for a mining rate of 4.5 million short tons per year yielding 3 million tons of dry ore and three times as much nickel, copper, and cobalt, but *no* manganese. This "three metal approach" eliminates manganese since the resultant 780,000 tons of manganese would far exceed the United States needs and very likely severely damage the world market for this metal. A third consortium planned to mine at about 1.5 million short tons annually, providing about one-half of the United States manganese needs but having far better prospects for profit as a "four metal" producer. Both "three" and "four metal" operations would probably extract relatively small quantities of molybdenum, vanadium, and zinc (and possibly other metals) from the nodules before disposing of the wastes to provide a 2 to 5 percent increase in revenues. In fact, even the "three metal" proponents have begun to consider some manganese revenues (as an ore or an intermediate) as the harsh economic "facts of life" become more apparent.

Recent (as yet unpublished) research for the National Oceanic and Atmospheric Administration involved the definition of a "typical three metal" operation mining 4.5 million tons of nodules using two mine-ships, three transports, a waterfront terminal, a twenty-mile-distant metal winning plant, using a reduction/ammonia leach process and disposing of the wastes on shore. Realistic capital and operating cost estimates for the total program (exploration to metal sales) and reasonable revenue projections (today's metal prices advanced to 1990) showed that a one and one-half billion dollar investment would be required. Preliminary pay-out analysis indicates that the expected annual revenues of 400 to 500 million dollars less operating costs (including depreciation) of 300 to 400 million dollars would yield an after-tax internal rate of return (discounted cash flow) based on a twenty-six year project life (six years construction and debugging, twenty years producing) between 2 and 3 percent. A rough extrapolation of these data suggests that a "four metal" operation would double these returns. Hardly the bonanza expected by the law of the sea debaters!

Legal/Political Considerations

In mid-1980, the Deep Seabed Hard Mineral Resources Act, Public Law 96-283, was signed by President Carter. The result of almost a decade of hearings, debate, compromise, and rewriting, the new law provides that the National Oceanic and Atmospheric Administration will:

- issue permits for American companies (or interests) to explore the seabed beyond the limits of national jurisdiction;
- issue licenses to qualified American companies to exploit man-

ganese nodule deposits in an environmentally sound manner;
- prepare a programmatic environmental impact statement and require each licensee to prepare a site-specific environmental impact statement;
- conduct a five-year research program to assure the environmental safety of manganese nodule mining, processing, and waste disposal;
- develop a regulatory regime to effectively manage deep seabed mining;
- recognize the interests of "like-minded" nations who wish similarly to exploit the seabed hard minerals; and
- delay commercial mining until 1988.

On the other hand, in spite of the often compelling arguments found in legislative history, the law does not provide:

- any form of subsidy for the developing industry;
- protection of investment from the terms or conditions of a treaty (such as a U.N. law of the sea treaty) entered into by the United States;
- continuity of operation (as the U.S. law yields to any contrary term of a treaty);
- depletion allowance (as the non-renewable resource is mined);
- credits or tax relief for payments made to an international agency.

In summary, Public Law 96-283 falls far short of encouraging private investment in deep-ocean hard mineral development but does provide a framework for future growth in two modes:

1. a viable U.S. industry resulting from a strong national recognition of the need for deep-ocean mining, supported by a realistic (minimal) regulatory regime with financial incentives rather than penalties; or
2. a foreign partnership/corporation yielding metal and money with diminished environmental restraints, no antitrust laws, and a markedly benign regulatory regime. In several instances, direct government support might further increase the likelihood of profitable operation.

As one disappointed ocean miner remarked: "They don't like us as much as the synfuel gang, but the act is a lot better than nothing." It remains to be seen if the act is good enough.

The United Nations Conference on the Law of the Sea work product is intended to be a comprehensive treaty to assure the orderly and equitable use of the world's oceans and their resources. It is nonsense to say that we have *no* problems in ocean use today—it is equally nonsense to claim that there is chaos at sea. We are paying tribute (blackmail) to free our tuna boats from certain South American nations while we are regularly navigating the straits (choke-points) of Hormuz and Malacca. Many foreign nations have entered into fishery agreements with the United States while Mexico has cancelled a bilateral shrimping agreement. Obviously, the real state of affairs is somewhere between "problem free" and chaos. There is no validity in the argument that ten years of debate (even under U.N. auspices) makes the terms of the "negotiating text" international law in the face of continuing deep-ocean manganese nodule deposit exploration and surveying (for instance), or that "the common heritage of mankind" is, in fact, common ownership with its propensity for infinite debate and mind-changing.

THE UNCLOS NEGOTIATING TEXT

The United States entered the UNCLOS preparatory committee discussions with an announced position on "freedom of passage" which essentially eliminated our negotiating strength in other areas. Our national attitude was apologetic, our negotiators were restrained and our "good guy" image was preeminent. Our performance/success is indicated by the degradation of expectations presented in the introduction to this paper. In the current version of the treaty, the Committee I output (addressing ocean mining) provides:

- full disclosure of technical exploration data for *two* mine-sites, with the "Authority" having first choice;
- mandatory "transfer of technology" to the Authority and to individual lesser developed countries;
- production controls to protect land producers of the key metals;
- punitive financial obligations (poorly defined) on all miners except the Authority;
- payments to "Liberation Organizations";
- mandatory renegotiation of the treaty terms with automatic loss of rights if a "satisfactory" revision is not reached;
- a monster bureaucracy with built-in delays.

On the other hand, the treaty draft does *not* provide:

- assured, continued access to a seabed mineral deposit;
- continuity of operation of the system (production control);
- security of investment;
- prompt (or even "timely") resolution of differences;
- profit incentives;
- protection from the Vienna Convention (the treaty on treaties).

The Vienna Convention, to which the United States is a party, could be a major obstacle to U.S. miners operating under U.S. (or reciprocating nation) legislation, as it provides that a signatory nation to a treaty must refrain from all actions contrary to the purpose of the treaty. Certainly deep-ocean mining under domestic law could be interpreted as contrary to the purpose of the law of the sea treaty as, for instance, no monies would accrue to the Authority or the less developed countries (LDCs). This concern alone suggests that the United States should hesitate to sign a United Nations Law of the Sea treaty until it is satisfied that the treaty is equitable and the bureaucracy is in position to act decisively.

The basic appeal of a comprehensive system of ocean law is the promise of order and fair treatment. The United States must objectively review the terms of the present treaty draft and decide if *all* its interests will be served by becoming a signatory nation. The sacrifice of a future source of essential metals in exchange for "comfort" in areas where our existing rights may be challenged is a questionable tradeoff for the nation. Unfortunately, a treaty (or contract) between parties with widely differing goals that depends upon obscure convoluted phrases to achieve its purposes usually becomes the basis for extended legal procedures rather than the solution of real or perceived problems. The goals of the United States may be confused, but the objective of the "other side" is the New World Economic Order, a fact that we should remember.

A Mineral Crisis?

In November 1980, *Newsweek* carried an article on ocean mining with a feature labeled "The Mineral Crisis" that included a table of major (high percentage) U.S. mineral imports and named the source nations. Although the ocean mining industry had been raising the issue for a decade, a State Department employee observed that the matter is now "serious" as the media is "aware." The strategic value of ocean mining is very real, with or without media attention.

If we eliminate the reuse of scrap and focus on the mineral *source* rather than nations that process ores and then ship metal to the United States, we have the following table:

METAL	U.S. IMPORT	MAJOR SOURCES
Manganese	100 percent	Gabon and South Africa
Nickel	90 percent	Canada and New Caledonia
Copper	30 percent	Chile and Zaire
Cobalt	100 percent	Zaire and Zambia

The percentages shown above differ from the U.S. Bureau of Mines data quoted by *Newsweek*, as scrap has been eliminated along with "toll processer" output. The United States has no manganese mines, although there are several known low-grade ore bodies in Maine ("bog ores") and in the Rocky Mountains. Our most extensive domestic deposits are the steel mill slag heaps, a non-economic source of manganese. Although we currently import only 30 percent of our copper (the level of petroleum imports in 1973 when OPEC appreciably raised our awareness of the power of cartels), our copper industry has several severe problems. One U.S. company now mines copper ore in Arizona, smelts the ore in Japan (which imports 100 percent of its energy), and ships finished product back to the United States more profitably than doing the work in the "good old USA!"

From the strategic perspective, manganese and cobalt are our most serious candidate metals. Cobalt is a by-product (of other metal mines) with most of the free world's supply coming from Zaire and Zambia in Central Africa. The metal is an essential alloy for producing heat-resistant high strength steel for jet engine turbine blades, for instance. The recent revolution in Zaire clearly indicated the importance of this source, with the price of cobalt increasing by five to ten times in a few months when Zaire's production ceased. U.S. Government stockpiles are supposed to provide cobalt to U.S. industry during short wars or brief interruptions of supply, but there is no realistic long-term alternate source for this metal. Similarly, the free world's source of manganese is Gabon and South Africa. Historic sources such as Brazil, Venezuela, India, and Morocco have either exhausted their deposits or have decided to restrict exports to provide for their expanding steel industries. Manganese is an essential element (used as a catalyst/cleaner) in the production of steel for which no known substitute exists.

OCEAN MINING IS CRITICAL

It is inconceivable that the United States will give up an alternate source of these critical metals to an organization dedicated to the "redistribution of the world's wealth" when our economic survival and military security depend on them. The Reagan Administration apparently shares this concern and is in the process of evaluating the law of the sea draft treaty in this regard.

A comprehensive law of the sea treaty providing real benefits and incentives to all parties is the ideal legal/political framework for development of ocean mining and minerals from the sea. A national will, supported by realistic application of legislation by the United States and/or like-minded nations, is a viable alternate approach. Reasonable financial incentives will enable international industry to develop and employ the existing technology base for successful and beneficial exploitation of this generous resource.

Ocean mining and minerals from the sea are essential to the long-term economic and strategic security of the United States of America.

Food from the Sea

Clarence P. Idyll

There is a mystique about the sea that has gripped the imagination of mankind since he first made contact with it. Its immensity, its rhythms, its strange inhabitants, its bounty—all of these have made the sea an area of special fascination, as that of an alien world.

Not the least of man's interest in the sea is the harvest that can be obtained from its waters. And this interest becomes sharpened to the point of urgency as people become frightened about the ability of the land to supply the food we need, now and in the future when our numbers double, and then double again. Partly through hope, partly through desperation, and partly through the realization that appropriate knowledge and action can produce significant results, mankind has turned to the sea with high expectations. These expectations are best examined on the basis of the scientific, economic, and social background and constraints which bear upon them.

Hunger has threatened mankind in one form or another since the beginning of our race. Famines can be traced back for centuries, but none has been more disastrous than some occurring in the last four decades. Food shortages in many parts of the world in 1947 caused widespread misery. But then came the "green revolution." The situation improved so dramatically that incautious statements were made asserting that man had at last found the key to adequate food supplies. Remarkable advances in plant genetics produced new strains of dwarf wheat and rice which raised the yields per acre 50 to 100 percent. But it was discovered that the new high-bearing strains of wheat and rice demanded much greater than normal amounts of fertilizers, pesticides, and skills, and these were missing or were too expensive in underdeveloped countries to be supplied in sufficient quantities.

Then, in 1972, disaster in the form of frost and drought struck farmers in many parts of the world. The worst was the terrible six-year Sahelian drought which devastated a 3,000-mile band of Africa south of the Sahara Desert, killing 100,000 people and huge numbers of livestock. Russia's food shortages prompted massive purchases of wheat from the United States, contributing to reduction of U.S. grain reserves to a few weeks' supply and thus weakening one of the world's buffers against famine.

Food from the sea was also reduced in 1972 when oceanographic changes in the Humboldt Current caused a collapse of the Peruvian anchovy fishery. This fishery, the world's largest, had produced about 20 percent of all fish caught in the ocean. The causes of the collapse were, first, a meteorological change that resulted in warming of the surface waters and a shift in the ocean current, and second, overfishing.

Prospects for World Agriculture

But if more food is needed now, the problem will be far greater in the future, because the human population is increasing at a rate of 203,000 a day, or 74 million a year, and four out of five of these new humans are born in poor countries, those with the least capacity to provide for more people.

The chance of the land producing more food is extremely uncertain. Apart from dwindling acreage for farms, shortages of fertilizers, environmental damage from urgently needed pesticides, and a dozen other problems, land farmers face the threat of long-term climate changes. In fact, the world may be sliding back into a new ice age. Since 1940 a cooling trend in the Northern Hemisphere has caused a temperature decline of 0.5 to 1.0 degrees centigrade. This has resulted, for example, in England's growing season being shortened by nine or ten days between 1950 and 1966. Then, there has been a significant shift in the world's monsoon belt, resulting in changes in the amounts and patterns of rainfall.

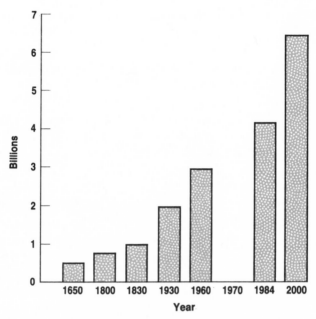

Fig. 1. Rise in Human Population

The ability of farmers to keep pace, more or less, with rising human population has been proven, some observers assert, by the steady rise in food production during the period from 1880 to 1940. But it now turns out that this was a time of significant warming of the world's climate, and it may have been abnormal. Thus, instead of the present new chill on many areas of the land being unusual, it may be that the earth is simply returning to a more normal state. It is disturbing to think what may happen to man's ability to keep farm production level with human population if we are faced with a long era of cold weather.

Yet, the evidence about climate changes is contradictory. A study by the National Academy of Sciences indicates that the greenhouse effect of carbon dioxide being added to the atmosphere by the activities of man "could have adverse, even catastrophic" effects around the world, possibly raising the average temperature 6 degrees centigrade by 2050 and causing dramatic reductions in agricultural production.

Short-term forecasts of food supplies by the Food and Agriculture Organization (FAO) of the United Nations are not encouraging. In a report issued in early 1981, the agency said that world grain production was continuing well below the long-term trend, and that a sharp decline in cereal grain reserves was expected because of likely increased import needs of the developing countries and the USSR. The former, for example, were expected to require 6 million metric tons (mmt) more grain in 1981 than in 1980. If FAO's forecast should prove accurate, global reserves of cereal grains will have diminished by the end of 1981 from 250 to 210 mmt, which is only 14 percent of world consumption compared to the 17 percent that is regarded as the safe minimum cushion against possible crop failure. This would leave the world in a situation similar to that of the hungry years of the early 1970s.

The many and often contradictory factors affecting our ability to produce food have resulted in differing opinions about the future. At one extreme, Paul Ehrlich, the distinguished California expert, says that the race is already lost. Some years ago he predicted that by 1985 vast famines would sweep the earth, involving hundreds of millions of people. Others say that it will take longer, but that after the year 2050, 500 million people could die of famine. On the other hand, Don Paalberg of the U.S. Department of Agriculture believes that barring unusually bad weather, food production can stay half a step ahead of demand for a few decades. After that, without population control, he believes that disaster will strike mankind. Thus, the most optimistic of predictions are not very encouraging, and the most pessimistic are terrifying.

Can the Sea Fill the Food Gap?

In the face of this uncertain future for agriculture, we turn to the question of whether the sea can take over from the land the task of feeding mankind. Some believe that the oceans can produce as much food as the land or even more.

This viewpoint is exemplified by Arnold Toynbee, one of the towering scholars of our time, whose book *A Study of History* has influenced Western thought and policy to a significant degree. In 1968, after the American orbiting of the moon, Dr. Toynbee pleaded that the United States should use the money spent on what he called the "dead end" of space exploration for the development of food from the sea. Said he, "Here is a vast accessible field for man's enterprise, and sure guarantee of our race's survival even if our descendants are going to be ten times as numerous as we are today. Even in these numbers our descendants will not starve, since the quantities of edible fish will have multiplied, in domestication, far more sensationally."

The supposition that the sea is rich seems to be confirmed by the immense swarms of fish and other life that can sometimes be seen in the ocean—great schools of herring in the Atlantic, seemingly endless numbers of tuna rolling in the central Pacific, hordes of salmon surging up the spawning streams of Alaska. Are these indeed proof of an inexhaustible ocean bounty, and is it therefore true that all we have to do to provide enough food for present and future generations is to work harder at harvesting this bounty?

The world catch from the ocean in 1979 was about 65 mmt. This amount is statistically insignificant since it provided only about 1-2 percent of the calories of food available to mankind. If this does not seem to be very much, the situation may appear better when it is recognized that fish is the source of about 13 percent of the world's animal protein—about three-quarters as much as is provided by beef, and more than three times that supplied by poultry.

SEA PLANTS POOR AS FOOD RESOURCE

One reason for the present small relative contribution of the sea to our food supply is the profound difference between land food and sea food,

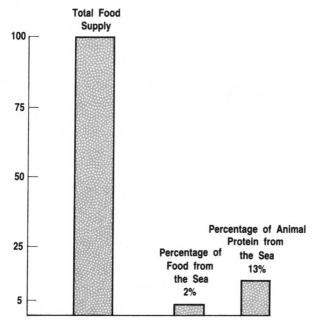

Fig. 2. Contribution of Sea to Supply of Food

especially the plants. On land, plants supply between 40 and 85 percent of human food, depending on the culture in which people live. The remainder of land food is supplied by herbivores, the plant eaters, with land carnivores providing virtually none. By contrast, the ocean plants are not food-bearing grasses and trees, but mostly one-celled microscopic, floating specks. The rest are the primitive algae—the seaweeds. Higher plants, which represent the great majority of vegetation on land, are nearly missing in the sea, and thus there are no seeds, nuts, fruits, or tubers to be harvested. Some of the seaweeds are edible, but only the leaves are eaten. Substantial quantities of seaweed are consumed in Japan and some other countries, but they are poor sources of energy and their use is more traditional than nutritional.

The situation in the sea is not much better with the herbivores, which supply the remainder of the food on land. On land the herbivores we eat are cattle, pigs, and sheep. In the sea the main herbivores are very small crustaceans, principally copepods, plus fish larvae, molluscs, arrowworms, jellyfish and many other small animals. We eat a few marine herbivores, but their contribution to our diet is small. What we do eat from the sea are the carnivores, two or more steps up the food chain.

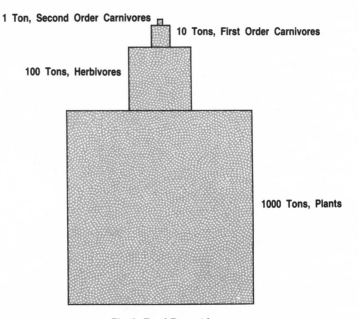

Fig. 3. Food Pyramid

LAND FOOD AND SEA FOOD ARE DIFFERENT

The significance of this difference between land food and sea food is that every time we pass from one trophic or nutrient level to another in the food chain—that is, from plants to the small animals floating in the plankton, from animal plankton to first level carnivores, and so on—we lose 80-90 percent of the substance and energy. Hence, if we start with 1,000 tons of sea plants, when these are consumed by animal plankton organisms we are left with 100 tons of body substance, the rest having been spun off as waste and energy. When these 100 tons are consumed by the first level carnivores, only 10 tons are left. These losses explain why many agriculture experts argue for less cattle farming, believing that the land should be used for raising grains and other plants, thereby reaping up to ten times as much food. Yet, on land the loss of energy is suffered only once, in the transformation of grass or grain to cattle. By strong contrast, in the sea we usually start to harvest only at the 10-ton level of the first order carnivores or the one-ton level of the second order carnivores—the cod, mackerel, and salmon. These are the equivalents of the lions and wolves on land. We do not eat lions and wolves, but not because of their taste or nutritional value; it is only because it would be too inefficient in terms of energy. Thus, sea food and land food are indeed different, and the contrast is enormously important to a world struggling to find new ways to feed itself.

We now turn to estimates of the potential food harvest of the sea. In the sea, as on land, the total amount of food available depends on the amount of organic chemicals produced by plants through photosynthesis. These plants are eaten by animals, and thus we proceed up the food chain. The amount of carbon fixed by photosynthesis in the sea is about 230 billion tons a year—approximately half that on land. By calculating the amount of living material at each trophic level above this, we arrive at a range of values somewhere between 100 and 1,000 mmt of edible material available to man per year. The reasons for this wide range are the uncertainty of our data base and the variety of definitions as to what to include as edible and economically available.

"PLANKTON SOUP"

Another kind of calculation is based on past catches and on estimates of fishery scientists of the sizes of fish populations. Widely accepted values range from about 90 to 100 mmt, if we include only the traditional kinds of seafood, like salmon, cod, tuna, and shrimp. If we were to catch and use certain less familiar creatures, including krill, squids, and some deep-sea fishes, the total harvest could be much larger. But the barriers to this expanded use of the ocean's unconventional resources are formidable.

First, what of the dream of feeding the world with plankton soup? It would be extremely valuable if we could learn to use the plankton directly as human food, since it constitutes by far the greatest bulk of living material in the sea. In his book *Deep Range*, Arthur Clarke, one of the most imaginative and widely read science fiction writers today, describes a latter-day marine scientist "holding at bay the specter of famine which had confronted all earlier ages, but which would never threaten the world again while the great plankton farms harvested their millions of tons of protein. . . . Until the oceans froze, man would never be hungry again."

Unfortunately, the plant plankton are of little use as human food. In the first place they consist of very small individuals usually encased in glassy silica or other indigestible substances. Most animal plankton species offer only a little better hope since they are also small, and many have skeletons of indigestible chiton. Furthermore, the cost of harvesting plankton— plant or animal—would be very high. Estimates made several years ago were that it would cost from $5,000 to $8,000 per dry ton to collect plankton for food, and these costs would probably be far higher now.

OTHER NON-CONVENTIONAL SEA FOODS

A few of the planktonic herbivores are capable of providing human food. The most promising of these is the antarctic krill. These are small shrimp-like creatures, a maximum of two inches long and averaging less than that. They occur in enormous numbers in the Antarctic Ocean, where they are a major source of food for the great whales, seals, penguins, and many other animals. The Soviets started gathering krill experimentally in the 1960s; Japan, West Germany, Poland, and Chile are also engaged in krill fishing. The annual catch has been about 125,000 tons in recent years. A catch of a million tons a year is said to be a possibility in the near future. Sustained annual catches of 100 to 200 mmt may be possible compared with the 65 mmt catch of all species combined in 1979.

But it may be some time before krill are useful as human food, since it is hard to process them into an acceptable item. Their chitonous shells are hard to remove, and as the delicate little animals spoil quickly, they must be processed almost immediately after capture—an expensive shipboard operation.

Squids constitute a second non-conventional group of animals available in large quantities in the sea. They are eaten by the Japanese and Southern Europeans but are not generally acceptable to most people. However, they provide fine food, with little waste. When better markets are developed and efficient harvesting methods invented, catches of oceanic squids can be increased.

Another example of unconventional sea foods with great potential are certain deep-sea species, including the lantern fishes. Some of them are among the most numerous of all fishes in the ocean, but since they live in deep water, coming near the surface only at night, if at all, they are rarely encountered. But with suitable gear it may be possible to harvest several million metric tons a year.

These and other resources not now used might yield 400 to 600 mmt or more a year. The upper limit is nearly ten times the present total catch from the sea. But it may be a long time before this day arrives, and whether it ever does will depend on our ability to devise cheap ways of catching, processing, and marketing some very strange creatures.

The "Promise of the Sea"

Among conventional fish stocks, few are unexploited, and a rapidly diminishing number are underexploited. We have learned to our chagrin that it takes only a few years of the kind of intensive fishing done by modern fleets to deplete virgin stocks.

Besides fishing harder, there are some other ways of increasing our fish yields. One, paradoxically, is to fish less hard—that is, to control fishing effort by rational management to restore depleted stocks so that eventually they yield higher catches. Another way is through fish farming, or aquaculture. For many observers this is the real promise of the sea. Logically it seems that we should abandon the hunting culture represented by fishing, and substitute fish culture, the equivalent of land farming. To quote Dr. Arnold Toynbee again, we should "abandon the practice of skimming the sea by the paleolithic method of hunting" in favor of "farming the sea by cultivating edible seaweed and by breeding and shepherding fish as we breed and shepherd sheep."

At present the world produces about 5 to 6 mmt of fish by culture, an amount something less than 10 percent of the fish produced. This quantity is considerably larger than it used to be, especially in several Asian countries, in Israel, and in a few others. Aquaculture is less important proportionately in the United States. This country produced about 90,000 metric tons of fishery products by culture in 1979, which is only 3 percent of the nation's fish production. Most of this was catfish, salmon, trout, and oysters. But we have the technology to raise a number of other species, including mullet, rabbitfish, shrimp, freshwater prawns, lobsters, clams, scallops, mussels, and abalone. The difficulty is that we cannot yet raise most of these animals at a cost that would allow them to be sold at a profit. Moreover, there are legal and political constraints that make it hard to expand aquaculture in our country. If we are able to overcome these constraints, there seems little doubt that we could increase farming production tenfold in a decade.

Thus, it appears that most of the food we get from the sea for many years in the future will come from what Dr. Toynbee called "the paleolithic method of hunting." That being the case, we should examine the status of the world's fisheries.

COMMERCIAL FISHING

The search for fish has been so thorough over virtually the whole ocean that nearly every major stock that can be caught and sold profitably has been discovered and exploited. Among the few exceptions are some populations of small herring-like fishes of the Gulf of Mexico and Caribbean region, and it may be that improved methods of fishing and expanded markets will make it profitable to fish these in the future. Other examples of unexploited stocks are hard to find.

There are a fair number of underexploited fish populations, the skipjack tuna of the Pacific being one of these. But most of these populations are being subjected to increasing fishing pressure, and are joining the great majority of fish stocks that are either fully exploited or over-fished. Salmon is one of these, catches now being about half as large as those of the 1930s.

Among the severely depleted stocks is the California sardine. The collapse of the California sardine fishery in 1952 haunts everyone interested in the conservation of natural resources. For many years the California sardine represented by far the largest United States fishery, constituting 500,000 to 680,000 tons per year from 1934 to 1945. Then this enormous fishery crashed; in 1952 almost no catch was made. It recovered briefly from 1954 to 1959, then collapsed again. It no longer exists, except for small catches incidental to other operations.

Few fish in the world have been as thoroughly studied as the California

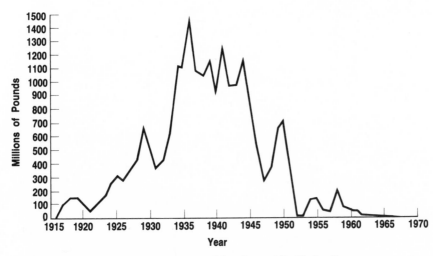

Fig. 4. California Commercial Landings of Pacific Sardines

sardine, and the reasons for the failure of its fishery have been determined: a change in the marine ecosystem concurrent with simultaneous overfishing. In the 1940s and 1950s the average ocean temperature off California dropped about 2 degrees centigrade. This was just enough to depress the spawning of sardines, which requires water temperature above 13 degrees centigrade. The unfortunate coincidence of this environmental change with very heavy fishing produced a dramatic reduction of the population, and turned Cannery Row into a derelict.

BIOLOGICAL COMPETITION OF SPECIES

In the twenty-odd years since this event, the ecosystem returned to its previous condition, and the sardine population has had no commercial fishery to influence it. In spite of these two encouragements, the population has not recovered. One suspected reason is that the anchovy population has increased as the sardines declined, with the anchovies filling the ecological vacuum created when the sardine population collapsed. The rise in numbers of anchovies has been as dramatic as the fall of the sardine population. Biologists estimated that 180,000 tons of anchovies existed in 1951 in the central stock (on which most of the fishing takes place), just before the sardine population fell, and that this rose to about 3 million tons by 1962. Since then the anchovy population has continued to prosper and its size is now believed to fluctuate between 3 and 4 million tons.

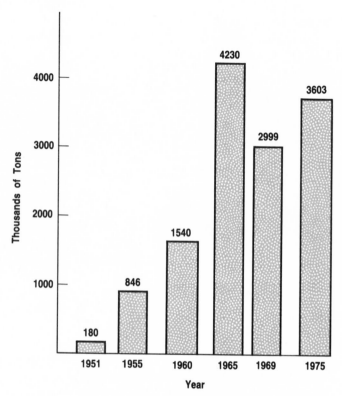

Fig. 5. Increase in Anchovy Population (Central Stock)
Since Collapse of Sardine Population

Sardines and anchovies have similar ecological requirements, especially for food, and the ecosystem apparently cannot simultaneously
support large populations of both. Historical evidence, derived from
successive layers of the scales in the mud sediments of the Santa Barbara
Channel, reveals that the dominance of sardines and anchovies has
shifted several times over many thousands of years, following changes in
ocean temperature patterns. Presumably, therefore, when one species
gets a toehold on the ecosystem, it will prevent the other from increasing
in abundance until a change in ocean temperature gradually tips the
balance again and another slow reversal in dominance takes place. But it
may be that the present anchovy dominance could be reversed more
quickly through fishery management by harvesting some of the anchovies, thus hastening the normal biological process. And even if the numbers of sardines did not increase as a result of this fishery, a rich industry

could be created on anchovies. In pursuit of this idea, a fishery management plan developed by the Pacific Fisheries Management Council authorized an annual catch of 166,400 tons of anchovies.

This proposal was vigorously opposed by sport fishing interests. The opposition was based largely on the fact that anchovies supply food for many of the larger fishes that sport fishermen catch—albacore, bonito, salmon, yellowtail, barracudas—and for several species of sea birds and mammals. It was feared that a commercial fishery on anchovies might so reduce the population that a decline would take place in game fishes. Further, anchovies are a favorite bait for sport fishing, and there was concern that the supply of this bait might be jeopardized by a commercial industry. The opposition was so strong and effective that instead of a 166,400-ton quota, the state of California has authorized only an 80,000-ton catch.

The issue in the anchovy puzzle is how to achieve what fishery managers and administrators call "optimum yield." This is a complex exercise attempting to ensure, in the first place, that the stock will not be damaged biologically by action of man, and after that, that the harvest will be divided among competing users in a way that results in maximum benefit to society. This is an ill-defined and elusive concept, and the results will obviously not be accepted by all competitors—probably not fully by any of them.

Fishery Management

It may be that ecological changes will prevent fishery managers from restoring the California sardine stock, but recent changes in the political situation have created a climate more favorable for the wise management of other fisheries in the United States. The changes resulted from a worldwide extension seaward of national jurisdiction over fisheries, usually out to 200 miles. Once hotly debated, this action has become generally accepted, and in 1976 the United States Congress passed the Magnuson Fishery Conservation and Management Act. While the opportunity for better management of our fisheries has been the most valuable outcome of this act, one of the principal stimulants to its passage was a desire to stop foreign fishing off the coasts of this country.

PRESSURES FROM FOREIGN FISHING

Few ocean issues of recent years have generated more heated emotion than the presence of foreign fishing vessels off the shores of other nations.

United States tuna vessels have been seized off Peru and Ecuador; British trawlers were rammed by Icelandic patrol boats in the famous "cod war;" the presence of Japanese tuna vessels in every ocean in the world has caused abrasive reaction in the affected nations. And United States fishermen and the public in general have been alarmed and angered by foreign fishing vessels off American coasts. In this country, inflammatory terms like "fish pirates" and "vacuum cleaner fishing" have been flung freely in the press. Most or all ills of the commercial and sport fishermen have at one time or another been blamed on foreign fleets.

Obviously that position overstates the case, since excessive exploitation by our own fishermen, as well as pollution and a great many other economic and social problems, are also responsible for the general lack of growth and economic viability of the United States fishing industry. Yet foreign fishing has certainly been one significant factor. Foreign catches off American coasts were small before 1960, but they rose so fast thereafter that they reached 4.4 mmt in 1975—nearly twice the U.S. commercial catch. In 1976, seventeen foreign nations operated more than 2,700 vessels off the United States; most were from Japan and the Soviet Union.

This fishing has had damaging effects on some fish stocks. For example, on the Atlantic coast very heavy Russian and Polish fishing was the major factor in the collapse of the haddock stocks, which had previously

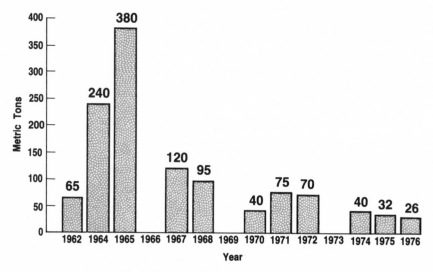

Fig. 6. Rise and Fall of Pacific Ocean Perch

supported a large fishery. Off the California coast, the incidental catch of halibut by foreign trawlers has reduced its abundance to such low levels that the results of careful management by the United States and Canada over forty-five years are jeopardized. Then, Soviet, Japanese, and other vessels off the coasts of Washington, Oregon, and California have fished so hard on ocean perch and other rockfishes that these species are now depleted. The Alaska pollock, one of the greatest stocks of fish in the world, was reduced to an overfished state in the space of ten years, between 1964 and 1974, entirely by foreign fishing.

Who Owns the Sea?

So the concerns that are felt so deeply about the presence of foreign fishing vessels off our shores have been to a large extent justified. But it is important to note that this fishing was perfectly legal since it was conducted outside our twelve-mile fishery conservation zone (aside from occasional deliberate or accidental incursions inside that limit). This leads us to one of the most difficult issues in all of ocean affairs, namely, who owns the sea? The dispute involves a bewildering complex of problems, including freedom of passage for ships; access to mineral resources of the ocean floor, such as oil and manganese nodules; control of pollution; freedom of scientific research—and not least, the right to exploit fishery resources and the responsibility to conserve them. A long series of United Nations conferences on the law of the sea has been held in attempts by the nations of the world to resolve these issues, but they have been so complex and intertangled that no agreement has been reached.

Interestingly, as complex as it is, the issue of fishing rights has been one on which agreement has come closest. This is partly because the disputes have been thoroughly aired, and partial solutions have been arrived at by forthright unilateral actions of many countries. This has resulted in what amounts to de facto, if not universally accepted, international practice. One of the most important of such actions has been the very widespread assumption of coastal nation control over fisheries out to 200 miles. This was started as early as 1947 by Peru, Chile, and Ecuador, and by now most principal maritime nations have either extended their jurisdiction over fisheries or have accepted this concept, however reluctantly in some cases. The United States action in adopting its own 200-mile conservation zone in 1976 changed the character of our fisheries more profoundly than any other event in the history of our country. This placed fisheries under

U.S. control in 2.2 million square miles of ocean, containing 10-20 percent of the world's fishery resources. The significance of this comes through partly when you realize that our fishermen catch only 4-5 percent of the world's fish harvest.

THE 200-MILE FISHERY CONSERVATION ZONE

Pressures in addition to those imposed by foreign fishing helped persuade the United States to proclaim its 200-mile fishery conservation zone. These were associated with the inadequacy of fishery management and conservation in this country, one result of which was that while the world as a whole had tripled its fish catch in the thirty years since 1945, the United States harvest had been stuck at virtually the same level. From second rank among the world's fishing nations, the United States had sunk to fifth or sixth. The United States lacked any unified management, the states being left to their own individual conservation action or inaction. But most fish stocks are shared by more than one state, and the general lack of cooperation among states has resulted in most cases in inadequate conservation, or none at all. This problem has been especially damaging on the Atlantic coast, where so many states are involved, but the Pacific states have not escaped the unfortunate consequences of this policy.

Hence the Fishery Conservation and Management Act of 1976 not only provided the tools for controlling foreign fishing; it established for the first time in United States history the means to provide regional fishery management. Many people think that this aspect of the act will eventually be more important than its control of foreign fishing. Domestic conservation is being carried out chiefly through eight Regional Fishery Management Councils, whose responsibility is to develop management plans for the nation's fisheries. The councils consist predominantly of local people with knowledge of regional conditions. The plans they develop are reviewed by the Secretary of Commerce to ensure that certain national standards enunciated in the act are met. Already evidence shows that management plans developed by the councils are beginning to restore and stabilize damaged fish stocks.

PRINCIPLES CONTROLLING FOREIGN FISHING

But let us return to the control of foreign fishing. The new act does not prohibit such fishing, but it does establish strict limits and regulations.

The act operates under three principles. The first and most important of these is that regulations must provide for the conservation and restoration of fish stocks. This means that limits will be placed on the amount of fish caught by U.S. and foreign fishermen *combined*. In most cases this has meant smaller catches for foreign fishermen than in previous years, both because conservation rules have reduced allowable harvests in most fisheries and because Americans are catching more fish.

A second principle is that in any fishery where Americans can catch the total quota, they will be allowed to do so. Only if they do not reach the quota will any fish be available to foreign fishermen.

A third principle under which the Fishery Conservation and Management Act operates is that the level of exploitation must take into account more than simply the maximum weight of fish that the stock can supply without biological damage. Economic and social factors must also be considered, including the maximum economic return to society from this activity, along with recreational satisfaction. The result to be sought is called "optimum yield," as opposed to the older concept of "maximum sustainable yield." One clear winner from this concept is the sport fishermen, whose activities and needs must be taken into account in an explicit and assertive way.

INTERNATIONAL COOPERATION

The fact that the new law does permit foreign fishing is evidence that the United States is adhering to the principles expressed by nearly all nations in the U.N. law of the sea negotiations, which state clearly that international fishery conservation regimes should provide for the fullest possible use of fish for food and other purposes, and that if the nation off whose coast the fish reside cannot exploit them fully, other nations must be allowed to do so. At the same time, under our new law, foreign fishing is permitted only under strict rules. The foreign country desiring to fish in the U.S. 200-mile zone must sign an agreement in which it acknowledges the authority of the United States to control fishing in the zone. Second, the foreign vessels must pay fees. Third, foreign vessels must adhere to all conservation regulations, including the reporting of catches and levels of fishing effort.

In the first years of the act the system has operated reasonably smoothly, considering its newness and complexity. Certainly there have been crises and delays, and vigorous complaints by some sectors of the

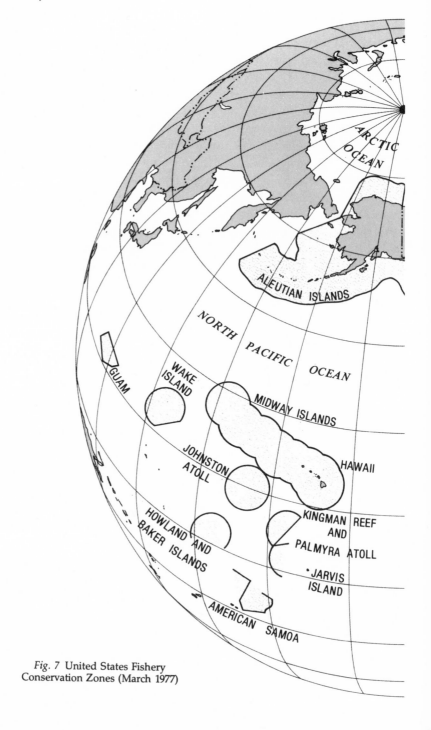

Fig. 7 United States Fishery
Conservation Zones (March 1977)

industry about government actions. The regulating process has been slow, and there is a feeling that federal authority may be too pervasive—a feeling shared by many federal people themselves. But on the whole, the intent of the act is being carried out.

In the first place, overfishing has diminished. The foreign catch in 1979 was 1.6 mmt, and this compares with catches of 2.72 mmt in 1974 and 3.63 mmt in 1972. In 1980 between $12 million and $13 million was collected from foreign fleets in fees, compared with $11 million in 1979. Fines in 1980, most assessed for reporting smaller amounts than actually caught or for mis-identifying the species caught, totaled $3,755,000; this compares with $958,500 in 1979.

American catches increased to a record high of 2.8 mmt in 1979, and that year the United States ranked fourth among fishery nations.

How Much Food from the Sea?

In summary, it appears that we will *not* be able to get as much food from the sea as from the land. This will not be because of lack of trying, but because of the way in which the marine ecosystem operates, producing relatively smaller amounts of usable food than the land. Yet the ocean can yield far more fish and other food than we take now. From traditional species alone, a maximum of perhaps 100 mmt can be harvested— compared with approximately 65 mmt at present. The upper limit of non-traditional species may be something like 600 mmt, nearly ten times current world harvests. The amount to be derived from aquaculture is even harder to guess than the other numbers, since the total depends to an important degree on the amount of effort and investment we are willing to expend, and on our ability to solve complex social and economic problems. The worldwide yield from aquaculture in the next decade or so could be about 60 mmt, close to the present world fish catch.

Whether we ever reach these potentials depends on several things:

- how we rank the priorities of our society;
- whether we are willing and able to protect the ocean environment so that the food fish stocks are not destroyed;
- whether we can develop the necessary skill and determination to conserve our living ocean resources; and
- whether we can find an appropriate balance between production and use of the fishery resources.

I am optimistic that we can achieve at least part of this difficult and complex set of goals. I am encourged by events of recent years, principally the development of a new ethic demanding better guardianship of our environment and its creatures. I am hopeful that this is leading us closer to achievement of optimum use of the sea, which will simultaneously maintain its beauty, protect its living populations, use its resources rationally, and distribute these resources fairly.

Finally, I am hopeful that this new ethic is leading not only to a greater measure of multiple benefits to our own people, but to greater gifts to all mankind.

Images of the Sea: The Ocean and Culture

John P. Craven

Break, break, break,
On thy cold gray stones, O Sea!
And I would that my tongue could utter
The thoughts that arise in me.[1]

The ocean—the other world of our earthly planet.

The physical characteristics of this wet, fluid, salty, opaque environment are so different from the characteristics of the land that the behavior of every living creature must dramatically adapt in order to survive in the watery element.

As we begin to understand the physical nature of the ocean, we begin to understand the weather, the climate, the limits on ships and submarines and floating structures, the ocean's yield of animal and vegetable protein, its harvest of minerals, its potential for recreation and living.

Should we not also be able to derive the nature of the culture of those who live in harmony with the sea—their music, their art, and their poetry?

What are the characteristics of the sights and sounds of the sea that make them instantly identifiable as born of the ocean? What are those unique properties of the ocean that constrain, shape, and motivate artists and artisans to a creativity that incorporates that strange melancholy and sense of loneliness of the sea?

> . . . From the long line of spray
> Where the sea meets the moon-blanched land,
> Listen! you hear the grating roar
> Of pebbles which the waves draw back, and fling,
> At their return, up the high strand,
> Begin, and cease, and then again begin,
> With tremulous cadence slow, and bring
> The eternal note of sadness in.[2]

What awesome force and power exists in the ocean environment that men's impotence before its perils is uppermost in the mind of the poet and the artist?

> Roll on, thou deep and dark-blue ocean, roll!
> Ten thousand fleets sweep over thee in vain;
> Man marks the earth with ruin, his control
> Stops with the shore.[3]

What rewards and riches does the ocean yield that men will leave home and family to experience months, even years of loneliness, and will risk the perils of pirates, of way and of the storm? And why is this theme so important to poets and artists?

> Quinquereme of Nineveh from distant Ophir,
> Rowing home to haven in sunny Palestine,
> With a cargo of ivory,
> And apes and peacocks,
> Sandalwood, cedarwood, and sweet white wine.
>
> Stately Spanish galleon coming from the Isthmus,
> Dipping through the Tropics by the palm-green shores,
> With a cargo of diamonds,
> Emeralds, amethysts,
> Topazes, and cinnamon, and gold moidores.
>
> Dirty British coaster with a salt-caked smoke stack,
> Butting through the Channel in the mad March days,
> With a cargo of Tyne coal,
> Road-rails, pig-lead,
> Firewood, iron-ware, and cheap tin trays.[4]

Why are the artistic themes of the ocean so few and so intense? Against the perils of the sea, the riches of the sea, the beauty of the sea, the loneliness of the male society of seamen, and their delayed returns and sudden departures from wives and sweethearts, all other themes seem secondary. And yet the ocean is but a place, just as the land is a place, and all the vocations and avocations of mankind on land have their counterpart in the ocean. Oceanography, for example, is not a unique science, but the oceanic application of all earth sciences. Ocean engineering is the sum of mechanical, civil, electrical, and chemical engineering. Ocean law is simply ordinary law applied to ocean conditions. Food from the sea employs the same range of techniques and husbandries as food from the land; the fisherman is but a hunter; the farmer of the sea cultivates seaweeds and sea vegetables, oysters, clams, catfish, prawns, trout, and yellowtail.

Shelter is no different. The ocean has its shacks and shanties—the raft and pole communities of the Philippines; its mobile homes—the Chinese junk; and its condominiums—the luxury yachts of the affluent.

Transport by sea parallels transport by land in variety; if not as fast, it is the most economical and carries the largest cargoes. Its variety ranges from the supertanker of 500,000 tons through that endangered species, the majestic ocean liner, through the new breed of hydrofoil, hovercraft, and swath ships, to the timeless sailboat and outrigger canoe.

Truly oceanic peoples, such as the Hawaiians, have recognized this commonality between land and sea. Its fundamental truth is embodied in *The Kumulipo,* the Hawaiian chant for the origin of life:

> Man for the narrow stream, woman for the broad stream.
> Born was the tough seagrass living in the sea,
> Guarded by the tough landgrass living on land.

> Man for the narrow stream, woman for the broad stream.
> Born was the ko'ele seaweed living in the sea,
> Guarded by the long-jointed sugarcane, the ko'ele'ele,
>   living on land.

> Man for the narrow stream, woman for the broad stream.
> Born was the Long-one living at sea,
> Guarded by the Long-torch living on land.

Since all of man's activities can be carried out on land or sea, then the uniqueness of the sea must be found in something other than the occupations and avocations of the water society. It must be found in the dramatically different physical properties of the sea—the absence of hills, of a firm foundation; the abundance of water, the presence of salt; the colors, the sounds; the weather.

Let us examine these unique physical properties of the sea as they relate to its art, its music, its poetry, and its literature.

Constraints of Nature on Art

Visually, the oceanic stage is stark and spare: the surface of the sea, the horizon, the sky, the clouds, the sun or the moon. The lighting is simple and direct: the single floodlight of the sun or its reflection from the moon.

> All in a hot and copper sky
> The bloody Sun, at noon,
> Right up above the mast did stand,
> No bigger than the Moon.[5]

LIGHT AND COLOR

In fact, the sun is not bloody or red, but is an intense globe of radiant energy, emitting a full spectrum of radiation, all the optical spectrum at an intensity too great to be viewed by the naked eye and extending well beyond the ultraviolet and infrared at intensities which can sear the skin and alter genes.

To the astronaut, the sun is a single bright spot in a black sky, but to earth-bound mortals, the atmosphere, the clouds, the land, and the sea refract, reflect, scatter, and absorb the sun's rays to produce the full panoply of light and color that characterizes our planet.

As we look at the cloudless sky, it appears blue. This is because our atmosphere contains oxygen molecules that are just the right size to scatter randomly the blue, and only the blue, portion of the sun's light. Thus the basic lighting of our set is a combination of diffuse blue light and a white spotlight.

The atmosphere consists of molecules of oxygen, nitrogen, carbon dioxide, and water vapor. In addition, it contains fine particles of matter, some generated by man's industries. But the greatest quantity of atmospheric particles is the oceanic salts which are carried into the air by seaspray. These particles provide the nucleus on which molecules of water vapor condense to form droplets of water or crystals of ice. In the aggregate, these droplets form the clouds of the sky and act as both reflectors and screens to re-radiate the direct light of the sun. As a consequence, daytime clouds are white or gray depending on the amount of light transmitted and the orientation of the sun.

The surface of the sea is illuminated by both sun and sky; a portion of the light is reflected and a portion is refracted into the water. The reflected light is blue from the light of the sky. Also contributing to the color of the sea is the light that is backscattered from the ocean depth. However, water is highly absorbent of the full spectrum except for a narrow band of blue-green. As very little of this returns from the deep ocean, the surface of deep ocean is dark blue. If the bottom is shallow, as for the coral reef or the sand bar, the light so reflected will give a green color to the water; or, if the wake of a ship places bubble reflectors at a depth of ten to twenty feet below the surface, the water will appear green; the face of a wave through which sunlight has been transmitted will also appear green. We can thus distinguish between shallow and deep water by the color of the surface. The color of the ocean can also be changed by biologics, as is the case for the "red tide," but most biologics reflect yellow or yellow-green. Thus the color of water that is highly eutrophied is that of green pea soup.

MOTION AND SHAPE

Equally dominant in determining the optical constraints on our oceanic picture is the shape of the sea surface. In sheltered bays or lakes where there is no wind, the calm and undisturbed surface of the water acts as a perfect reflector. The artist who depicts a mountain lake has but to depict the appropriate reflected image (this is not a mirror image) in order to simulate the surface of the lake. When there is wind and a stretch of water over which it can act, then the surface will be disturbed, and reflected images will be distorted or disappear.

The first wavelets to appear are capillary waves. These give a satin sheen to the water surface. At higher wind velocities, small gravity waves or ripples appear. Each ripple or wave has concave and convex surfaces. The concave surface acts as a spherical mirror to concentrate the light from the sun. As each wavelet changes slope and phase, a glitter phenomenon is produced in which the sea seems to explode with light, a brilliant shimmering glaze. When the fetch is large and the winds moderate, then the waves are too long to be effective as sun mirrors. At such times, the sea presents a monochromatic, monolithic appearance, with the deep dark blues modulated by the blue-green of the faces of the waves. When the wind velocity exceeds fifteen knots—not uncommon in the open ocean—the crests of the waves become unstable and break in a cascade of droplets. These droplets, like the droplets in a cloud, form multiple reflectors for the sunlight, and thus appear white.

The ocean world for the daytime artist is thus blue/blue-green/white and gray. Pictures of our world from space clearly demonstrate this monochromatic feature of the ocean. We are all so familiar with this feature that we are surprised by ocean pictures in which the photographer has changed the blues to reds or yellows or browns or some other combination of non-oceanic color in order to achieve an interpretive effect.

OPTICAL PHENOMENA

This monochromatic aspect of the sea changes dramatically at sunrise and sunset. Artists and mariners are transfigured by the rosy-fingered dawn and blood-red sunset.

> Red sky at night, sailors' delight.
> Red sky at morning, sailors take warning.[6]

The very feature of "scattering," which makes the sky blue by day, eliminates this color at sunrise and sunset. At sunset we view the sun through an ever-increasing thickness of atmosphere. Almost all the blue light has been scattered forward to the west. As the sun sets, the remaining yellows and oranges are absorbed by the thicker layers of atmosphere, and only the reds and a small part of the green spectrum remains.

The light from the sun is further distorted by refraction in the atmosphere. The velocity of light is reduced in the dense atmosphere. Because of its wave-like nature, the wave front is bent as the light passes from one medium to another, and as a consequence the rays are bent. The green waves are bent less than the red. As a result we see a series of overlapping suns of differing color—a green sun at the top and a red sun at the bottom, with orange and yellow in between. As the sun sinks below a clear horizon, the upper limb can be seen as a green flash.

Many other optical phenomena are produced in atmospheres of layered density and in the presence of the rising or setting sun: when the sky is filled with clouds, the high cirrus and the low cumulus to serve as reflector and screen; when there are clouds of dust to scatter the red light of the sun; when the earth's shadow draws a curtain over the vault of heaven, and the oceanic set is an artist's delight, featuring crepuscular rays of the setting sun—layers of red and orange, rims of purple, and flashes of green over a darkening and deepening blue sea. When a distant island is on the horizon, diffracted by the atmosphere and wreathed in orographic clouds as it disappears and reappears in reality and mirage, then the perceptive but uneducated painter and poet can only ascribe God-like properties to the total scene.

> Hail, Sacred Isle, Dear land
> For distant shining.
> The mists beguiled by thy sunny strand
> From ocean chaplets to the gods are twining.[7]

COLORS ASHORE

Just as the basic colors of the ocean are blue and green, the basic colors of the seashore are white and brown and gray. The sands of the seashore are mostly composed of weathered rocks, primarily quartz, which, rounded and polished by years of erosion, are now translucent reflectors giving a pinkish white cast to the beach. Calcareous fragments of seashells and coral skeletons are a major fraction of many beaches. Some greens in the form of glauconite or reds from iron oxide will appear, but with rare exception the weathering, polishing, and mixing of sands give an overall whiteness to the beach which the greens, browns, and reds of individual grains may belie.

The bright, man-introduced colors of painted boats, piers, and wharves do not last long under bleaching sun and saltwater, and the driftwoods—the flotsam and jetsam of the shore—are bone gray. The uneroded rocks jutting into the sea—basalts, shales, sandstones—are themselves black or gray or reddish brown.

THE SEA SHAPES THE SHIP

Thus the nature of color and light of the sea and seashore constrains the artist in the temper and tone of his palette. It is no wonder that the artist will quickly introduce the ship to provide opportunities for variety and freedom. But even sketches or caricature figures reveal that the shape of the ship is itself constrained by characteristics of the sea. The raked bow, full hull, and square transom have been dictated by the ocean and not by the artist. True, signal flags and pennants provide opportunities for color and line, but the overriding feature of the ship is that its form and color are determined by the physics of the sea. Sails must be airfoils which curve into a form that induces a rotation or circulation of the wind. Our eye finds these esthetic, but the shape of the topgallant, the direction in which flags and pennants point, and the catenaries that are assumed by ropes and cables are determined by the physics of the sea, not by the artist.

Of most significance is that ship stability requires the largest and heaviest portion of the ship to be at the ocean surface, and, to avoid topheaviness, masts and sails and superstructures must be of light and skeletal construction. These characteristics, added to the spot character of the sun, result in pyramidic drawings and paintings.

Sea Themes in Painting

When these optical constraints of the ocean are coupled with the themes of peril, reward, and loneliness, then the artist is ready for canvasses that are the quintessence of the sea. To demonstrate the commonality of such art, we recall three well-known paintings from different cultures and different eras: *The Great Wave* by Hokusai, one of Japan's most famous woodblock printers, a work of the early nineteenth century; *The Raft of the "Medusa"*, an equally famous painting of the Napoleonic era, by Gericault; and the modern painting *The Seafarer* (often called "Sinbad the Sailor") by Paul Klee. Each painting can be described in almost identical words.

The overall structure of Hokusai's *The Great Wave* is pyramidic, the ocean forming the base of the pyramid, the crest of the wave its apex, the pyramid reinforced by the profile of Mount Fuji. Boats engulfed by the wave form the mid-portion of the pyramid. The overriding theme is the peril and discomfiture of the men who have set out to reap the rewards of the sea and find themselves in a situation where the expectation of reward is replaced by the hope of survival.

The overall structure of *The Raft of the "Medusa"* is likewise pyramidic, the ocean forming the base of the pyramid, the mast and seaman's head forming the apex, the bodies of the living and the dead forming the upper mid-section, and the great wave and the engulfed raft forming the lower mid-section of the pyramid. Again the theme is the piteous plight of men whose expectation of reward from the sea has been replaced by the desperate hope of survival.

In *The Seafarer*, the ocean again forms the base of the pyramid, the top of Sinbad's spear and his hat form the apex, the ship and the predators of the deep form the lower mid-section, and the great wave engulfing the boat forms the upper mid-section of the pyramid. Once more the search for adventure and reward is counter-balanced by the struggle for survival.

These three pictures are not unique. Rembrandt's classic *Storm on the Sea of Galilee* is another for which the description is the same. Here again the artist has caught the terror of men who fear they will not survive, and, like the storm-tossed seamen in the other paintings, would seem to appeal in their anguish, "O Lord, Thy ocean is so big and our raft is so small."

Sea Themes in Music

The music of the sea is no less constrained. The composer is forced to imitate the sounds of the sea and the rhythms of the sea, if he or she is to achieve an identifiable effect.

The most prominent sound of the seashore must be the call of the seagull. Its high frequency cry results from the small size of its vocal apparatus and the resonant cavity which the bird employs to amplify its sounds. Nevertheless, other marine creatures capable of making low frequency sounds, such as the whale and the dolphin, frequently emit cries in the frequency range of the gull. These calls solve a basic problem for gulls in navigating at sea. In the water or in fog, visibility is nil, and it is necessary to resort to sound instead of sight for object avoidance and navigation. Low frequency sounds travel long distances but the direction from which they come is uncertain. High frequency sounds travel but a short distance, but the direction of their origin can be more precisely determined. Thus, the whale and the porpoise use both high frequency sound for localization and the lowest sounds of which they are capable for long distance communication. Man has intuitively imitated the whale in the foghorn and bell buoy. The low frequency of the foghorn is a long distance warning of impending danger, while the high frequency sound of the bell buoy precisely locates the limits of the channel. Similarly, the Navy employs low frequency and high frequency sonars for detection and localization.

IMITATION OF SEA SOUNDS

The most obvious use of these sounds in music is through direct imitation. This has been done by Richard Rodgers in his score for the 1952 film *Victory at Sea*, where the sounds of seagulls, of sonar, and of guns are employed as part of the musical composition. A more sophisticated and exotic use of the vocal sounds of the sea has been employed in Hovhaness' symphonic tone poem *And God Created Great Whales*. The actual songs of the great whales are employed by him as an integral part of this impressive work.

We do not need to observe water very long to discover that the sounds and rhythms of water are a function of the size and scale of the physical phenomena. Small bubbles of air or of water, such as raindrops, make high frequency sounds. Thus, the bubbles of the brook are high-pitched, and the belches of great whales are low-pitched. The rhythms are similarly altered. We should expect that composers would intuitively simulate the frequencies and rhythms of the water environment when composing programmatic music. Sure enough, Saint-Saëns's "Aquarium," depicting little fish making little bubbles, utilizes high frequency sound and rapid rhythms. Schubert's "Trout" replicates the leap of that spirited fish from a stream.

The decrease in pitch and tempo as we move from a small body of water to a large one is superbly accomplished by Smetana in his depiction of the River Moldau. The bubble and splash frequencies of the upper reaches of the stream are marvelously simulated in the opening bars. Then the tempo changes to an ever-slowing, majestic theme: the river forming broad, sullen eddies as it grows ever wider and deeper.

WIND SOUNDS

The sounds of the wind are as important as the sounds of the sea itself in musical portrayal, but they are quite different. The least musical is turbulence noise like blowing on a microphone. Termed "white noise" by sound engineers, it contains all frequencies. The most musical sounds are the Aeolian sounds of wind in the rigging. As the wind passes over a taut rope, it generates vortex trails whose frequency is a function of the diameter of the rigging and the velocity of the wind. A one-inch rope in a ten-knot wind will produce a vortex sheet having the frequency of the orchestra concert A. A doubling of the velocity will raise the sound an octave. As winds gust from ten to sixty knots in a gale, the one-inch rigging will hum a song ranging over six octaves. This song will be amplified when the lanyards are in tune with the vortex frequency, or when the vortices are shed over the openings of hatches or ports in the ship. Numerous Helmholtz resonators (or "little brown jugs") exist on ships or in the cavities of limestone cliffs to amplify the siren song of the wind. Music which rises and falls over the octaves as in gusts are often characterized as "storm or tempest pieces." Examples: the Chopin etude called "The Winter Wind" and Beethoven's "Tempest" sonata.

Quite clearly, the sound of wind and wave are different, the wave being periodic and rhythmic with a modest range in pitch frequency, and the wind occurring in bursts and gusts and ranging over a broad spectrum of frequencies. This dialogue between wind and wave is captured by Debussy in the third movement of the most famous piece of ocean music ever written—*La Mer*.

Words and Music

When composers attempt to range beyond these imitations of sea sounds to depict other oceanic themes, they run into great difficulty. It is not surprising, therefore, that many, if not most, serious symphonic pieces about the ocean employ voices and poetry as essential elements of the composition. Vaughan Williams' *Sea Symphony* features the epic poems of Walt Whitman, *Sea-Drift* and *Passage to India*. Delius employs the same poetry in his tone poem, *Sea-drift*. Sir Edward Elgar invokes the poetry of Elizabeth Barrett Browning in his *Sea Pictures*. And Samuel Barber has set his *Song of the Sea* to Matthew Arnold's *Dover Beach*.

SEA CHANTEYS

Sea songs and sea poetry are intermingled with the rhythm of work tasks at sea; the raising of sail and the turn of the windlass are themselves matched to the motion of the sea and the natural frequencies of the ship. Poetry of the sea naturally sings itself, and the sea chantey is as good spoken as sung. Indeed, in the sea chantey, opportunity exists for expressing the themes of the sea.

Although many of the sea chanteys relate to work tasks or to life at sea, the great majority are concerned with the male-female relationships of the seaman. The chantey "Haul Away, Joe" decries the cultural idiosyncracies of the girl in each port—a Dutch girl, an Irish girl, and so on, and the frustration of competition with "the Portugee." "Blow the Man Down" vents the frustrated aggression of the sailor lured by feminine wiles only to discover that he has been shanghaied to another ship for another voyage to a new culture and a new clime. "Leave Her, Johnny, Leave Her" describes those conditions in which the seaman voluntarily leaves his sweetheart to go to sea:

> Oh, the times are hard and the wages low.
> I'll pack my bags and go below.

Variations on these themes appear in "Shenandoah," "Johnny Baker," "The Rio Grande," and "Nancy Lee." The other side of the relationship is expressed in "Tom's Gone to Ilo":

> Oh, I love Tom and he loves me;
> He thinks of me when on the sea.

The conditioning process of transiency develops a salty independence well-expressed in one of the earliest of sea chanteys, written by William Shakespeare for his play *The Tempest:*

> The master, the swabber, the boatswain and I,
>   The gunner and his mate
> Loved Mall, Meg and Marion and Margery,
>   But none of us cared for Kate;
>   For she had a tongue with a tang,
>   Would cry to a sailor, Go hang!
> She loved not the savour of tar nor of pitch,
> Yet a tailor might scratch her where'er she did itch:
>   Then to sea, boys, and let her go hang!

SEAMEN'S HYMNS

The sea chantey developed and died in the eighteenth and nineteenth centuries. The latter decades of the nineteenth century saw religious revival, and in every port a seaman's mission became haven for sobering up after the first night ashore, and a place for food and nourishment for the body and the soul. The chantey was replaced by the seaman's hymns, all analogizing heaven as a safe port, Jesus as the pilot, and death as the last journey out to sea. Others were more reverent.

> Jesus, Savior, pilot me
> Over life's tempestuous sea;
> Unknown waves before me roll,
> Hiding rock and treacherous shoal;
> Chart and compass come from thee;
> Jesus, Savior, pilot me.

> When at last I near the shore,
> And the fearful breakers roar
> 'Twixt me and the peaceful rest,
> Then, while leaning on thy breast,
> May I hear thee say to me,
> "Fear not, I will pilot thee."[8]

Some were even literary; Tennyson's "Crossing the Bar" is the epitome of the seaman's anthem.

> Sunset and evening star,
>   And one clear call for me!
> And may there be no moaning at the bar,
>   When I put out to sea,
>
> But such a tide as moving seems asleep,
>   Too full for sound and foam,
> When that which drew from out the boundless deep
>   Turns again home.
>
> Twilight and evening bell,
>   And after that the dark!
> And may there be no sadness of farewell
>   When I embark;
>
> For tho' from out our bourne of Time and Place
>   The flood may bear me far,
> I hope to see my Pilot face to face
>   When I have crost the bar.

The Sea in Literature

The salty, "scurvy tune" from Shakespeare's *The Tempest* referred to earlier is complemented in that same play by one of the most perceptive poems of the deep that has ever been written—a poem that could have equally well been written by a modern deep-sea diver.

> Full fathom five thy father lies;
>   Of his bones are coral made;
> Those are pearls that were his eyes:
>   Nothing of him that doth fade
> But doth suffer a sea-change
> Into something rich and strange.
> Sea-nymphs hourly ring his knell:
> Hark! now I hear them—Ding-dong, bell.

These poems were the forerunners of Kipling and Masefield and Tennyson. The full flavor of ocean themes is captured in Kipling's last verse of *The Bell Buoy:*

> I dip and I surge and I swing
>   In the rip of the racing tide,
> By the gates of doom I sing,

On the horns of death I ride.
A ship-length overside,
Between the course and the sand,
Fretted and bound I bide
Peril whereof I cry.
Would I change with my brother
    a league inland?
(Shoal! 'Ware shoal!) Not I!

The sampling of great poems of the sea could continue: John Donne's *The Storme*, epitomizing dread and seasickness ("So violent, yet long these furies be / That though thine absence sterve me, I wish not thee"); or John Milton's *Lycidas*, an elegy for a friend lost at sea ("Look homeward Angel now, and melt with ruth. / And, O ye Dolphins, waft the hapless youth. / Weep no more, woeful Shepherds weep no more / For Lycidas your sorrow is not dead, / Sunk though he be beneath the watry floor, / So sinks the day-star in the Ocean bed.")

Or Coleridge or Tennyson or Masefield or Longfellow, or Oliver Wendell Holmes: ("Build thee more stately mansions, O my soul, . . . Till thou at length art free, / Leaving thine outgrown shell by life's unresting sea!")[9]

The oceanic themes of the painter, the musician, and the poet are replicated over and over in the literature of the sea. The Biblical story of Jonah; the cry of the Psalmist ("Out of the depths have I cried unto thee, O Lord. . . . They that go down to the sea in ships, that do business in great waters, these see the works of the Lord and his wonders in the deep"); and the saga of Ulysses, the voyager exposed to the seductive songs of the Sirens, to the terrible jaws of Scylla and the caves and whirlpools of Charybdis, to storm and tempest, fire and foe, to endless wanderings condemned—from earliest times the sea has inspired the singer of songs and the teller of tales.

These themes continue in the plays of Shakespeare, in *The Tempest* and *The Merchant of Venice*, and in modern times in the stories of Melville. His *Moby Dick* is nought but a collection of 125 of the finest essays on life at sea. Variations of the yarns of these greatest of all sea stories are found in Hemingway's *Old Man and the Sea*, in the Nordhoff and Hall trilogy *Mutiny on the Bounty*, *Men Against the Sea*, and *Pitcairn's Island*, in Richard Henry Dana's autobiographical *Two Years Before the Mast*, in Kipling's *Captains Courageous*—the list is endless, even though the themes are finite.

Blending the Arts of the Sea

If one looks for an art form in which the music, art, and poetry of the sea would come together, it is to be found in the opera. Indeed, it has there occurred, but the technical difficulties of reproducing a stormy sea and a pitching ship on a landlocked stage have limited this art form to tales of the port. Wagner's *The Flying Dutchman* is the one oceanic opera that has most influenced artists and poets, but it has not been until modern times that the true opera of the sea has appeared in Benjamin Britten's great works *Billy Budd* and *Peter Grimes*.

Peter Grimes is a classic tale of a socially isolated mariner who must interact with the citizens of his land-oriented borough in order to obtain a young apprentice. At the outset and at the conclusion of the opera, one and then another of his novitiates are claimed by the sea, as is Peter Grimes himself in his final exile from a society which, save for one caring female, does not understand his obsession.

Britten binds the scenes of the opera by a series of interludes. These "Four Sea Interludes" have been rearranged as a tone poem which tells in music the eternal story of the sea. The imaginative reader may thus create in his mind's ear and eye the synthesis of the music, art, and literature of the sea.

As one listens to the music of Britten, its theme is all too obvious—that of the tempest. The imagined story must be of a ship laden with rich cargoes from a distant land, among its crew a man whose destiny is tragedy. The ship is caught in a storm just short of its home port, and is wrecked upon its native shore. From that strand, wives, sweethearts, and friends watch helplessly. Other brave souls also of tragic proportion put to sea in a heroic but fatal attempt at rescue. All the terror, pathos, helplessness of man against the sea is depicted in the music.

As one listens, the mind also recalls the great paintings of the sea, and one can visualize the prescient calm of Whistler's mist-clouded seascapes, one can feel the surge of the oncoming storm in the paintings of Winslow Homer, its fury in the struggles between ship and sea depicted by Turner, and its final all-destroying wrath in the sun-russeted furies of Ryder.

The effect can be heightened by reading aloud a storm scene from the pen of one of the writers of the sea. Any author could be chosen— Shakespeare, Cooper, Melville, Conrad, Wouk—but a most dramatic reading comes from the works of Dickens, whose poetic Victorian prose captures the rich imagery required to focus the imagination on the terrors of the sea.

On reading aloud, one will find that the storm scene from *David Copperfield* is in near perfect synchronism with the music from *Peter Grimes*. Begin with the last six minutes and nine seconds of the Britten work. The sostenuto calm before the storm (except when ominously interrupted by the metronomic sound of a bell buoy or a distant flash of lightning) suspends apprehension until the sudden onset of the storm hits with cascading crescendoes of "wind" music. In the words of Charles Dickens:

> The tremendous sea itself, when I could find sufficient pause to look at it, in the agitation of the blinding wind, the flying stones and sand, and the awful noise, confounded me. [*Violins in stairstep ascent and descent through the octaves, overlaying the compulsive pounding of percussion.*] As the high water walls came rolling in, and at their highest, tumbled into surf, they looked as if the least would engulf the town. As the receding wave swept back with a hoarse roar, it seemed to scoop out deep caves in the beach, as if its purpose were to undermine the earth. When some white-headed billows thundered on, and dashed themselves to pieces before they reached the land, every fragment of the late whole seemed possessed by the full might of its wrath, rushing to be gathered to the composition of another monster. [*No less a description of the rushing of orchestral sound.*] Undulating hills were changed to valleys, undulating valleys (with a solitary storm-bird sometimes skimming through them) were lifted up to hills; masses of water shivered and shook the beach with a booming sound [*to the ceaseless pounding of the bass drum is added the bray of trombones, which pass their brazen cascade of sound to the horns and trumpets*]; every shape tumultuously rolled on, as soon as made, to change its shape and place, and beat another shape and place away [*the comma and semicolon cadences of the story match the measure and phrasing cadence of the sound*]; the ideal shore on the horizon, with its towers and buildings, rose and fell; the clouds flew fast and thick; I seemed to see a rending and upheaving of all nature. . . .
>
> "What is the matter?" I cried.
>
> "A wreck! Close by! . . . A schooner from Spain, or Portugal, laden with fruit and wine. Make haste, sir, if you want to see her! It's thought, down on the beach, she'll go to pieces every moment." . . .
>
> In the difficulty of hearing anything but wind and waves [*the music now presto fortissimo*] and in the crowd, and the unspeakable confusion, and my first breathless efforts to stand against the weather, I was so confused that I looked out to sea for the wreck, and saw nothing but the foaming heads of the great waves. A half-dressed boatman, standing next to me, [*the music relents*] pointed with his bare arm (a tatto'd arrow on it, pointing in the same direction) to the left. Then, O great heaven [*three musical exclamation points*] I saw it, close in upon us!

One mast was broken short off, six or eight feet from the deck, and lay over the side, entangled in a maze of sail and rigging [*a stilted staggering reel of violins*]; and all that ruin, as the ship rolled and beat—which she did without a moment's pause, and with a violence quite inconceivable—beat the side [*tympani*] as if it would stave it in. Some efforts were even then being made, to cut this portion of the wreck away; for, as the ship, which was broadside on, turned towards us in her rolling [*the music moderates, maintaining a sustained rumble in the bass*] I plainly descried her people at work with axes, especially one active figure with long curling hair, conspicuous among the rest. But, a great cry [*the music intensifies*] which was audible even above the wind and water, rose from the shore at this moment; the sea, sweeping over the rolling wreck, made a clean breach, and carried men, spars, casks, planks, bulwarks, heaps of such toys, into the boiling surge.

The second mast was yet standing, with the rags of a rent sail, and a wild confusion of broken cordage flapping to and fro. [*The music subsides again.*] The ship had struck once, the boatman hoarsely said in my ear, and then lifted in and struck again. I understood him to add that she was parting amidships, and I could readily suppose so, for the rolling and the beating were too tremendous for any human work to suffer long. As he spoke, there was another great cry of pity from the beach [*the interlude now surges, now pulsates to the deathly rhythms of castanets*]; four men arose with the wreck out of the deep, clinging to the rigging of the remaining mast; uppermost, the active figure with the curling hair. [*For a moment there is a lull, an epitaphic calm.*]

There was a bell on board; and as the ship rolled and dashed [*the storm music reinterpolates*] like a desperate creature driven mad, now showing us the whole sweep of her deck, as she turned on her beam-ends toward the shore, now nothing but her keel, as she sprung wildly over and towards the sea [*the penultimate quiet of spent fury*], the bell rang; and its sound, the knell of those unhappy men, was borne towards us on the wind. [*The music rises.*] Again we lost her, and again she rose. Two men were gone. [*The episode intensifies.*] The agony on shore increased. [*A tumultuous wail.*] Men groaned, and clasped their hands; women shrieked, and turned away their faces. [*One last uncontrolled orgasm of sound.*] Some ran wildly up and down along the beach, crying for help where no help could be. [*Four thunderclaps of doom—then silence.*]

The surviving mariner leaves these scenes of imagination, or—too often—these scenes of reality, vowing never to return to the sea again. The immutable physical forces of the ocean will forever doom the seaman to a life of peril and tragedy. But ever he will return, drawn by the remembered call of a young lad's uninhibited song:

> I must go down to the seas again,
> to the lonely sea and the sky,

And all I ask is a tall ship
and a star to steer her by,
And the wheel's kick and the wind's song
and the white sail's shaking,
And a grey mist on the sea's face,
and a grey dawn breaking.[10]

NOTES

1. Alfred, Lord Tennyson, "Break, Break, Break."
2. Matthew Arnold, "Dover Beach."
3. George, Lord Byron, "Childe Harold," Canto vi, st. 179.
4. John Masefield, "Cargoes."
5. Samuel Taylor Coleridge, "Rime of the Ancient Mariner."
6. Maxim derived from the Bible, Matthew 16:2–3.
7. Eduard Mörike, "Weyla's Song."
8. Edward Hopper and John E. Gould, "Jesus Savior, Pilot Me."
9. Oliver Wendell Holmes, "The Chambered Nautilus."
10. John Masefield, *"Sea Fever."*

The Yankee Mariner in the Next Two Decades

Don Walsh

"Futuristics" is a risky business. The futurist—or, indeed, anyone looking ahead and trying to foresee changes on the basis of present trends (as I do in this summing-up chapter)—is bound to be a prisoner of his or her own circumstances. As a result, virtually all prediction of the future is inaccurate to some degree. Only the degree is unknown. By the same token, some prediction will be *right* to some degree. So fear of being wrong is not a good argument for inaction. The implications of ongoing activities, contemplated in an orderly way, can suggest improvements in our present condition and perhaps help to bring about a more promising future than might have been expected.

The construction of a "perfect world scenario" is a useful drill. Undertaken properly, with help from the best experts, it can be a structured way of thinking beyond the short term. It is done all the time in the business world, where it makes the difference between tactical and strategic planning. The issue here is our nation's ocean future in the next two decades, for we know that much of what will happen in this area by the year 2000 will be the result of actions taken in the early 1980s.

Curiously enough, twenty years is hardly a future in uses of the sea. Twenty years is about the average life of a ship; military vessels often last up to twenty-five years. Nearly ten years are needed to develop an offshore oil and gas field and bring it into full production; its active producing lifetime, of course, depends on size of the field. An ocean mining system cannot be brought into being in less than five to seven years; once in service, it will have a life of about twenty years. In short, much of the American sea industry and sea power for the next two decades is being designed now; a twenty-year forecast has greater validity than might be thought.

Sea Power: Components and Foundations

As others have said earlier, this book is a study and analysis of the elements of national sea power, "sea power" meaning the sum total of our uses of the sea. Its essence is national security for the United States. One component is a balanced, healthy maritime trade, both import and export, with a substantial use of American-flag ships. Another is less reliance on foreign sources for materials needed to support our economy, and more reliance on oceans as the source of these materials; examples are gas and oil, food and drugs, and mineral resources. A third and major element, of course, is a strong navy that will protect American interests throughout the world.

Since the beginning of the republic, the United States has been a sea power. Often it has not done as well as it should, and the consequences have been traumatic. As several of our contributors have emphasized, the nation is currently in one of its down periods in this respect. Before exploring the future, we need to consider the sequential steps that make for sea power.

MARINE SCIENCE AND TECHNOLOGY

Essentially there are four steps. The first is marine science, the development of organized knowledge about the marine environment. The end point of marine science activity is predictive information that will serve the users of ocean space. This is true whether the information concerns commercially important fish stocks or the prediction of maritime weather to permit safer ship passages. This vital underlying foundation of sea use is often the first to be eliminated in periods of budget cutting. The reason is simple: marine science tends to deal in payoffs that may be several years away. It is more convenient to "mortgage the future" than to reduce present activity. That is part of the human condition and a tendency that will always be with us.

The second step is marine technology or ocean engineering—application of the engineering arts to ocean science and development of the technology to build machines that work in the oceans. It is interesting to note that almost every major field of engineering is found in the oceans. Even aeronautical engineering has its place; an advanced hydrofoil ship or surface-effect (air cushion) ship has aircraft aerodynamic structures, power plants, and flight control systems. The ocean is a hostile environment for both man and machine. The engineering challenges in ocean equipment and design are formidable.

ECONOMIC VIABILITY

But simply building machines to work in ocean space does not assure effective use of the sea. Work may be done, but whether the work is worthwhile depends on the economics of marine enterprise. This is the third step in sea power development—determining economic viability. It is essential to determine whether a certain ocean use will yield a product or service that is uniquely important or is economically competitive with a land equivalent. An example of the first is offshore gas and oil, which compete successfully with onshore energy development; we have seen the fraction of ocean production rise to about 20 percent of total production, and this fraction will increase as land resourses diminish. An example of the latter is the harvest of saltwater fish; in most places the ocean harvest is able to compete with terrestrial foods in the marketplace.

Since ocean use industries are businesses, their utility is determined by the marketplace. Better knowledge of resource locations, value, and renewability (where applicable) comes from marine science. The development of effective and efficient capture machines comes from ocean technology.

The forward march of these two fields bids the entrepreneur continuously to reevaluate resource development activity. Something that may have been unproductive and uneconomic becomes important and a source of profit as better harvesting techniques emerge.

Thus it is vital that we never fail to make the necessary investments to insure a healthy science and technology base for national uses of the ocean. Many will say this is the responsibility of the private sector. This is only partially true. Many basic research areas properly call for government participation—areas where risk is high or where the economic payoff is remote or ill-defined, or even where the capital expense is simply too great for private venture; in such areas, the risk must be shared by government and the private sector. The determination of proper programmatic balance is the stuff of which lively arguments are made. Needless to say, it is a dialogue that will never be laid to rest. And it should not be, since appropriate government/private sector relationships determine effective uses of ocean space.

PUBLIC POLICY AND OCEAN POLITICS

The role of government brings us to the fourth and final step in the development of sea power. This is public policy and ocean politics. One could simply define this area as "manmade constraints on uses of the sea." Constraints to this point have been determined by more or less immutable factors involved with science, technology, and economics. This makes them more easily subject to analysis than are the imperfections of how one (and one's government) governs these activities through policy decisions originating all the way from local to international authorities.

At the risk of irreverence I would suggest that we who are involved with the oceans know far more how to do things in the sea than we know about governing those actions. Our abilities in science and technology and our economic understanding are ten to fifteen years ahead of our political sophistication. For this reason, many of us who are in marine science, oceanography, and the economics of ocean use now devote many of our energies to ocean politics and policies. This is our "choke point" in national marine development, and as such we feel it should be the focus of greater energies.

Why a National Policy for Ocean Use?

Ocean policy consists of decisions, plans, and programs as well as an executive mechanism to develop and carry them out. It can exist at many levels, from local to international, and from highly developed maritime states to impoverished developing countries. But to a large extent, far-reaching national ocean policy is a fiction in the world today. This being the case, why should it be suggested that such a thing is needed by the United States? The answer lies in two broad areas. First, world dependence upon uses of the sea is increasing rapidly. There are ever more "players on the stage," and the occasions for international friction are becoming more frequent. Second, the diversity of ocean use has continuously grown since World War II, and this growth suggests many levels of conflict and competition at all levels of government.

"ROADMAP" OF SECTORAL POLICIES

Essentially, a national ocean policy provides a harmonizing "roadmap" of sectoral policies for determining priorities and resource allocations to ensure the greatest good for the most people. In international affairs, a nation's ocean policy can help assure its rights and the peaceful use of ocean space in harmony with other coastal states. This is done in the formulation of national foreign policies by the world's states, but by and large, such a comprehensive policy framework does not exist for the oceans. And as noted earlier, comprehensive national ocean policies are virtually non-existent in the world today. Some countries, such as Japan and the Soviet Union, come close. Others, such as the United States, France, and the United Kingdom, have sets of sectoral policies that deal with national ocean uses *in sum*, and there are many micro or sectoral policies in most other maritime states. These deal with matters of fisheries, maritime trade, and so on, and many are quite good and effective. Some even deal with both domestic and international concerns of that sector. But for the most part, sectoral policies are largely uncoordinated both within and without the nation originating them, and more and more frequently sectoral interests collide, resulting in conflict.

For example, the Georges Bank off northeastern United States presents a domestic conflict between fishing interests and offshore gas and oil operations. Both uses are essential to our nation, but lack of a national ocean policy has made difficult the adjudication of their respective complaints. This illustration involves not simply a national issue affecting adjacent U.S. coastal states. Foreign nations having treaty agreements to fish in our waters are also concerned about the future use of this most important fishing area. Canada is alert to any major pollution incident that might affect its nearby fishing grounds.

The existence of a U.S. national ocean policy would not necessarily prevent such conflicts, but it could help to anticipate the problems, and would certainly greatly help to resolve those difficulties that do arise. In other words, greater efficiencies in both national and international uses of the oceans could be achieved through development, maintenance, and implementation of a national ocean policy system for the United States.

PREDICTIONS AND PRIORITIES

Of overriding importance to the national interest, however, is yet another benefit to be gained from a national ocean policy structure, namely, its usefulness in allowing us to project and predict where the United States should be going, and helping to set priorities for getting there—the setting of goals and development of programs to achieve those goals. The simple fact is that we must realistically address our ocean future before that future arrives. Ocean activities require long lead time and require strategic planning that cannot be rushed. Since governments tend to be populated with short-term people at policy levels (presidential appointments and elected officials), long-term planning is difficult. But it has been done, with varying degrees of success, in the conduct of our nation's foreign policy, and it is to be hoped the same thing can be accomplished in ocean affairs.

EXECUTIVE MECHANISM ESSENTIAL

It should be emphasized here that a national ocean policy is not a fixed conceptual framework. It is a living, dynamic thing, and while the development of its fundamental shape and scope is important, even more important is the executive framework that will help it to develop and adjust to an ever-changing world environment involving other national sea powers. The executive mechanism must be shaped to ensure that policy decisions are carried out by the responsible agencies of government and that interagency and international conflicts are resolved swiftly and fairly.

No matter how complete our scientific knowledge of the marine environment, how elegant our engineering solutions, how rigorous our economic analysis, it is the political process that ultimately decides the issue in almost every case. If this process is in the hands of people lacking in understanding of the importance and manifestations of sea power, and if there is no ocean policy "roadmap" for guidance, then the quality of the decisions will, more often than not, be bad.

Fortunately, there is evidence of increasing intellectual concern with issues of ocean policy, how it is formulated, executed, and maintained. Scholars from the social sciences who specialize in analysis of policy, together with forward-thinking members of the "ocean community," are now beginning to form a cutting edge of thought in this area. This is not a phenomenon in the United States alone; it is emerging in other major sea powers as well. Within the United States we have seen development of an academic field of training in marine policy studies. The Institute for Marine and Coastal Studies at the University of Southern California, with which I am associated, now has a master's degree program in this area, and there are perhaps a half-dozen other such programs in this country. So both research and academic training are actually being done at a modest level. Much more, of course, remains to be done.

If this has seemed to belabor the question of national ocean policy and the interaction between science, technology, economics, and government, it comes from the absolute conviction that the future of the United States as a sea power demands that proper policy decisions be made *now*. To a large extent, these decisions are being deferred—or ignored. Many hands reach for the federal/public dollar. The national development of ocean activities is not and will not be exempt from competition within national priorities. A well-considered and integrated "map" for national uses of the sea, in the form of policy and its executive framework, will help insure that our nation remains a major sea power. Only thus will Yankee Mariners increase and prosper as the United States enters the twenty-first century.

Present and Future of American Sea Power

To understand where our nation should be going in the future, one must know where it stands today. Previous chapters have traced the development of the United States as a sea power from the historical point of view. Specific ocean uses have also been detailed by specialists who have made study of those uses their life work. Some of that information is repeated here only as context for predictions of the future.

THE U.S. NAVY

In national defense at sea, our Navy has suffered badly since the end of the Vietnam conflict. In 1968 the Navy had nearly 1,000 ships; by 1980 it had dropped in size to about 450 ships. This was the smallest U.S. fleet since the late 1930s, and hardly the sort of force that could look after national interests over the 71 percent of the globe that is covered by the seas. In the late seventies we faced threats, such as the taking of hostages in Iran, the Soviet invasion of Afghanistan, and continuing international conflict in Southeast Asia, with an inadequate number of seagoing assets. Those we had were overworked, with the result that both men and machines wore out.

The Reagan Administration has promised to rebuild the Navy, but the initial emphasis must be on maintaining its trained manpower pool and in restoring the worn-out or aging fleet. The President has stated that he intends to see a return to a 600-ship Navy, the size that the military joint chiefs of staff have urged on presidents for several years. Some are now questioning whether even 600 ships will be enough to meet the ever-increasing challenges faced on every ocean in the world. Nevertheless, it appears that the corner has been turned: the policy has been established, and, if the current fiscal climate in the American economy can be accommodated and mitigated, we should see a modern U.S. Navy that will be capable of meeting national security needs.

MARINE TRANSPORTATION

In our "other fleet," the merchant marine, the situation is not so promising. Since the end of World War II, the U.S. merchant fleet has slowly become a withered arm of our national security system. Where in the early 1950s American-flag ships carried nearly 50 percent of our national imports and exports, today it carries only about 4 percent. This means that we put our trade lifelines into the hands of foreigners. Since the overwhelming percentage of raw materials needed to run our economy comes from overseas, the future consequences are worth considering. In times of regional, international, or even global conflicts, how will these foreign ships be bound to serve U.S. economic needs? Recent years of Middle East conflicts have seen painful examples of political pressures reducing or terminating shipping services to various states in that area. Could the United States expect the same thing if its political policies were found to be unacceptable to the nations whose ships service our economy? It is hard to answer such questions, but it should be emphasized that international shipping is basically not a free market system in most respects. It is highly political, and it involves the activities, directly and indirectly, of foreign governments.

It is ironic, in view of the present American position in marine transportation, that most advanced technology now employed in shipping, such as containerization, roll-on roll-offs ships, and barge carrying vessels, came from U.S. developments. Even the mass production of ships origi-nated as a highly developed U.S. industry. For example, in World War II, a Kaiser shipyard produced a Liberty Ship in four days and eleven hours—from laying of the keel to launching of the completed vessel.

To bring the U.S. merchant fleet back to the healthy state in which it would carry 40–50 percent of U.S. trade would require a massive ship construction program with enormous amounts of capital—virtually a wartime-type shipbuilding push. Such an undertaking is unlikely at present. But it is crucial that some steps be taken to raise the percentage of U.S. commerce carried on U.S. ships, to insure the health of our economy as it relates to national security. Most experts in maritime affairs agree that the 40–50 percent level is an optimum ratio.

Crisis in Maritime Industry

There has been much speculation about how the United States got into this situation: labor has been unproductive; our tax and antitrust laws make it difficult to compete; our labor and material costs are too high compared with foreign sources; Americans do not know how to compete in the "maritime free market"; our government's policies have not helped promote a healthy maritime industry; and more. In fact, there is a little bit of truth in each of these statements. But there is no one, convenient scapegoat. All share the blame. An integrated national ocean policy would have helped greatly to anticipate and avoid the critical situation we now face. It is almost too late when one considers the size and cost of the remedies needed to correct the situation.

Candidate Reagan made public statements that indicated he recog-nized the critical issues; it remains to be seen if President Reagan is able to do something about them. The recent transfer of the Maritime Adminis-tration from the Department of Commerce to the Department of Trans-portation is evidence of some movement in the area. In any case, there is no escaping the fact that massive government involvement will be re-quired if the U.S. merchant marine is once again to be a major factor in our world trade activities.

One should note here that the merchant marine is also a naval auxiliary in times of national emergency, helping to support our overseas military forces through logistical transfer of supplies, fuel, and people. Therefore, defense planners must also have a strong interest in a large, viable merchant fleet. It is doubtful that the United States would be able to hire foreign-flag ships (unless from wartime allies) for these tasks in time of war.

SHIPBUILDING AND REPAIR

The outlook for the shipbuilding and ship repair industrial base in the United States is mixed at present. On the one hand, the buildup to a 600-ship Navy promises a generous orderbook for shipyards qualified to build warships—a somewhat different kind of business. This is a major improvement from Carter Administration days, when it appeared that the Navy would be held to about 450 ships; several U.S. shipyards projected layoffs and closings then—only a couple years ago.

On the other hand, there is no clear indication that even a modest buildup of the merchant fleet is planned. To be sure, there will still be orders for replacement of retiring vessels as well as special purpose ships that can qualify for construction subsidy. But it is clear that the Reagan Administration wishes to do away with the operating and construction subsidies that have aided survival of the merchant marine, and aims to make some fundamental policy changes that should lead to increased private sector investment in this area. The Merchant Marine Act of 1936 states that the U.S. merchant marine will carry a substantial portion of U.S. maritime trade. And though "substantial" has been defined by other government policy makers as being 50 percent, there is no present indication that the Reagan Administration understands the type of national investment required to meet that goal. To be fair, however, one should note that the defining of "substantial" was done some time before the present administration.

Labor Force Reductions

An interim problem faces shipyards: the size of orderbooks in the near future. Because of a world shipping glut, the lack of military orders, and a very low level of activity in merchant ship construction, American shipyards began to wind down their future plans about two or three years ago. They projected that perhaps eight of the thirteen major yards would face sizable labor force reductions, and that there might even be some closures. Indeed, in the last three years, two large yards have gone out of business and several smaller ones have had labor force reductions.

The new thrust for a 600-ship Navy will provide fairly full employment for that part of the industrial base that qualifies. However, there is a time lag—perhaps as much as three to four years—between Washington promises and the actual cutting of metal. The shipyards greet the former with delight, but they pay the bills with the latter. Their problem will be to hang on until the almost assured orders come in.

Meanwhile, one area of construction and repair is flourishing. This is in support of the offshore oil and gas industry, in the construction of oil drilling platforms, drillships, offshore logistics vessels, and specialized vessels such as pipeline lay barges. Not only does this industrial segment prosper; it is dominated by U.S. companies and U.S. technologies. Even in the face of ever-increasing foreign competition with all its alleged advantages (cheap labor, government subsidies, competitive restrictions, and so on), the U.S. offshore oil entrepreneur manages to keep the substantial share of the market.

OCEAN ENERGY

This leads us next to consider the offshore oil and gas industry in the United States or under U.S. corporate development worldwide. This is a healthy, growing industry with U.S. capital, technology, and management predominating in the world market. As the world's major consumer of energy (perhaps not a happy fact, but a fact indeed), the United States has suffered two "oil shocks" in the 1970s, and Americans seem to have learned that diversity of supply is a healthy thing. As noted earlier, more than 20 percent of U.S. oil and gas supplies come from offshore production today, an amount that will be even greater in the future.

While our national energy policies in the development of offshore assets may appear to be a jumble of confusion, they shine as a beacon of reason in comparison with sea power policies in other areas such as fishing, marine transportation, and mining. And, other than as oil and gas, the attainment of energy from the sea in economically viable amounts is still for the United States an achievement for the future. Renewable ocean energy resources such as thermal difference, tidal power, and wave energy remain largely in the domain of research and development. It is suggested, however, as a result of a considerable investment made by the Department of Energy (DOE) in this area, that there is some practical promise in ocean thermal energy (OTEC).

This system uses the thermal difference between the warm surface waters of the ocean and the deep cold currents to drive an ammonia "steam" turbine, which in turn drives an electrical generator. Enormous ocean-based floating facilities would be required, and much R&D remains to be done to establish their feasibility. It is thought, however, that for certain applications OTEC can produce energy more cheaply than conventional oil-fueled power plants. Examples are island sites in tropical latitudes—Guam, Hawaii, American Samoa, Puerto Rico, and the Virgin Islands—where the temperature difference between surface and deep water meets the requirements for OTEC, and the extra cost of importing conventional fuel makes an alternative energy source economically viable.

Other renewable ocean energy sources seem to be too far in the future for practical consideration by the year 2000. True, there are some ocean tidal energy plants in other parts of the world, but their application to U.S. needs is uncertain at this time. And even OTEC will probably not be found in use for commercial power generation until after the turn of the century, and only then if the U.S. government maintains some level of investment in its high risk and long-term development. Considering President Reagan's interest in dismantling or greatly reducing the Department of Energy, and proposed elimination of OTEC from federal funding, the situation is in doubt. The present administration does not dislike OTEC; it simply feels this developmental program is now mature enough to be handed over to the private sector, a view not shared by private industry.

MINERALS FROM THE SEA

Ocean mining is relatively new, but it could have a major impact on the supply of raw materials needed by the United States. However, it is an area that suffers heavily from lack of a national ocean policy.

Mining on the sea floor in shallow waters along seacoasts has been going on for some time, generally as an extension of simple dredging technology to the production of sands and gravels for construction materials. In the past ten to twenty years, other sands have been produced from shallow waters which contain such strategically important materials as gold, titanium, tungsten, and barite. In some areas of the world, tin and coal have been mined from the shallow sea floor. In almost all cases, these activities have taken place well within the territorial waters of the adjacent coastal state, and there have been no problems with respect to national ownership of the resource.

The major object of attention in ocean mining at present is the deep seabed where the best resources of manganese nodules are located. As Professor John Flipse indicates in his paper, the issue seems to be more one of international politics than of the ability to mine and market the resource. The latest law of the sea conference under United Nations sponsorship spent nearly ten years considering, among other issues, how these deep-sea resources should be produced and allocated among nations of the world; it is the issue that remains the major obstacle to conclusion of a treaty.

Mining and UNCLOS

The United States has participated actively in the law of the sea negotiations, but its effectiveness has been uneven over the years since 1958 when the first United Nations Conference on Law of the Sea (UNCLOS) was convened. I believe this reflects the absence of a national ocean policy that could help guide our negotiators through the many changes of U.S. government so they could operate in a uniform, coherent way. Many foreign delegations have done much better than ours in maintaining continuity of purpose.

So deep-ocean mining remains a problem that is more political than economic. The fundamental technologies have been proved and the economic analyses have been made. The copper, cobalt, nickel, and manganese available in this resource could be of great value to the United States in reducing dependence on foreign sources of these strategic minerals. At this time, it is not clear how the question will be finally resolved.

An interesting fact to note is that even with concurrence on deep-sea mining by the LOS conference, it will be some time in the late 1980s or into the early 1990s before the first commercial deep-ocean mining operations get underway. Full-scale use of the resource may not take place until the year 2000.

Polymetallic Sulphides

A more recent and perhaps more important event has been discovery of polymetallic sulphide deposits on the sea floor along certain crustal plate boundaries. The earth's crust is divided into six major crustal plates, and at many of the boundaries, the differential movement between two plates creates a focus for the sulphide deposits. Seawater leaching into the fractured seafloor structures is superheated and in turn forced upwards back to the sea floor. The superheated saltwater solution leaches metallic compounds out of the crustal rock, and as the hot water mixes with the near-freezing seawater at the bottom, these compounds are precipitated out. A wide variety of metallic compounds is found in these deposits, and many of them represent high quality, ore-grade deposits. It would appear that much of the deep-sea mining technology developed for the manganese nodules can be applied to these deposits.

The discovery of multiple sources of the sulphide deposits is so new that it is hard to make a present prediction as to their economic potential and availability. The first such deposits were seen in the Red Sea in the early 1960s, but it is only the discoveries of the past two years that have prompted great optimism about their economic value.

More important, some of the deposits have been found off the Oregon and Washington coasts within 200 miles of the United States. A 200-mile "exclusive economic zone" is part of the present UNCLOS treaty negotiations. It is obvious that final passage of the treaty would put such resources clearly within the complete jurisdiction of the United States. The United States does claim such a zone at present for fisheries, but for no other marine resources.

As with the manganese nodules, the polymetallic sulphide mining activity would probably not come into commercial-scale practice for at least ten to fifteen years. Much work needs to be done to map the deposits, determine their extent and economic value, determine ownership and conditions for their exploitation, and develop the appropriate technologies. But recent small samplings of at least four different locations in the Pacific Ocean and the Red Sea show great future promise.

LIVING MARINE RESOURCES

It has already been mentioned that the United States has a 200-mile-wide "Fishery Conservation and Management Zone" which gives it management and use rights over fish resources within the zone. Catch quotas are set for each stock on an annual basis, and stock in excess of what can be caught by U.S. fishermen can be licensed out to foreign fishermen whose governments have signed a fishing agreement with the United States. Despite the quotas, the United States still ranks as fifth largest fishing nation in the world, accounting for about 5 percent of the world's catch.

The guarantee of right-of-priority access to the 200-mile zone surrounding the United States and its possessions has helped to bring more capital to the American fishing industry to build boats, processing plants, and cooperative facilities. This was not the case when the more efficient foreign fishing fleets could work within twelve miles of our coastlines without any restrictions from the United States government.

It is interesting to note that since the United States declared this zone in 1976, the majority of fishing nations in the world have adopted similar fishery conservation zones. It is not simply a matter of keeping coastal stocks for the use of the adjacent coastal state; it is also a powerful tool for proper management of these resources, to ensure sustained yield.

Fishing for Export

It can be argued that Americans are not great fish eaters, but in 1980 the United States actually imported nearly $2.7 billion worth of fish products in addition to its own production. This figure represents about 10 percent of the U.S. international trade deficit for 1980! Yet our 200-mile fishing zone is estimated to hold about 20 percent of the world catch potential. If we produce only 5 percent of the world catch, then it seems the opportunity exists not only to reduce our import bill but actually to become a net exporter of fish. The world could use that food, and we could use the trade revenues.

In the chapter "Food from the Sea," Clarence Idyll makes the point that nearly 10 percent of the world's production of aquatic foods (both fresh and saltwater) comes from aquaculture, or fish farming. Yet in the United States, the figure is less than 4 percent, and little of this is saltwater "farming." There is a great potential in this area, but we are not exploiting it.

Why is the United States not doing better in the production of marine food and related fish products, such as fishmeal and oils? Again, it is the lack of vigorous, coherent policy in these areas, fisheries and aquaculture. More government attention must be given to the stimulation, incentives, and promotion of a competitive national fishing industry. The National Marine Fisheries service under the Department of Commerce has often been a source of disappointment to the commercial fishing industry; and although the 200-mile limit gives us assured access to the resource, our planning has not taken full advantage of it. In aquaculture we lack a national focus at the seat of government, with the Departments of Agriculture, Commerce, and Interior all jockeying to be the annointed lead agency. As a result, for the last four years no one of these agencies has been able to get the upper hand, and the nation has been the poorer for it.

PORTS AND HARBORS

Finally, in the coastal zones are found the most complex sets of ocean use problems. Ports and harbors facilitate trade from the interior to the sea and from the sea to the interior. No matter what flags fly on the ships that use them, American ports are the sea-land transition points for this, the world's largest trading nation. The advent of a coal-energy economy will find the United States playing a major role in the supply of this important commodity. With nearly 40 percent of the world's known coal reserves, this country is in an excellent position to supply much of the world's future energy needs. But this will require major and massive investments in U.S. ports to develop modern coal terminal facilities. Typically, a major harbor improvement project may require from ten to fifteen years from planning to completion. Even longer will be taken to recover the investment from coal sales. But it must be undertaken now because there is effective foreign competition in this market from such nations as Australia and South Africa.

At the same time that its ports must grow to take advantage of increasing world trade, the United States must also contend with the migration of its citizens to its coastal regions. By the year 2000 nearly 80 percent of the U.S. population will live within fifty miles of a coastline. This population will add to the pollution burden; compete for land that could be used for commercial development; stress limited recreational resources; and insist on environmental conservation programs that will add to the costs of coastal commercial activities.

COASTAL ZONE MANAGEMENT

Perhaps the most difficult ocean policy area for this country will be coastal zone management. The land/sea interface is a sharp convergence point among multiple uses of the oceans. It is here that the majority of disputes will take place. Good policy for the coastal ocean areas will result in good plans that can anticipate and ameliorate this stress. But while our government has encouraged and supported the coastal states to develop coastal zone management plans, these plans still leave much to be accomplished. Much has gone well and much has gone badly. By and large, a great deal of time and additional effort will be required; we may not see any real harmony in effective coastal planning for fifteen to twenty years.

It is clear that the federal government must keep its hand in the process to assist individual states to build coastal zone plans that are consistent with those of their neighbors and the federal government itself. Thus it is noted with some discomfort that the Reagan Administration is now shutting down the major part of the government's program in coastal zone management. Again the claim is that it is time for the states to take over the program. But as with OTEC, there is much disagreement with this assertion.

MARINE RECREATION

Perhaps the greatest growth industry in national uses of the sea is marine recreation. Despite inflation, recession, fuel crises, and all other forms of impediments, this area of the U.S. economy continues to grow at a rate exceeding the rate of population growth. Some recent figures put the contribution of marine recreation to gross national product at a level very close to that of the U.S.-flag merchant marine. In this context, marine recreation includes all activities associated with this area, from the manufacture of bathing suits and surfboards to the operation of ocean-going yachts. The only dampening factor that can be seen against this vigorous growth is the limits of space and facilities for docking boats. Furthermore, as more parts of the world begin to develop leisure-time activities and disposable income, the U.S. vendors of these goods and services should enjoy even greater market opportunities worldwide.

The Political Ocean: The Key to Sea Power Development

The theme emerging from all this is apparent: *effective national uses of the sea can come only through effective national ocean policy.* The United States, through present actions, is attempting to plan the state of its sea power for the beginning of the twenty-first century. And yet today, there are some severe deficiencies in this planning, deficiencies that can put our nation to a great disadvantage unless they are remedied.

The present administration in its budget cuts has reduced the level of much of American ocean activities (which are supported by federal funding) by something like 25 percent. By and large, these levels of support had been slowly losing to inflation during the past decade; added cuts of the magnitude of the administration's curtailments have a much more severe impact than might be surmised. On the other hand, some areas, such as the Navy, appear to be doing much better than just a year ago.

This is not to point the finger at any one group or organization. The administration has to get the U.S. economy back into good health, and the excesses of the past must be worked off. All constituencies will suffer in the near term. The ocean-oriented community is no exception. But this does not repair the added damage that surely will be done in the next three or four years while the nation's economic health is being treated.

Meanwhile, competition from foreign states increases. The United Nations Law of the Sea Conference has brought together some 156 nations for the largest international negotiation ever held, and they mean to develop a uniform legal code for 71 percent of the planet. In one way the LOS conference is a "macro-example" of the discontinuity between policy and man's abilities to work in the oceans. But it has also helped to sensitize many coastal states throughout the world to the importance of effective uses of ocean space. With 86 percent of the coastal nations being developing nations, the United States faces both a challenge and an opportunity as it moves towards the twenty-first century. Its ability to take full advantage of the opportunities and to avoid the pitfalls will depend largely upon the quality of its national ocean policy development. Because of the complexity of such an undertaking, it is not too soon to start.

Designing the Nation's Ocean Future

What can be done? Simply, the planning process for development of a national ocean policy framework can be started. This sort of activity costs very little and will have both a short-term and a long-term benefit.

In the short term, an integrated ocean policy roadmap will help allocate program reductions where they will have the least impact on our sea power development. Good decisions will avoid compound crippling of projects and programs through multiple budget reductions in several interrelated agencies. If the private sector is to assume more responsibility, negotiations must be conducted between government and the private sector to insure minimum disruption in the transition.

The longer-term benefit of having a national ocean policy framework has been amply emphasized earlier in this chapter. In my view, this will give the Yankee Mariner a competitive edge in the next two decades.

Was there ever a Yankee Mariner, and if so, can he come back? Contributors to this book have made the case for his existence. Although his history is somewhat uneven, there is no denying that he has done rather well on the whole. His reemergence in flourishing health is not guaranteed, but he *can* come back. Our nation can maintain itself and prosper as a great sea power if it has the will to seek out effective ways of planning and implementing its maritime programs. To do so requires the informed support of a concerned public, within and without the ocean-oriented community.

The ordinary citizen, whether a resident of Louisville or Los Angeles, must be made to understand the importance of the oceans to our nation. Congress must be informed and educated on sea power issues; few of our legislators can see the ocean from Capitol Hill. And those in the ocean community, from Navy to recreation, must seek opportunities to meet and to exchange ideas as well as to formulate plans to influence the government, not with the zeal of religious crusaders but simply with knowledgeable concern for the nation's future.

Sea power as an issue lacks the galvanizing impact of a moon shot or a "Sputnik." But we all depend on ocean space for our well-being on Planet Earth. Certainly that should be a far more persuasive incentive to galvanize our efforts to maximize our role in ocean space and to be sure our fellow citizens know its importance.

If the United States fails as a sea power, it will surely fail as a nation. It has just about run out of momentum in asserting and enhancing its place in the sea.

What we do in the next twenty years to reassert ourselves in ocean space may well determine our position in the world community for unknown decades beyond.

Glossary

AAW—antiair warfare

AEW—airborne early warning

ASW—antisubmarine warfare

CNO—Chief of Naval Operations

CVN—nuclear-powered aircraft carrier

ICBM—intercontinental ballistic missile

MCM—mine countermeasure ship

mmt—million metric tons

nm—nautical mile

RDF—rapid deployment force

SAC—Strategic Air Command

SLBM—submarine-launched ballistic missile

SLCM—sea-launched cruise missile

SLOC—sea lines of communication

SRF—strategic rocket force

SSBN—nuclear-powered ballistic missile submarine

SSG—diesel-powered missile-launching submarine

SSGN—nuclear-powered missile-launching submarine

SSM—surface-to-surface missile

SSN—nuclear-powered attack submarine

SUM—small sub underwater mobile

SURTAS—surveillance towed-array sonar

UNCLOS—United Nations Conference on the Law of the Sea

V/STOL—vertical and short takeoff and landing